TEXT READING PROGRAM

If it were not for these enlightening Text commentaries, we would still be floundering in an intellectual soup. The soup was mighty tasty, but was difficult to get our teeth into without these brilliant observations, comparisons, and analogies. We know this is a vast body of work that has been given us and we are grateful from the bottom of our hearts.
—SYLVIA AND CAP LYONS

A very powerful tool to keep me on track, reading and absorbing just a few pages each day. This process has been an invaluable source of inner peace during this past year.
—CONNIE PORTER

Robert Perry and Greg Mackie are experts at making the sometimes challenging Text not just understandable, but rich with meaning and poignancy. This is a priceless gift to anyone who wants to fully understand the awesome teachings of *A Course in Miracles*. I can think of no better form of support than this!
—JULIA SIMPSON

The Text commentaries offer insights I could not have had alone, because of the deep understanding Robert and Greg have.
—DIETRUN BUCHMAN

An amazing journey into the genius and magnitude of this material. Don't miss this opportunity.
—SHARON EDWARDS

Robert and Greg's insights illuminate Text principles like never before.
—LORETTA M. SIANI, PH.D

I have studied the Text and read it through at least once a year for the last 19 years. I thought I knew it pretty well. However this year has been a real eye-opener. Many of those little question marks I made in the margins have been erased. I shall be forever grateful for this year of Text study.
—WENDY FINNERTY

After 20 years with the Course, I now understand it on a much different level.
—ULLA WALLIN

Robert and Greg's intelligence, insight, and wit, create a fun climate of spiritual scholarship that helps make the Text more intelligible and alive. They're extraordinarily gifted.
—AMY ELLISON

The clear and down-to-earth commentary has helped me connect with the Text as never before.
—NANCY NEVITT

Robert and Greg have a tremendous comprehension of the Course and provide down-to-earth explanations. I know of no better way to learn the message of the Text than this program.
—JAN WORLEY

Translates the beautiful poetry of the Course's Text into everyday common language, making the valuable meaning of each sentence easily understood.
—KATHERINE LATORRACA

Previously, I had never succeeded in completely reading the Text. Participating was the best thing that I did for myself this year.
—DAVID COLWELL

There is nothing else in my years of studying the Course that has helped me so much!
—GEORGE PORTER

I can honestly say I'll finally complete the reading of the entire Text—
and I've been at this for 20 years!
—BARBARA OLSON

Robert and Greg's insights helped me understand and assimilate the
Course's otherwise complex and difficult passages. I will do this again
next year, and the next, and the next. This program is amazing.
—JO CHANDLER

Your program has been a revelation.
—DON DE LENE

I would like to say that this year has been too amazing to actually put
into words.
—KATHY CHOMITZ

Having studied the Course faithfully for 28 years, I never imagined the
insights and miracles I would receive from these commentaries on the
Text!
—MIRKALICE GORE

I can truly say that this program has made an incredible difference to
my life. I wholeheartedly recommend it.
—DAVID FLEMING

Nothing less than totally inspiring.
—REV. JERRY CUSIMANO

THE ILLUMINATED TEXT

Commentaries for Deepening Your Connection with
A Course in Miracles

Robert Perry & Greg Mackie

VOLUME 7

Published by Circle Publishing
A division of the Circle of Atonement
P.O. Box 4238 * West Sedona, AZ 86340
(928) 282-0790 * www.circleofa.org
circleoffice@circleofa.org

Cover design by Thunder Mountain Design and Communications
Design & layout by Phillips Associates UK Ltd
Printed in the USA

ISBN 978-1-886602-38-0

Library of Congress Cataloging-in-Publication Data

Perry, Robert, 1960-
 The illuminated text : commentaries for deepening your connection with A course in miracles / Robert Perry & Greg Mackie.
     p. cm.
 Includes bibliographical references.
 Summary: "Provides in-depth analysis of the Text of A Course in Miracles"--
Provided by publisher.
 ISBN 978-1-886602-38-0
1. Course in Miracles. 2. Spiritual life. I. Mackie, Greg, 1963- II. Title.
 BP605.C68P455 2010
 299'.93--dc22

                         2009039354

CONTENTS

Foreword ix

Commentaries on Chapter 27: THE HEALING OF THE DREAM

I. The Picture of Crucifixion 3

II. The Fear of Healing...13

III. Beyond All Symbols 25

IV. The Quiet Answer..31

V. The Healing Example 37

VI. The Witnesses to Sin...47

VII. The Dreamer of the Dream...53

VIII. The "Hero" of the Dream 65

Commentaries on Chapter 28: THE UNDOING OF FEAR

I. The Present Memory..77

II. Reversing Effect and Cause 88

III. The Agreement to Join 97

IV. The Greater Joining 104

V. The Alternate to Dreams of Fear 111

VI. The Secret Vows 117

VII. The Ark of Safety 122

Commentaries on Chapter 29: THE AWAKENING

I. The Closing of the Gap...129

II. The Coming of the Guest 135

III. God's Witnesses 142

IV. Dream Roles 149

V. The Changeless Dwelling Place 154

VI. Forgiveness and the End of Time 160

VII. Seek Not Outside Yourself 164

VIII. The Anti-Christ 170

IX. The Forgiving Dream 177

Commentaries on Chapter 30: THE NEW BEGINNING

Introduction 187

I. Rules for Decision 188

II. Freedom of Will 199

III. Beyond All Idols 204

IV. The Truth behind Illusions 212

V. The Only Purpose 218

VI. The Justification for Forgiveness 226

VII. The New Interpretation 234

VIII. Changeless Reality 241

Commentaries on Chapter 31: THE FINAL VISION

I. The Simplicity of Salvation 249

II. Walking with Christ 258

III. The Self-Accused 266

IV. The Real Alternative 272

V. Self-Concept versus Self 280

VI. Recognizing the Spirit 294

VII. The Savior's Vision 299

VIII. Choose Once Again 311

FOREWORD

The Text is the foundation of *A Course in Miracles*. Doing the Course is simply a process of learning and internalizing its thought system, and the Text is where that thought system is laid out. It is an unparalleled spiritual tour de force. Careful study of it will change your outlook in ways that perhaps nothing else can.

Many students, however, find the Text to be very hard going. Many do not finish it, and even those who make it through, perhaps repeatedly, wish they had a deeper grasp of what they were reading.

For this reason, in 2006, the Circle of Atonement offered the Text Reading Program. This was a year-long tour through the Text of *A Course in Miracles* with commentary on each paragraph, written by myself and Greg Mackie, both teachers for the Circle. Before each weekday, we would send out to all the participants via e-mail the reading for that day. This would usually consist of a single section from the Text, accompanied by our commentary as well as practical exercises.

We often supplemented these sections with material from the Urtext, the original typescript of the Course. Our experience was that, especially in the early chapters of the Text, material from the Urtext that was eventually edited out was very helpful and clarifying. So when we felt it was useful, we included this Urtext material in brackets, and let it inform our commentary. We also indicated where a word had been emphasized in the Urtext, as this too often added clarity.

Note: In this volume, words that were originally emphasized in the Urtext are <u>underlined</u>. So when you see an underlined word here, know that that word was emphasized in the Urtext, but that emphasis was not included in the eventual published Course, which included fewer emphasized words. Again, we did this because quite often that emphasis from the Urtext would add clarity.

The reason we developed this program has a bit of history to it. In 2000, we offered a local program in Sedona that included a daily Text class, using a schedule that took us through the entire Text in a year of weekday readings. (On the sixth and seventh days, we rested!) Our friend, student, and colleague John Perry attended that program. When it ended, he began guiding people through the Text using the same schedule, only doing so online. He sent out the Text material for a given day and interspersed it with his own clarifying comments. In fall 2005 he felt guided to suggest we do something similar. Our guidance told us to go ahead, and so that's what we did. Without John's suggestion, however, it is safe to say we never would have done this.

2006, the year of the program, was an intense one. I would write commentaries for three weeks. Then I got a breather for a week while Greg wrote the commentaries. And then the schedule started over. Each day we wrote the commentary that needed to go out the next day. In addition, we led a weekly phone class for participants, in which we summarized the previous week's sections. (The recordings are still available to students who sign up for the online version of the Text Reading Program.)

The response to our program far exceeded our expectations. We have included a few edited comments at the front of the book, but if you want to read the unadulterated student reactions, straight from the various horses' mouths, then go to www.circlepublishing.org and click on the link for the Text Reading Program. During the year of the program, and actually ever since, we have had consistent requests that we put this material into published form.

So here it is, presented in book form as a multi-volume set. We hope you find these commentaries illuminating, and that they do indeed deepen your understanding of the spiritual masterpiece, *A Course in Miracles*.

ROBERT PERRY
SEPTEMBER 2009
SEDONA, ARIZONA

Commentaries on Chapter 27

THE HEALING OF
THE DREAM

I. The Picture of Crucifixion
Commentary by Robert Perry

1. The wish to be unfairly treated is a compromise attempt that would <u>combine</u> attack and innocence. Who can combine the wholly incompatible, and make a unity of what can <u>never</u> join? Walk you the gentle way, and you will fear no evil and no shadows in the night [a reference to the twenty-third Psalm: "Yea, though I walk through the valley of the shadow of death, I will fear no evil"]. But place no terror symbols on your path, or you will weave a crown of thorns from which your brother and yourself will <u>not</u> escape. You <u>cannot</u> crucify yourself alone. And if you are unfairly treated, he <u>must</u> suffer the unfairness that you see. You <u>cannot</u> sacrifice yourself alone. For sacrifice is total. If it could occur at all it would entail the whole of God's creation, and the Father with the sacrifice of His beloved Son.

We actually have a wish to be unfairly treated. It's true, isn't it? Something in us secretly celebrates when we seize upon proof that we have truly gotten a raw deal. The delight we take in this, says Jesus, is that in this state of blame we get to combine innocence and attack. We get to attack while still being completely innocent. This is the beauty of being the outraged victim.

I saw a great example of this recently. A young Texan woman is suing British Petroleum for the death of her two parents, who were killed in a refinery explosion for which BP has admitted responsibility. As I watched, her quiet anger at them seemed not only valid, but righteous. She was smoldering with anger, yet absolutely innocent. We actually *wish* to see ourselves as unfairly treated because it grants us that privilege of being innocent while angry, innocent *because* we are angry.

The fallout from this, though, is horrific. It makes our brother into a symbol of terror, and places that terror symbol right in our path. As we approach this symbol, we then weave a crown of thorns, place it on our own head, and then point to the symbol, saying, "How could you do this to me?!" The fact remains, as the last section said, that we force this sacrifice on ourselves. But when we do, we are not the only one who

3

suffers. For we blame our brother for the crucifixion that we imposed on ourselves.

> 2. In your <u>release</u> from sacrifice is <u>his</u> made manifest, and shown to be his own. But every pain you suffer do you see as proof that <u>he</u> is guilty of attack. Thus would you make yourself to be the sign that he has <u>lost</u> his innocence, and need but look on you to realize that <u>he</u> has been condemned. And what [loss] to <u>you</u> has been unfair will come to <u>him</u> in righteousness. The unjust vengeance that you suffer now belongs to <u>him</u>, and when it <u>rests</u> on him are <u>you</u> set free. Wish not to make yourself a living symbol of his guilt, for you will <u>not</u> escape the death you made for him. But [Ur: and] in <u>his</u> innocence you find your own.

This is why it is so crucial to stop imposing sacrifice and loss upon ourselves. For every time we do, we assign someone else the responsibility for it. We thus kill two Sons of God with one stone. The martyr never suffers alone. Everyone around her has to bear the burden of guilt for her crucifixion.

In one way or another, we all play the role of martyr. Each bit of our suffering is intended as the sign of someone else's guilt. He made us this way unjustly, and now he deserves to be paid back in kind. And the loss that to us "has been unfair will come to him in righteousness." And only then are we made free. According to Jesus, this is a recipe for suicide, "for you will not escape the death you made for him."

> 3. Whenever you consent to suffer pain, to be deprived, unfairly treated or in need of <u>anything</u>, you but accuse your brother of attack upon God's Son. You hold a picture of your crucifixion before his eyes, that he may see his sins are writ in Heaven in your blood and death, and go before him, closing off the gate and damning him to hell. Yet this is writ in hell and <u>not</u> in Heaven, where you are <u>beyond</u> attack and prove his <u>innocence</u>. The picture of yourself you offer him you show yourself, and give it all your faith. The Holy Spirit offers you, to give to him, a picture of yourself in which there is <u>no</u> pain and <u>no</u> reproach at all. And what was martyred to his guilt becomes the perfect witness to his innocence.

If you think that writing someone's sins against you in your blood is a rather extreme image, think again. I encountered a website which relates some unbelievable practices at the community of a famous American guru. When this guru has been offended by the actions of a student, he at times apparently has messages written in fake blood on the walls of that student's rooms, messages such as "Traitor." This fake blood is understood by all to be the guru's "blood," which was "spilled" by the student's offense. These messages come very close to being a literal example of Jesus' gruesome image in this paragraph. More comments on this paragraph below.

> 4. The power of witness is beyond belief because it brings conviction in its wake. The witness is believed <u>because</u> he points beyond himself to what he <u>represents</u>. A sick and suffering you but represents your brother's guilt; the witness that you send lest he forget the injuries he gave, from which you swear he never will escape. This sick and sorry picture *you* accept, if only it can serve to punish him. The sick are merciless to everyone, and in contagion do they seek to kill. Death seems an easy price, if they can say, "Behold me, brother, at your hand I die." For sickness is the witness to his guilt, and death would prove his errors <u>must</u> be sins. Sickness is but a "little" death; a form of vengeance not yet total. Yet it speaks with certainty for what it represents. The bleak and bitter picture you have sent your brother *you* have looked upon in grief. And everything that it has shown to him have you believed, <u>because</u> it witnessed to the guilt in him which you perceived and loved.

Notice that the principle Jesus has been elucidating applies to *all* forms of suffering. It applies to any case where we suffer pain, any instance in which we feel deprived, any situation where we feel unfairly treated, and even any sort of need we believe we have. It even applies to physical illness. All of these forms of pain have a single source: our "consent to suffer."

Application: Think of some form of suffering going on in your life right now. Then ask yourself, "Whom do I hold responsible for this?" Notice how, in subtle or not-so-subtle ways, you have tried to *show* this person your suffering. Think of one of the ways in which you did so.

Then visualize this as you holding a picture before this person's eyes, a picture of your crucifixion.

Now say to him, "Behold me, brother, at your hand I die."

"I am the silent witness of your guilt."

Notice the reaction that you hope to obtain.

Now see yourself holding up a second picture to his eyes, the inevitable result of the first.

This is a picture of the gate of Heaven, on which is posted a large sign.

The sign is labeled "The Sins of [name]" and lists his sins against you, one after another.

It was written in your blood by an angel of God.

It shows that when this person reaches Heaven's gate, it will be closed, and he will be damned to hell.

Now realize that *you* wrote this sign, from blood you drew, and it is false.

And you falsely posed for the picture of your crucifixion.

You staged the whole thing.

Realize, too, that for every second you showed this phony picture to your brother,

you have spent hours gazing on it, in total conviction.

Realize that in the real Heaven, you have never been wounded.

Indeed, you cannot be.

And that your shining wholeness is the proof of your brother's innocence.

5. Now in the hands made gentle by His touch, the Holy Spirit lays a picture of a <u>different</u> you. It is a picture of a body still, for what you <u>really</u> are cannot be seen nor pictured. Yet <u>this</u> one has <u>not</u> been used for purpose of attack, and therefore never suffered pain at all. <u>It</u> witnesses to the eternal truth that you cannot <u>be</u> hurt, and points <u>beyond</u> itself to both <u>your</u> innocence and <u>his</u>. Show <u>this</u> unto your brother, who will see that every scar is healed, and every tear is wiped away in laughter and in love. And he will look on his forgiveness there, and with healed eyes will look <u>beyond</u> it to the innocence that he beholds in you. Here is the proof that he has <u>never</u> sinned; that <u>nothing</u> which his madness bid him do was ever done, or ever had effects of any kind. That <u>no</u> reproach he laid upon his heart was <u>ever</u> justified, and <u>no</u> attack can ever touch him with the poisoned and relentless sting of fear.

Application: Continue the same visualization you were doing above:

As your brother gazes on the picture of your crucifixion, see the tears on his face.

See his grim acceptance that his future will be spent in hell.

Is this what you want?

Ask the Holy Spirit to touch you and give you His gentleness.

Now in the hands made gentle by His touch, see Him lay a picture of a different you.

This you has never suffered pain, having never attacked.

In this picture, your head is thrown back in happy laughter.

Your arms are extended as if in universal welcome.

You are wholly joyous, literally incapable of feeling grief or pain.

You are standing on a bright green lawn, and in your extraordinary happiness your feet hardly seem to touch the ground.*

This is the symbol of the real you.

Now show this picture to your brother, and say, "Behold me, brother, at your hand I live.

I am the proof that you never sinned, that nothing your madness bid you do had effects of any kind."

Now see a look of healing relief spread over your brother's tear-stained face.

The two of you begin to gently laugh as you wipe away his tears.

How foolish it was to think that he had sinned!

Now he knows that no reproach he laid upon his heart was ever justified.

And now you know the same is true of you as well.

* Drawn from *Absence from Felicity: The Story of Helen Schucman and Her Scribing of 'A Course in Miracles,'* Kenneth Wapnick, Ph.D. [Roscoe, NY: Foundation for "A Course in Miracles"], first edition, p. 117).

6. Attest his innocence and <u>not</u> his guilt. <u>Your</u> healing is his comfort and <u>his</u> health <u>because</u> it proves illusions are not true. It is not will for life but wish for death that is the motivation for this world. Its <u>only</u> purpose is <u>to prove guilt real</u>. No worldly thought or act or feeling has a motivation other than this one. These are the witnesses that are called forth to be believed, and lend conviction to the system they speak for

and represent. And each has many voices, speaking to your brother and yourself in different tongues. And yet to both the message is the same. Adornment of the body seeks to show how lovely are the witnesses for guilt. Concerns about the body demonstrate how frail and vulnerable is your life; how easily destroyed is what you love. Depression speaks of death, and vanity of real concern with anything at all.

"It is not will for life but wish for death that is the motivation of this world." What a line! This certainly does not appear to be the case. Look at the tenacity with which every living thing clings to survival. How, then, does Jesus explain this? He says we use everything in the world to prove guilt real, and thus prove that we deserve death. How can we be constantly trying to prove that we deserve death unless we really wish to die?

We do this by trying to turn all things into witnesses for guilt. We especially make our body into such a witness. Our body is there to be the visible picture of what our brother has done to us. All of our attitudes around the body, then, are really attitudes about its role as witness for guilt. When we are concerned about our body's health and safety, we are saying, "Look how easily that guilty world can hurt me and even destroy my life." When we are depressed, we are saying, "Oh, what's the use? The world is going to destroy me eventually no matter what I do." When we dress up the body, we are saying, "A witness for guilt is a lovely thing to behold, an object worth celebrating." We are like a woman striding into a courtroom in a stunning red dress, right before she delivers the testimony that sends the defendant to the chair.

Yet of course, as we bring to the stand more and more witnesses to our brother's guilt, we believe more and more in our own guilt—and thus believe that we deserve death.

> 7. The strongest witness to futility, that bolsters all the rest and helps them paint the picture in which sin is justified, is sickness in whatever form it takes. The sick have reason for each one of their unnatural desires and strange needs. For who could live a life so soon cut short and <u>not</u> esteem the worth of passing joys? What pleasures <u>could</u> there be that will endure? Are not the frail <u>entitled</u> to believe that every stolen scrap of pleasure is their righteous payment for their little lives? Their death will pay the price for all of them, if they enjoy their benefits or

not. The end of life must come, whatever way that life be spent. And so take pleasure in the quickly passing and ephemeral.

This paragraph so adeptly captures a pervasive attitude, yet its real message can be easy to miss. It says that the best witness to how the world has screwed us is sickness. It is the most convincing proof that life has given us a raw deal. And since life has been unfair to us, we then have a tremendous amount of license. "So I have strange needs and unnatural desires? So I'm a little demanding? So I'm ignoring you as I indulge in my stolen scrap of pleasure? Don't I have a right? After all, look at what life has done to me—and will ultimately do to me. I'm going to lose this battle. I might as well enjoy myself before the end comes." This reminds me of that old Peggy Lee song, "Is That All There Is?":

> If that's all there is my friends, then let's keep dancing.
> Let's break out the booze and have a ball.
> If that's all there is.

In summary, when I am sick (especially if I'm chronically sick), then the fact that life is in the process of killing me gives me the right to turn into a demanding, idiosyncratic, self-absorbed person. I've earned the right to make it all about me. I'm being sinned against (even to the point of death), so I have the right to sin in return.

> 8. These are _not_ sins, but witnesses unto the strange belief that sin and death are real, and innocence and sin will end alike within the termination of the grave. If this were true, there _would_ be reason to remain content to seek for passing joys and cherish little pleasures where you can. Yet in this picture is the body _not_ perceived as neutral and _without_ a goal inherent in itself. For it becomes the symbol of reproach, the sign of guilt whose consequences still are there to see, so that the cause can _never_ be denied.

The self-absorbed pleasures that we feel are our right, given what life has done to us, are not sins. They are just the sad witnesses to our depressing view of life. And if our view were right, if life really were slowly killing us, then we *would* have a right to make it all about our vintage wine and favorite ice cream, our stamp collections and our quest for that perfect cup of coffee. Yet even if we decide that we are right, we need to face that this view automatically turns our body into a weapon. Our body becomes the mute witness of what the world has done to us. It becomes the corpse on display in the museum of the world's atrocities.

> 9. Your function is to show your brother [Ur: to *prove* to him that] sin can <u>have</u> no cause. How futile <u>must</u> it be to see yourself a picture of the proof that what your function <u>is</u> [your function of saving your brother] can never be! The Holy Spirit's picture changes not the body into something it is not. It only takes away from it <u>all</u> signs of accusation and of blamefulness. Pictured <u>without</u> a purpose, it is seen as neither sick nor well, nor bad nor good. No grounds are offered that it may be judged in <u>any</u> way at all. It has no life, but neither is it dead. It stands apart from <u>all</u> experience of love or fear. For now it witnesses to <u>nothing</u> yet, its purpose being open, and the mind made free again to choose what it is <u>for</u>. Now is it not condemned, but waiting for a purpose to be <u>given</u>, that it may fulfill the function that it will receive.

As the previous section said, our sense of futility comes not from living in a futile world, because we aren't. Rather, it comes from accusing our brother of treating us unfairly. For our real purpose is to save him, to walk him up to the pearly gates and happily let him through. But our accusation says that those gates are forever barred to him. We are like a doctor who keeps saying, "This patient is hopeless; there is nothing I can do here." And so he doesn't even try to save them, and then he feels that his life is futile.

Application: To show your brother that other picture, you need to first remove the purposes that you have laid on the body. If you can, find a mirror and stand in front of it, looking over your body, while repeating these lines to yourself.

> *I picture my body without a purpose.*
> *It is therefore neither sick nor well, nor bad nor good.*
> *It has no life, but neither is it dead.*
> *It stands apart from all experience of love or fear.*
> *Now it witnesses to nothing yet, its purpose being open, and my*
> *   mind made free again to choose what it is for.*

Now is it not condemned, but waiting for a purpose to be given,
that it may fulfill the function that it will receive.

10. Into this empty space, from which the <u>goal</u> of sin has been removed, is Heaven free to be remembered. Here its peace can come, and perfect healing take the place of death. The body can become a sign of life, a promise of redemption, and a breath of immortality to those grown sick of breathing in the fetid scent of death. Let it have healing as its <u>purpose</u>. Then will it send forth the message it received, and by its health and loveliness proclaim the truth and value that it represents. Let it receive the power to represent an endless life, forever unattacked. And to your brother let its message be, "Behold me, brother, at your hand I live."

Application: Again look at your body in the mirror, while repeating these words:

Into this empty space, from which the goal of sin has been
removed, is Heaven free to be remembered.
Here its peace can come, and perfect healing take the place of
death.
My body can become a sign of life, a promise of redemption, and
a breath of immortality to those grown sick of breathing in the
fetid scent of death.
Let it have healing as its purpose.
Then will it send forth the message it received, and by its health
and loveliness proclaim the truth that it symbolizes.
Let it receive the power to represent an endless life, forever
unattacked.
And to my brother let its message be, "Behold me, brother, at
your hand I live."

11. The simple way to let this be achieved is merely this; to let the body have no purpose from the past, when you were sure you <u>knew</u> its purpose was to foster guilt. For this insists your crippled picture

is a lasting sign of what it represents. This leaves no space in which a different view, another purpose, can be given it. You do *not* know its purpose. You but gave illusions of a purpose to a thing you made to hide your function from yourself. This thing without a purpose cannot hide the function that the Holy Spirit gave. Let, then, its purpose and your function both be reconciled at last and seen as one.

This paragraph reiterates and expands on the themes of the ninth paragraph. To let our body receive a new purpose and give our brother that beautiful message "Behold me, brother, at your hand I live," we need to clean the slate. We need to cleanse the body of purposes based on our past, for in that past we were sure we *"knew* its purpose was to foster guilt" (Urtext version). To really clean the slate, then, we need to get in touch with the fact that we wanted it to show our brother how he injured us. If you doubt that you have held this purpose for the body, ask yourself, "Have I ever been sick?"

Then we need to realize that we don't know the body's purpose. We simply fashioned a neutral, purposeless form, and then we painted on it *illusions* of a purpose, the purpose of showing our brother how guilty he is. And we did all this to obscure our own purpose, the purpose of showing our brother how *holy* he is. Yet this purposeless body cannot really hide our purpose. Therefore, the only solution is to give it the same purpose as our own. "Let, then, *its* purpose and *your* function both be reconciled at last and seen as one" (Urtext version).

II. The Fear of Healing
Commentary by Robert Perry

1. Is healing frightening? To many, yes. For accusation is a bar to love, and damaged bodies <u>are</u> accusers. They stand firmly in the way of trust and peace, proclaiming that the frail can <u>have</u> no trust and that the damaged <u>have</u> no grounds for peace. Who has been injured <u>by</u> his brother, and could love and trust him still? He <u>has</u> attacked and will attack again. Protect him not, because your damaged body shows that *you* must be protected <u>from</u> him. To forgive may be an act of charity, but <u>not</u> his due. He may be <u>pitied</u> for his guilt, but <u>not</u> exonerated. And if you forgive him his transgressions [as an act of pity for his guilt], you but <u>add</u> to all the guilt that he has really earned.

This paragraph has a simple but challenging message: We are afraid of having our body healed because our damaged body is an effective accuser, and we want to remain an accuser. As the last section said, we see a sick body as a powerful witness to our brother's sins. It is the key evidence in our case against him.

Application: Think of some infirmity of yours and ask yourself, "Whom do I hold responsible for this, at least partly?" Then ask yourself, "Is it possible that I resist being healed of this because that would mean giving up proof of this person's guilt?"

2. The unhealed <u>cannot</u> pardon. For they are the witnesses that pardon is unfair. They would retain the <u>consequences</u> of the guilt they overlook. Yet no one <u>can</u> forgive a sin that he believes is real. And what has consequences <u>must</u> be real, because what it has <u>done</u> is there to see. Forgiveness is <u>not</u> pity, which but seeks to pardon what it thinks to be the truth. Good cannot *be* returned for evil, for forgiveness does not first <u>establish</u> sin and <u>then</u> forgive it. Who can say and <u>mean</u>, "My brother, you have injured me, and yet, because I am the <u>better</u> of the two, I pardon you my hurt." <u>His</u> pardon and <u>your</u> hurt can<u>not</u> exist together. One <u>denies</u> the other and <u>must</u> make it false.

We cannot convincingly forgive someone as long as we carry in our body the hurt that that person supposedly inflicted. This is a hard message, but the logic is clear:

> "No one can forgive a sin that he believes is real."
> "What has consequences must be real."
> Therefore, no one can forgive a sin that has consequences.

As long as the consequences of your brother's sin are still there in your body, your forgiveness is going to be half-hearted and unconvincing. You will be forgiving him out of pity, out of feeling sorry for this person, which also implies feeling above him. It will amount to this: "My brother, you have injured me, and yet, because I am the *better* of the two, I pardon you my hurt" (Urtext version). The statement "you have injured me," along with "I am the better of the two," renders the "I pardon you" insincere.

> 3. To witness sin and yet forgive it is a paradox that reason cannot see. For it maintains what has been done to you <u>deserves</u> no pardon. And by <u>giving</u> it, you grant your brother mercy but retain the proof he is not <u>really</u> innocent. The sick remain accusers. They cannot forgive their brothers <u>and</u> themselves as well. For no one in whom true forgiveness rests <u>can</u> suffer. He holds not the proof of sin before his brother's eyes. And thus he <u>must</u> have overlooked it and removed it from his own [eyes]. Forgiveness <u>cannot</u> be for one and not the other. Who forgives <u>is</u> healed. And in his healing lies the <u>proof</u> that he has truly pardoned, and retains no trace of condemnation that he still would hold against himself or any living thing.

I must admit that I struggle with the message in this section. It seems unfair to say, "You can't really forgive unless you are healed of your illness." This paragraph, however, helps me. What I get from it (combined with the previous paragraph) is this: Forgiveness means letting go of the belief that my brother really sinned. This in turn means accepting that his "sin" was absolutely powerless, and so unable to have effects. If I fully accept that, then the effects it *seemed* to have (i.e., my injury) will disappear.

The example that comes to mind, of course, is Jesus. The effects that his body carried were pretty extreme—it was dead. Yet a couple of days later, it was resurrected. Besides whatever else the resurrection was,

14

then, it was a statement of forgiveness toward his attackers.

What this also says to me is that real, full, total forgiveness only takes place at the level that Jesus was at. The forgiveness we practice now is valuable, but it falls far short of the real thing.

> 4. Forgiveness is not real <u>unless</u> it brings a healing to your brother <u>and</u> yourself. <u>You</u> must attest his sins have no effect on <u>you</u> to demonstrate they are not real. How else <u>could</u> he be guiltless? And how <u>could</u> his innocence be justified <u>unless</u> his sins have no effect to <u>warrant</u> guilt? Sins are beyond forgiveness just <u>because</u> they would entail effects that <u>cannot</u> be undone and overlooked entirely. In their <u>undoing</u> lies the proof that they are merely errors. <u>Let</u> yourself be healed that you may be forgiving, offering salvation to your brother <u>and</u> yourself.

Perhaps we should broaden this message. To really forgive means to demonstrate that our brother didn't hurt us, and this means letting any form of hurt that seemed to result from his attack be healed. If he hurt my feelings, I let that be healed. If he hurt my bank account, I let that be healed. If he hurt my reputation, I let that be healed. If he hurt my body, I let that be healed. I don't want to get caught in the contradiction of being forgiving while hanging onto the proof of his guilt. For his sake and mine, I want to show him that his attack had no effect on me.

Application: Think of someone whom you think has hurt you. Try to get in touch with your desire to show this person the hurt he or she caused you. Then realize that this is unforgiveness, and say:

> *I cannot be hurt, and do not want to show my brother anything except my wholeness (based on T-5.IV.4:4).*

> 5. A broken body shows the mind has <u>not</u> been healed. A miracle of healing proves that separation is <u>without</u> effect. What you would prove to him you will believe. The power of witness <u>comes</u> from your belief. And everything you say or do or think but testifies to what you teach to him. Your body can be means to teach that it has never suffered pain because of him. And in its healing can it offer him mute testimony of his innocence. It is <u>this</u> testimony that can speak with power greater than a thousand tongues. For here is his forgiveness <u>proved</u> to him.

Application: Again think of an infirmity of yours that you hold someone else (at least partly) responsible for. Then say,

In its sickness my body has shown my brother that he has injured me and does not deserve forgiveness.
But in its healing my body can offer him mute testimony of his innocence.
It is this testimony that can speak with power greater than a thousand tongues.
*For here is his forgiveness **proved** to him.*

6. A miracle can offer nothing <u>less</u> to him than it has given unto you. So does your healing show your mind is healed, and has forgiven what he did <u>not</u> do. And so is <u>he</u> convinced his innocence was never lost, and healed along with you. Thus does the miracle undo all things the world attests can never <u>be</u> undone. And hopelessness and death <u>must</u> disappear before the ancient clarion call of life. This call has power <u>far</u> beyond the weak and miserable cry of death and guilt. The ancient calling of the Father to His Son, and of the Son unto his own [his brothers], will yet be the last trumpet that the world will ever hear. Brother, there is no death. And this you learn when you but wish to show your brother that you had no hurt of him. He thinks your blood is on his hands, and so he stands condemned. Yet it is given you to <u>show</u> him, by your healing, that his guilt is but the fabric of a senseless dream.

The miracle of forgiveness, then, frees both of you. By affirming the powerlessness of your brother's sin, it frees you from the effects of that sin. Then it shows him proof that he didn't really do anything, and so frees him from guilt. Jesus then says, in a line of great power, "Thus does the miracle undo all things the world attests can never *be* undone" (Urtext version). We do such brutal things to each other in this world. Some of them seem as if they can never, ever be undone. Wouldn't it be wonderful if a miracle could come along and undo all the hurt on both sides? This power of life to replace death will be the last thing this world sees. Reminiscent of St. Paul's passage about the overcoming of death at the last trumpet (I Cor 15:52-55), Jesus says that "the last trumpet the world will ever hear" will be "the ancient clarion call of life."

7. How just are miracles! For they bestow an equal gift of full deliverance from guilt upon your brother <u>and</u> yourself. <u>Your</u> healing saves <u>him</u> pain as well as you, and <u>you</u> are healed <u>because</u> you wished him well. This is the law the miracle obeys; that healing sees no specialness at all. It does <u>not</u> come from pity but from love. And love would prove <u>all</u> suffering is but a vain imagining, a foolish wish with <u>no</u> effects. Your health is a result of your desire to see your brother with no blood upon his hands, nor guilt upon his heart made heavy with the proof of sin. And what you wish is <u>given</u> you to see.

The practical import of this section, in my eyes, is that we need to *want* to show our brother that his attack had no effect—not to prove how tough we are, but to prove how innocent he is. Can we answer this challenge? Can we actually desire to show our brother that his attack had no consequences?

Application: Again think of someone you believe has hurt you, and say,

> *My health is a result of my desire to see [name] with no blood upon his/her hands, nor guilt upon his/her heart made heavy with the proof of sin.*
> *[Name], I wish you well. I wish you freedom from guilt.*

If we can say this and really mean it, we invite the miracle. And when the miracle walks onto the scene, it doesn't pick and choose who is worthy of it. It heals both us and our brother, without discrimination. For it is just, and justice is completely impartial.

8. The "cost" of your serenity is his. This is the "price" the Holy Spirit and the world interpret differently. The world perceives it as a statement of the "fact" that your salvation <u>sacrifices</u> his. The Holy Spirit knows <u>your</u> healing is the witness <u>unto</u> his, and <u>cannot</u> be apart from his at all. As long as he consents to suffer, <u>you</u> will be unhealed. Yet you can show [Ur: to] him that ["that" was added by the editors to make the meter work; they had apparently forgotten that the original Urtext had "to" before "him"] his suffering is purposeless and wholly without cause. Show him <u>your</u> healing, and he will consent no more

17

to suffer. For his innocence <u>has been</u> established in your sight <u>and</u> his. And laughter will <u>replace</u> your sighs, <u>because</u> God's Son remembered that he *is* God's Son.

If you were to say, "The cost of my serenity is my brother's," what would you mean by that? From the world's perspective, you would mean that your serenity costs your brother his, that if you have serenity, he can't have it. From the Holy Spirit's perspective, you would mean that his serenity is what purchases yours, that unless he is serene, you can't be.

That message—unless he is serene, you can't be—sounds like a statement of doom. It sounds like you're doomed until he is healed. But that is not so, for you can heal him, by showing him you weren't hurt. "Show him your healing, and he will consent no more to suffer." Then you will be laughing instead of heavily sighing, because both of you remembered that you are God's Son.

> 9. Who, then, fears healing? Only those to whom their brother's sacrifice and pain are seen to represent their own serenity. Their helplessness and weakness represent the ["the" was added by the editors to make the meter work] grounds on which they justify his pain. The constant sting of guilt he suffers serves to prove that he is slave, but they are free. The constant pain <u>they</u> suffer demonstrates that they are free *because* they hold him bound. And sickness is desired to prevent a shift of balance in the sacrifice. How could the Holy Spirit be deterred an instant, even less, to reason with an argument for sickness such as this? And need <u>your</u> healing be delayed because you pause to listen to insanity?

Now we return to the opening question of the section: "Is healing frightening?" Only now it has changed to "Who fears healing?" The answer is: Those who interpreted the statement in the previous paragraph ("The 'cost' of your serenity is his") in the world's way—those who think that *their* serenity costs their brother *his*. They think that if they can make him suffer guilt, they have serenity, they are free. Of course, the way they make him suffer guilt is by retaining the injury that he (supposedly) caused them. Even though this is obviously a sacrifice on their part, they consider it worth it, because it causes him to sacrifice even more. This is why they fear healing, because it would remove the proof of his guilt, and thereby lift his guilt, and thus take away their serenity. Now the balance of sacrifice has shifted—their brother is completely off the hook and they are doing all the sacrificing.

It all seems to make a certain twisted sense. But let's face it—this is crazy. Why should we punish ourselves just so we can punish someone else? And even if we have been doing just that, why should we delay our healing an instant longer?

Application: Ask yourself, "Is there some way in which I have been punishing myself just so that I can show someone else the proof that he or she has sinned against me?" If so, say to yourself,

> *This is insanity.*
> *Yet does my healing need to be delayed an instant because I*
>   *paused to listen to insanity?*

What follows is the second half of "The Fear of Healing," yet it is really its own new section. What happened was that the first three paragraphs of this new discussion (10-12) inadvertently dropped out in process of the Course being retyped. This left the final four paragraphs. These were a bit short to be labeled their own section, and by depriving them of the context of the three missing paragraphs, they were rendered utterly opaque. At that point I assume that the most natural thing to do was to just treat them as the final confusing paragraphs of "The Fear of Healing," even though the whole theme of the fear of healing has disappeared in them, and has been replaced by a whole new set of themes.

10. Correction is <u>not</u> your function. It belongs to One Who knows of fairness, <u>not</u> of guilt. If you assume correction's role, you <u>lose</u> the function of forgiveness. No one can forgive until he learns correction is <u>but</u> to forgive, and <u>never</u> to accuse. Alone, you <u>cannot</u> see they are the same, and therefore is correction <u>not</u> of you. Identity and function are the same, and <u>by</u> your function do you know yourself. And thus, if you confuse your function with the function of Another, you <u>must</u> be confused about yourself and who you are. What is the separation but a wish to take God's function from Him and <u>deny</u> that it is His? Yet if it is <u>not</u> His it is not <u>yours</u>, for <u>you</u> must lose what you would take away.

We are faced on a daily basis with the errors of others—which really means the *attacks* of others—and we tend to see two possible responses to these errors: "correct the attackers" or "forgive the attackers." These two seem like total opposites. To correct the attacker, in our mind, means to let him know how awful his deeds have been, so that his guilt will provoke him to change. To forgive the attacker obviously seems like the opposite end of the spectrum from this.

From the Holy Spirit's perspective, however, things look entirely different. He knows that, on some level, this person is already aware that he has attacked, and is already punishing himself with guilt. The Holy Spirit therefore sees only *one* response: to correct this person's error of thought by letting him know that he is forgiven, because his attack had no effect.

We don't know this, not really. Only the Holy Spirit does. Therefore, we need to take forgiveness as our function for now, and leave correction to the Holy Spirit. If we try to take His role of correction, then we are trying to play God. We are trying to usurp the functions of God, which, after all, is the essence of the separation.

> 11. In a split mind, identity <u>must</u> seem to be divided. Nor can anyone perceive a function unified which has conflicting purposes and different ends. Correction, to a mind so split, <u>must</u> be a way to punish sins you think are <u>yours</u> in someone else. And thus does he become your victim, <u>not</u> your brother, <u>different</u> from you in that he is <u>more</u> guilty, thus in need of your correction, as the one <u>more innocent</u> than he. This splits <u>his</u> function off from yours, and gives you both a <u>different</u> role. And so you <u>cannot</u> be perceived as one, and with a single function that would <u>mean</u> a shared identity with but <u>one</u> end.
> 12. Correction *you* would do <u>must</u> separate, because that is the function given it *by* you.

The notions of identity, function, and goal/end/purpose are all bundled together. Therefore, once you perceive your *identity* being split off from your brother's, then you will also see your *function* and your *goal* as different from your brother's as well.

This leads to a very familiar perspective: While my identity is pretty innocent, my brother's is far more guilty. Therefore, my function is to correct him (i.e., rub his nose in his sins), while his function is to take his forty lashes, repent, and then change. Finally, given our fundamental differences, it is hard to believe that we will end up in the same place, that we are heading toward the same end.

This scenario should already be suspect, but it gets worse. For remember, this brother is a split-off part of our own Identity, which makes him a convenient dumping ground for split-off parts of our own ego. Thus, the sinfulness we see in him and want to correct (i.e., punish) is really our own.

> When you perceive correction is the <u>same</u> as pardon, then you also know the Holy Spirit's Mind and yours are one. And so your <u>own</u> Identity is found. Yet must He work with what is <u>given</u> Him, and you allow Him only <u>half</u> your mind. And thus He represents the <u>other</u> half, and seems to have a <u>different</u> purpose from the one you cherish, and you <u>think</u> is yours. Thus does your function seem <u>divided</u>, with a half <u>in opposition</u> to a half. And these two halves appear to represent a split within a self perceived as two.

Ultimately, our function is the same as the Holy Spirit's: to give the Atonement, which is described both as correction and as forgiveness. And when we realize that correction and forgiveness are one, we will also realize that our mind and the Holy Spirit's Mind are one. Then we will finally be in touch with our whole Identity.

Right now, though, we identify with only half of our mind. (Is this Jesus' way of saying that we have only half a brain?) The phrase "other half" seems to refer to *both* the Holy Spirit *and* our brother. In other words, the Holy Spirit "represents the other half" both in the sense of "*stands for* the other half" and in the sense of "*speaks on behalf of* the other half." Seeing the other half as both the Holy Spirit and our brother makes a certain amount of sense, for isn't the Holy Spirit always stumping for our brother? Isn't He always saying, "Love your brother. Look out for your brother"? And isn't this why we feel split off from Him? Because He constantly chirps "love your brother" while we know that, to get by in this world, we need to knock some heads.

> 13. Consider how this self-perception <u>must</u> extend, and do not overlook the fact that <u>every</u> thought extends because that is its purpose, being what it really <u>is</u>. From an idea of self <u>as two</u>, there comes a <u>necessary</u> view of function split <u>between</u> the two. And what you would correct

is only <u>half</u> the error, which you think is <u>all</u> of it. Your <u>brother's</u> sins become the central target for correction, lest your errors and his own be seen as one. <u>Yours</u> are mistakes, but <u>his</u> are sins and <u>not</u> the same as yours. <u>His</u> merit punishment, while yours, in fairness, should be overlooked.

If we think we are split in two, then we will (as noted above) see a different function for each half. We become the corrector, the punisher, while our brother becomes the corrected, the punished. We treat our errors as innocent mistakes that should be overlooked, while we treat our brother's errors as sins that should be punished. All of this is a desperate attempt to mask the fact that, since the two of us are one, our errors are, in essence, exactly the same.

14. In <u>this</u> interpretation of correction, your own mistakes you will not even <u>see</u>. The <u>focus</u> of correction has been placed <u>outside</u> yourself, on one who <u>cannot</u> be a part of you while this perception lasts. What is condemned can never be returned to its accuser, who had hated it, <u>and hates it still</u> as symbol of his fear ["as symbol of his fear" is not in the Urtext]. This is your brother, focus of your hate, unworthy to be part of you and thus <u>outside</u> yourself; the other half, which is denied. And only what is left <u>without</u> his presence is perceived as <u>all</u> of you. To this remaining half the Holy Spirit must represent the <u>other</u> half until you recognize it *is* the other half. And this He does by giving you and him [Ur: *both* of you] a function that is one, <u>not</u> different.

This whole thing is a ploy designed to keep two things outside of us: our sins and our brother. As long as we attack his mistakes, onto which we have projected our own sense of sinfulness, our mistakes are off the table. They are not part of the conversation. They don't need addressing and they certainly don't need healing. And as long as he is so infected with sin, then he must be outside of us. He can't be part of us. The Holy Spirit's job in this situation is to "represent the other half," until we realize that it *is* our other half.

Application: Think of someone you are in conflict with. Note how the two of you seem to have different identities, one innocent and one guilty. Note also how you have different functions—you are meant to deliver correction and she is meant to accept correction. Finally, note that the issue here is her errors. Yours are mistakes, but hers are sins and not the same as yours. Hers merit punishment, while yours, in fairness, should be overlooked. Now say silently to this person,

> *My errors are the same as yours; only the forms are different.*
> *My function is the same as yours.*
> *My identity is the same as yours; both of us are equally holy.*
> *I forgive you, that I may accept that you are my other half, the*
>   *part that I have denied.*

15. Correction <u>is</u> the function given both, but neither one alone. And when it is fulfilled as <u>shared,</u> it <u>must</u> correct mistakes in you and him [Ur: both of you]. It <u>cannot</u> leave mistakes in one unhealed and set [Ur: make] the other free. <u>That</u> is <u>divided</u> purpose, which can not <u>be</u> shared, and so it cannot be the goal in which the Holy Spirit sees His Own [Ur: *cannot* be the function which the Holy Spirit sees as His]. And you can rest assured that He will <u>not</u> fulfill a function that He does not see [Ur: that He cannot understand,] and recognize as His. For only thus can He keep <u>yours</u> preserved intact, <u>despite</u> Your [Ur: your] separate views of what your function <u>is</u>. If He <u>upheld</u> divided function, you were lost indeed. His <u>inability</u> to see His goal divided and distinct for you and him [Ur: for each of you], preserves yourself from the awareness of a function not your own [Ur: preserves your Self from being made aware of any function *other* than Its Own]. And thus is healing given you and him [Ur: *both* of you].

Because one mind by itself—being only half a mind—can't understand the real nature of correction, the Holy Spirit gives that function to two minds, to carry out together. For only together do they represent a whole mind. This shared function leads to the correction of mistakes in both minds, not just one. To correct just one mind, while leaving the other's mistakes intact, would be divided purpose. If the Holy Spirit supported such a division, He would be supporting separation. There is even a suggestion (in the Urtext version) that He would be splitting up your very Self and dividing It into different functions.

Yet what does it mean for two people to carry out the function of correction together? This is difficult to understand. It reminds me of these lines from an earlier section:

For no one alone can judge the ego truly. Yet when two or more join together in searching for truth, the ego can no longer defend its lack of content. (T-14.X.9:5-6)

How, then, do we actually uncover the ego's lack of content together? How do we actually correct mistakes in both of us together? We will get our best clue in the final line of the section.

16. Correction <u>must</u> be left to One Who knows correction and forgiveness <u>are</u> the same. With <u>half</u> a mind this is <u>not</u> understood. Leave, then, correction to the Mind that <u>is</u> united, functioning as one <u>because</u> it is not split in purpose, and conceives a single function as its <u>only</u> one. Here is the function <u>given</u> it conceived to be its own, and <u>not</u> apart from that its Giver [the Holy Spirit?] keeps *because* it has been shared. In His [the Giver's, the Holy Spirit's] <u>acceptance</u> of this function lies the means whereby your mind is unified. His <u>single</u> purpose unifies the halves of you [you and your brother] that you perceive as separate. And each forgives the other, that he may accept his <u>other</u> half as <u>part</u> of him.

This whole section has been hard to understand, and this paragraph is no exception. To really make sense of this paragraph, I believe that we need to interpret "the Mind that is united," as being both the Holy Spirit and our mind and our brother's united as one. The reason is that this "Mind that is united" is identified with the Holy Spirit (we are told to leave correction to this Mind and to the Holy Spirit) and yet this Mind has also been given a function by Someone Else, by a "Giver," Who appears to be the Holy Spirit.

So here is my best guess at what this paragraph means: Only a whole mind, a mind not split into "me" and "my brother," can understand that correction and forgiveness are the same. Only a whole mind can refrain from splitting up correction and forgiveness into two different things. This Mind is the Holy Spirit, but it is also your mind and your brother's mind joined as one. The Holy Spirit's unified Mind unifies your two minds. He inspires each one of you to forgive the other. And when both of you do this, when each forgives the other, correction moves through you as one, and corrects you both in a way that neither one of you could accomplish on your own.

III. Beyond All Symbols
Commentary by Robert Perry

1. Power can<u>not</u> oppose. For opposition would <u>weaken</u> it, and weakened power is a contradiction in ideas. Weak strength is meaningless, and power used to weaken is <u>employed</u> to limit. And therefore it <u>must</u> be limited and weak, because that is its purpose. Power is <u>un</u>opposed, to be itself. No weakness <u>can</u> intrude on it without changing it into [Ur: changing what it *is*, to] something it is not. To weaken <u>is</u> to limit, and impose an opposite that <u>contradicts</u> the concept that it attacks. And <u>by</u> this does it <u>join</u> to the idea a something it is not, and make it unintelligible. Who can understand a double concept, such as "weakened-power" or "hateful-love"?

This is simply a masterful bit of philosophical reasoning on Jesus' part. It reflects a train of thought that runs throughout the Course—that the existence of opposites is a logical contradiction and therefore an impossibility. I see two arguments in this paragraph:

If a power is opposed by another power, it is not infinitely powerful.
If it is not infinitely powerful, it contains weakness.
Yet a weakened-power is a contradiction in terms.
Therefore, it cannot exist.

When a power opposes another power, its purpose is to weaken that other power.
A thing's *purpose* is an extension of its *nature*.
Therefore, a power whose *purpose* is to weaken must have a *nature* that is weakened.
Yet a weakened-power is a contradiction in terms.
Therefore, it cannot exist.

A weakened-power is like a square circle—a contradiction that cannot exist. Would you ever expect to actually *find* a square circle, even if you searched the entire world; indeed, the entire universe? No, square circles are logically impossible. They cannot exist. Jesus is saying the same thing about weakened-powers, or hateful-love. They cannot exist.

Yet everything in this world is a mixture of opposites. All powers in this world are opposed. All love is mixed with not-love. Jesus' argument, therefore, leads directly to the conclusion that this world, in its entirety, is a logical impossibility.

> 2. You have decided that your brother is a symbol for a "hateful-love," a "weakened-power," and above all, a "living-death." And so he has no meaning to you, for he stands for what is meaningless. He represents a double thought, where half is cancelled out by the remaining half. Yet even this is quickly contradicted by the half it cancelled out, and so they both are gone. And now he stands for nothing. Symbols which but represent ideas that cannot be must stand for empty space and nothingness. Yet nothingness and empty space can not be interference. What can interfere with the awareness of reality is the belief that there is something there.

As usual, Jesus takes his lofty idea and brings it right down to practicalities. Think of someone you know. You see her as a power that opposes and is opposed by other powers, right? You see her as a symbol of weakened-power. That means you think she stands for a contradiction. You see this person as loving at times, but also unloving and even hateful at times, right? You see her as a symbol of hateful-love. In your eyes, then, she stands for a contradiction. Finally, you see this person as possessing life, but also being affected by life's opposite, which causes her to get sick, to age, and ultimately to die. You see her as a symbol for a living-death. Again, in your eyes, she stands for a contradiction. This is not surprising. We often talk about other people as a bundle of contradictions.

But contradictions cannot be real. Square circles cannot exist. The picture you see of her stands for empty space. It's like a photo of the twin towers of the World Trade Center. It's a picture of something that is not there. Yet this picture can only interfere with the awareness of her reality if you think that it stands for something that really *is* there.

The next paragraph just draws out the implications of this. Please choose someone (maybe the same person you have been thinking about) and read paragraph 3 slowly, applying everything you read to your picture of this person and inserting his or her name where indicated.

3. The picture of your brother [name] that you see means nothing. There is nothing to attack or to deny; to love or hate, or to endow with power or to see as weak. The picture has been wholly cancelled out, because it symbolized a contradiction that cancelled out the <u>thought</u> it represents. And thus the picture has no cause at all [no reality that supports it]. Who can perceive effect [the picture] <u>without</u> a cause [the reality it pictures]? What can the causeless [the picture] <u>be</u> but nothingness? The picture of your brother [name] that you see is wholly absent and has never been. Let, then, the empty space it occupies be <u>recognized</u> as vacant, and the time devoted to its seeing be perceived as idly spent, a time unoccupied.

4. An empty space that is <u>not</u> seen as filled, an unused interval of time <u>not</u> seen as spent and fully occupied, become a silent invitation to the truth to enter, and to make itself at home. No preparation <u>can</u> be made that would enhance the invitation's real appeal. For what you leave as vacant <u>God</u> will fill, and where <u>He</u> is there <u>must</u> the truth abide. Unweakened power, with <u>no</u> opposite, is what creation <u>is</u>. For this there are <u>no</u> symbols. Nothing points <u>beyond</u> the truth, for what can stand for <u>more</u> than everything? Yet true undoing must be kind. And so the first replacement for your picture is <u>another</u> picture of <u>another</u> kind.

We may fear the full acknowledgment of how meaningless and vacuous our picture of our brother is. We may fear the empty space this leaves. Yet we should welcome it. For this empty space becomes a silent invitation for God to enter our minds. It becomes the most sincere invitation to Him that we could ever make. If we truly leave this space blank, the truth will rush into our mind. And we will know the reality of unweakened power, power that is utterly unopposed and unconstrained.

However, there are no symbols that can truly capture this formless truth. "And so the first replacement for your picture is another picture of another kind."

5. As nothingness cannot <u>be</u> pictured, so there <u>is</u> no symbol for totality. Reality is ultimately known <u>without</u> a form, unpictured and unseen. Forgiveness is not yet a power known as wholly free of limits. Yet it sets no limits <u>you</u> have chosen to impose. Forgiveness is the means by which the truth is represented <u>temporarily</u>. It lets the Holy Spirit make <u>exchange</u> of pictures possible, until the time when aids are meaningless and learning done. No learning aid has use that can extend <u>beyond</u> the goal of learning. When its aim <u>has been</u> accomplished it is functionless.

Yet in the learning interval it <u>has</u> a use that now you fear, but yet will love.

You can't have an accurate picture of nothingness, can you? What would that picture be? Yet you also can't have an accurate picture of totality (understood as formless infinity). What would that picture look like? Thus, we cannot really symbolize the truth. Yet we need symbols. We need pictures, at least for now. We need them until we pass beyond the world of form into the formless, into direct knowing, without pictures or symbols.

Forgiveness is what gives us the best, truest picture that we can have of our brother while we are still in this world. It is still just a finger-painting—it is not our brother as he really is—but it is painted by the finger of the Holy Spirit. Forgiveness can give us this picture because, even though it is not the unlimited power of Heaven, "it sets no limits *you* have chosen to impose" (Urtext version), and so it leaves the door open to the unlimited power of Heaven.

> 6. The picture of your brother <u>given</u> you to occupy the space so lately left unoccupied and vacant will not need defense of <u>any</u> kind. For you will give it <u>overwhelming</u> preference. Nor delay an instant in deciding that it is the <u>only</u> one you want. It does <u>not</u> stand for double concepts. Though it is but <u>half</u> the picture and <u>is</u> incomplete, <u>within</u> itself it is the same. The other half of what it represents remains unknown, but is <u>not</u> cancelled out. And thus is God left free to take the final step Himself. For this you need <u>no</u> pictures and <u>no</u> learning aids. And what will ultimately take the place of <u>every</u> learning aid will merely *be*.

First, we empty our mind of our current picture of our brother, realizing it stands for nothing. This emptying is forgiveness, for our picture is essentially that of a sinner. Then, into this empty space, the Holy Spirit places a new picture. It is a picture that is not composed of conflicting elements. "Within itself it is the same." We will find this new picture overwhelmingly preferable to the old one.

True, this picture is limited, as all pictures are. No picture can be blown up to infinity, and so no picture can capture the infinity of what our brother is. Therefore, this picture is not the *whole* picture. But it does not oppose what lies outside of it. And so it does not close the door on infinity, as the old picture did. Thus, it leaves God free to take His final step.

7. Forgiveness vanishes and symbols fade, and nothing that the eyes have ever seen or ears have heard remains to be perceived. A Power wholly limitless has come, not to destroy, but to receive Its Own. There is no choice of function anywhere. The choice you fear to lose you never had. Yet only this appears to interfere with power unlimited and single thoughts, complete and happy, without opposite. You do not know the peace of power that opposes nothing. Yet no other kind can be at all. Give welcome to the Power beyond forgiveness, and beyond the world of symbols and of limitations. He would merely be, and so He merely is.

When God takes His final step, "Forgiveness vanishes and symbols fade, and nothing that the eyes have ever seen or ears have heard remains to be perceived." This is a reference to a line from I Corinthians: "Eye hath not seen, nor ear heard, neither have entered into the heart of man, the things which God hath prepared for them that love him" (I Cor 2:9). In other words, when God takes the final step, we at last discover the things that He has prepared for us, the things that cannot be perceived, only known. A Power comes to us that opposes nothing and is opposed by nothing, that merely *is*. And thus It comes bringing perfect peace. How insane it was for us to fight this peace because we were attached to using our "power" to oppose. Now, abiding in this Power, we realize we never had a choice about what our function is. Our function could never be opposition; it could only be extension. We finally realize that, like this Power, we ourselves merely *are*.

Application: Choose someone and apply the following series of thoughts to that person:

Realize that a contradiction cannot be true.
Just like a square circle cannot exist, it is impossible that a weakened-power or a living-death or a hateful-love can exist.

Realize that your picture of your brother is just such a contradiction.
Do you see both strength and weakness in this person? If so, then that is a contradiction and makes no sense.
Do you see both hate and love in this person? If so, that is a contradiction and is unintelligible.

29

Do you see both life and death in this person? If so, that is a contradiction and cannot be true.

Realize that your picture of your brother, being a contradiction, must stand for nothing.
It does not stand for who this person really is.
See the space it occupies in your mind as being vacant.
See the time devoted to seeing it "as idly spent, a time unoccupied."

"An empty space that is not seen as filled, an unused interval of time not seen as spent and fully occupied, become a silent invitation to the truth to enter, and to make itself at home."
Into this space, let a new picture of this person come into your mind.
Let the Holy Spirit place in you a new picture.
You may want to ask Him, "Show me this person in a form that reflects his or her reality."
It will still be a picture, so let it have form and color.
But let this picture not be a bundle of contradictions.
Instead, let it reflect only one idea—only life, only love, only power.

This picture does not depict this person's reality, which cannot be pictured.
But it does not cancel out his or her reality, either. It does not oppose it.
And so it makes way for God's final step, where God will reveal to you at last who this person really is.

IV. The Quiet Answer
Commentary by Robert Perry

1. In quietness are all things answered, and is every problem quietly resolved. In conflict there can be no answer and no resolution, for its purpose is to make no resolution possible, and to ensure no answer will be plain. A problem set in conflict has no answer, for it is seen in different ways. And what would be an answer from one point of view is not an answer in another light. You are in conflict. Thus it must be clear you cannot answer anything at all, for conflict has no limited effects. Yet if God gave an answer there must be a way in which your problems are resolved, for what He wills already has been done.

We all know what it's like to solve problems when those problems involve conflicts between two parties. No answer will satisfy everyone. And the more your "solution" satisfies one party, the more it will dissatisfy the other.

We are quite familiar with this kind of situation, but little do we know that this very kind of situation exists within us. We are in conflict on the inside. And so, no matter what solution we come up with, it will not be experienced as a solution by all of our mind. Further, since our conflict cannot be limited, it infects everything we encounter, making no solution, in any area of life, truly and fully acceptable to us.

2. Thus it <u>must</u> be that time is not involved and every problem can be answered *now*. Yet it must also be that, in your state of mind, solution is impossible. Therefore, God must have given you a way of reaching to <u>another</u> state of mind in which the answer is <u>already there</u>. Such is the holy instant. It is here that <u>all</u> your problems should be brought and <u>left</u>. Here they <u>belong</u>, for here <u>their</u> answer is. And where its answer is, a problem <u>must</u> be simple and be easily resolved. It <u>must</u> be pointless to attempt to solve a problem where the answer cannot be. Yet just as surely it <u>must</u> be resolved, if it is brought to where the answer <u>is</u>.

If our conflict-ridden mind makes solution impossible, the answer must be for us to rise above our normal state of mind into another state, a state that transcends conflict, that is quiet, the state of the holy instant. In this state lies God's Will that this problem be solved. And since God's Will takes no time, in this state the problem is already solved. By taking our problem to the holy instant, then, we bring the problem to its answer. And we connect with that answer, so that even if the solution unfolds over time on the outside, that solution is already fully realized within us. For us, the problem is over.

> 3. Attempt to solve no problems but within the holy instant's surety. For there the problem *will* be answered and resolved. Outside there will be no solution, for there is no answer there that could be found. Nowhere outside [of the holy instant] a single, simple question is ever asked. The world can only ask a double question. One with many answers can have no answers. None of them will do. It does not ask a question to be answered, but only to restate its point of view.

We need to start thinking of problem solving as reaching that place of quiet, that place above the battleground, reaching the holy instant. On the battleground, each captain is asking his own question: "How can my platoon's interests be served?" What therefore greets the peacemaker is not really one question, but an amalgam of different, competing questions. And there is no solution that can successfully satisfy all of them. Only in the holy instant can a simple, unified question be asked, a question that does not assume the conflict, but is truly seeking a way out of it.

> 4. All questions asked within this world are but a way of looking, not a question asked. A question asked in hate cannot be answered, because it is an answer in itself. A double question asks and answers, both attesting the same thing in different form. The world asks but one question. It is this: "Of these illusions, which of them *is* [Ur: are] true? Which ones establish peace and offer joy? And which can bring escape from all the pain of which this world is made?" Whatever form the question takes, its purpose is the same. It asks but to establish sin is real, and answers in the form of preference. "Which sin do you prefer? That is the one that you should choose. The others are not true. What can the body get that you would want the most of all? It is your servant and also your friend. But tell it what you want, and it will serve you lovingly and well." And this is not a question, for it tells you what you want and where to go for it. It leaves no room to question its beliefs, except that what it states takes question's form.

32

I have always felt this was a masterful dissection of the world's questions. According to this, all of the world's questions are like an alcoholic asking, "Do I want scotch or bourbon?" The real question— "Should I drink at all?"—is not even asked. Instead of asking it, this question *answers* it, with an implied but clear, "Of course!" Having (incorrectly) answered the only real question, this question now aims only to choose between different options within its answer. Another example is, "Should we go to war with this country or that country?" The question "Should we go to war at all?" is not asked; the answer is simply assumed. All we are doing now is choosing among options within that assumption.

> 5. A pseudo-question has no answer. It <u>dictates</u> the answer even as it asks. Thus is all questioning within the world a form of propaganda for itself. Just as the body's witnesses are but the senses from <u>within</u> itself, so are the answers to the questions of the world contained within the questions that are asked. Where answers represent the <u>questions,</u> they add nothing new and nothing has been learned. An <u>honest</u> question is a learning tool that asks for something that you do <u>not</u> know. It does <u>not</u> set conditions for response, but merely asks what the <u>response</u> should be. But no one in a conflict state is free to <u>ask</u> this question, for he does not *want* an honest answer where the conflict <u>ends</u>.

I love that line: "Thus is all questioning within the world a form of propaganda for itself." Have you ever gotten this feeling when you look at the world? Have you ever felt like the problem is the *questions*, and not just the answers? That the questions are themselves *already* answers? Yet if you see that happening out in the world, you can be sure it is happening in your own life as well.

A real question is a powerful learning tool. It is not a pseudo-question. It is really seeking something new, something you don't already know. Our questions tend to assume that conflict is a given, that hate is justified, that sin is real, that the body can fetch for us things of value. But a real question opens the door to stepping completely outside that familiar framework, which is why we have such a hard time asking one.

> 6. Only within the holy instant can an honest question honestly be asked. And from the meaning of the <u>question</u> does the meaningfulness

33

of the answer come. Here is it possible to separate your wishes <u>from</u> the answer, so it [the answer] can be <u>given</u> you and also be <u>received</u>. The answer is provided everywhere. Yet it is only here it can be <u>heard</u>. An honest answer asks <u>no</u> sacrifice because it answers questions truly asked. The questions of the world but ask of whom is sacrifice demanded, asking <u>not</u> if sacrifice is meaningful at all. And so, <u>unless</u> the answer tells "of whom," it will remain unrecognized, unheard, and thus the <u>question</u> is preserved intact because it gave the answer to <u>itself</u>. The holy instant is the interval in which the mind is still enough to hear an answer that is <u>not</u> entailed within the question asked. It offers something new and <u>different</u> from the question. How <u>could</u> it be answered if it but repeats itself?

Only in the holy instant, when our mind is out of the conflict, can we ask an honest question, a question that asks for an answer that is new and different, rather than confirms the assumptions implicit in the question.

Outside the holy instant, the mind is caught up in conflict, both within itself and between itself and others. In that state, the mind's questions can only amount to, "In order for this to be resolved, who needs to pay?" That is why the Holy Spirit's answers often don't seem to really address the question. He never demands that anyone pay, and so His answers often tempt us to exclaim in frustration, "Answer the question!"

7. Therefore, attempt to solve <u>no</u> problems in a world from which the answer has been barred. But bring the problem to the only place that holds the answer lovingly <u>for</u> you. Here are the answers that will <u>solve</u> your problems because they stand <u>apart</u> from them, and see what <u>can</u> be answered; what the question *is* [Ur: *question* is]. Within the world the answers merely raise <u>another</u> question, though they leave the first unanswered. In the holy instant, you can bring the question <u>to</u> the answer, and receive the answer that was <u>made</u> for you.

Application: Try to think of a "normal" problem in your life, a problem with your work life, or your money, or your living situation, or your love life.

Now realize that in contemplating this problem and what its solution might be, you are in conflict within yourself. You are pulled in the direction of God and in the opposite direction, that of your ego. Realize also that you see your interests in conflict with the interests of others.

You see yourself on the battleground. And realize that even your own preferences are in conflict with each other.

Realize that no solution can satisfy all the sides of this conflict in your mind, for each side will see the solution from its own vantage point. There is no solution that will satisfy them all.

In fact, the mind does not want the conflict to end. It wants to stay in conflict. It assumes that the only answer is battle, war, hate. It therefore only wants an option *within* this answer.

And so it does not ask an honest question. It asks a question that assumes the validity of the conflict and then favors one of the options within the conflict.

The question always takes this form: "What illusion out here in the world will make me happy?" Can you see your mind asking a question like this in the context of your problem? Any question that seeks an external solution as the way to peace is a form of this question.

This question really amounts to: "Which sin do I prefer? Which one is true?"

The sin that you prefer always asks someone else to sacrifice (which is what makes it a "sin"). The question, then, amounts to: "Who will have to make a sacrifice so that I can be happy? Who needs to pay in order to balance the scales of justice and solve this problem? Can you see this element in your question? Can you see yourself contemplating solutions that will ask for sacrifice from someone else?

These questions are really questions asked in hate—they are about gaining from someone else's loss. And hate is not a question, but a point of view. These questions assume the validity of war. Another way to look at it is that these questions affirm that sin is real. That again is a statement, not a question.

Can you see how the questions that have come out of your problem are really "a form of propaganda" for the world?

This section says that the answer lies in a state of mind that is beyond the conflict, a state of mind that has reached to quietness. In this state the answer lies waiting for you. In this state your mind is quiet enough to ask an honest question, and to hear an answer that is not just a repeat of the assumptions behind the question.

This state is the holy instant. To enter this state, quiet your mind. Forget about the past, forget about the future.

Remember that this instant is the only time there is.

Try to drop all of your preconceptions about the situation.

Go through various aspects of it and realize that you don't know what they mean.

You don't know what your best interests are.

You don't know what anything in the situation is for.

Set aside all of your beliefs about what the problem really is and what the solution must be.

Now you are ready to ask an honest question, a simple question, one that asks for an answer that is truly new and different.

Ask, "How do You want me to find happiness in this situation?"

"How do You want me to give happiness in this situation?"

"How can I leave the battleground, and take everyone with me?"

V. The Healing Example
Commentary by Greg Mackie

This section is about the amazing effects that follow from the simple decision to accept a miracle for yourself. It sketches a process that could be summarized as follows:

1. The Holy Spirit offers you a miracle.
2. You accept the miracle by entering a holy instant in which you love without attack.
3. As a result of the miracle, you are healed.
4. As a result of your healing, you become a miracle worker. The miracle extends from you and heals others, both mentally and physically.
5. As a result of healing others and the gratitude they give you for their healing, your own healing is reinforced and made complete.

> 1. The only way to heal is to be healed. The miracle extends without your help, but you are needed that it can begin. Accept the miracle of healing, and it will go forth because of what it is. It is its nature to extend itself the instant it is born. And it is born the instant it is offered and received. No one can ask another to be healed. But he can let *himself* be healed, and thus offer the other what he has received. Who can bestow upon another what he does not have? And who can share what he denies himself? The Holy Spirit speaks to *you*. He does not speak to someone else. Yet by your listening His Voice extends, because you have accepted what He says.

The process begins when we accept a miracle from the Holy Spirit. This is the prerequisite for miracle working; as that famous earlier line in the Text says, "*The sole responsibility of the miracle worker is to accept the Atonement for himself*" (T-2.V.5:1). Until we accept the Atonement for ourselves we cannot give it, for who can give what he doesn't have? But once we do that—once we accept the Atonement and receive the miracle of healing for ourselves—it will naturally extend to others. As we

37

are healed, we become healers. And once we get that snowball of healing rolling down the hill, it will keep rolling and grow until it encompasses everyone and everything.

> 2. Health is the witness unto health. As long as it is unattested, it remains without conviction. Only when it has been demonstrated is it proved, and must provide a witness that compels belief [Ur: Only when *demonstrated* has it *been* proved, and *must* compel belief]. No one is healed through double messages. If you wish <u>only</u> to be healed, you heal. Your single <u>purpose</u> makes this possible. But if you are <u>afraid</u> of healing, then it cannot come through you. The <u>only</u> thing that is required for a healing is a lack of fear. The fearful are <u>not</u> healed, and cannot heal. This does <u>not</u> mean the conflict must be gone forever from your mind to heal ["to heal" was apparently added by the editors]. For if it were, there were no <u>need</u> for healing then [Ur: anymore]. But it <u>does</u> mean, if only for an instant, you love without attack. An instant is sufficient. Miracles wait not on time.

We all say we want healing, but the fact is that we're ambivalent about it. Part of us really does want healing, but the part of us that is still invested in the ego is afraid of being healed. This conflict between the desire for healing and the fear of healing ("double messages") prevents us from accepting the miracle of healing that turns us into miracle workers.

Must we, then, completely eradicate fear from our minds to work miracles? No. All that is needed is an instant of love without attack—a holy instant in which we temporarily call off the dogs and love our brothers without reservation. This reminds me of an earlier line in the Text: "It is essential, however, that the miracle worker be in his right mind, however briefly, or he will be unable to re-establish right-mindedness in someone else" (T-2.V.3:5). This brief instant of love without reservation is an instant of desiring *healing* without reservation; this singleness of purpose heals us, and thus lets the miracle flow through us to heal others.

And when we heal others, their healing serves as a witness to our own healing—it is a demonstration that proves our own healing to us. This, I believe, is what the first sentence means: The health of those we heal is the witness unto our own health.

> 3. The holy instant is the miracle's abiding place. From there, each one is born into this world as witness to a state of mind that has <u>transcended</u>

conflict, and has reached to peace. It carries comfort from the place of peace into the battleground, and <u>demonstrates</u> that war has no effects. For all the hurt that war has sought to bring, the broken bodies and the shattered limbs, the screaming dying and the silent dead, are gently lifted up and comforted.

That holy instant in which we set aside attack and love without reservation is what sets the entire miracle-working process in motion. That moment of single-minded desire for healing brings the miracle of healing to us, and from there it extends from us to everyone in the battleground of our world. (Have you noticed how many times that battleground image has come up?)

The battleground is a metaphor, of course, but I think the imagery here points to something crucial: Just as battleground medics treat actual "broken bodies and shattered limbs," we miracle working medics are meant to not only heal people mentally (though this is the ultimate source of all healing), but to actually heal physical pain and suffering. We are to tend to the wounded and even, as Jesus did, raise the dead. This demonstration "that war has no effects" is the ultimate witness to the peace of God that we have found above the battleground.

> 4. There <u>is</u> no sadness where a miracle has come to heal. And nothing more than just <u>one</u> instant of your love <u>without</u> attack is necessary that all this occur. In that <u>one</u> instant <u>you</u> are healed, and in that single instant is <u>all</u> healing done. What stands <u>apart</u> from you, when you accept the blessing that the holy instant brings? Be not afraid of blessing, for the One Who blesses you loves all the world, and leaves nothing within the world that <u>could</u> be feared. But if you <u>shrink</u> from blessing, will the world indeed seem fearful, for you have <u>withheld</u> its peace and comfort, leaving it to die.

So often in the Course, Jesus speaks of how one seemingly ordinary moment can have huge effects beyond anything we could have dreamed of. The prototype is Helen and Bill's joining in seeking a better way, a seemingly ordinary event that led to a course that has blessed countless people. Here, he says again that all we need is "just one instant of your love without attack." In everyday terms, this might look like nothing more than a brief moment when you smile and wave at the driver who just cut you off instead of cursing her. But this one tiny instant is enough to get that miracle snowball rolling down the hill. It is enough to bring about *all healing*. Is not one instant of kindness worth it, when this instant will lead to the end of all fear and the recognition of universal blessing?

> 5. Would not a world so bitterly bereft be looked on as a condemnation by the one who <u>could</u> have saved it, but stepped back because he was <u>afraid</u> of being healed? The eyes of all the dying bring reproach, and suffering whispers, "What is there to fear?" Consider well its question. It is asked of you on <u>your</u> behalf. A dying world asks only that you rest an instant from attack upon <u>yourself</u>, that it be healed.

The last paragraph said that when we are afraid of blessing, the world will look like a terrifying place because we have withheld blessing from it. This makes a lot of sense if you think about it. If we're unwilling to love without attack for just an instant, it means that we prefer to attack. And if we attack the world instead of heal it, what else *could* the world look like except a place that condemns us and punishes us for our "sin" of withholding healing from it?

That statement that "the eyes of all the dying bring reproach" is especially poignant. It sounds like another one of those extreme Course images with no counterpart in everyday life, but Robert shared with me a real-life version of it that I found tremendously moving. The following are the opening lines from an episode of the PBS show *Frontline* called "The Ghosts of Rwanda." They are the words of the commander of the United Nations Assistance Mission for Rwanda, General Romeo Dallaire:

> Rwanda will never ever leave me. It's in the pores of my body. My soul is in those hills. My spirit is with the spirits of all those people who were slaughtered and killed that I know of. And lots of those eyes still haunt me. Angry eyes or innocent eyes. No laughing eyes. But the worst eyes that haunt me are the eyes of those people who are totally bewildered. They're looking at me with my blue beret and they're saying, "What in the hell happened? How come I'm dying here?" Those eyes dominated. And they're absolutely right. How come I failed? How come my mission failed? How come as the commander I did not convince, I lost soldiers, and 800,000 people died?

Application: The eyes of Rwanda and the eyes of the suffering and dying everywhere are asking us plaintively, "What is there to fear?"—in other words, "Why fear healing?" This paragraph asks us to consider well this question, so let's do that now. Remember, though: the purpose of this is not to instill guilt in yourself, but simply to open your heart to compassion. In that spirit, repeat the following lines:

Why fear healing?
Why keep attacking myself?
Is not my heart willing to bring my weary brothers rest? (based on W-pI.191.10:8)
Why not accept the miracle of healing so I can bring that miracle of healing to everyone, including those whose dying eyes are pleading for me to rest an instant from attack upon myself, that they may be healed?

6. Come to the holy instant and be healed, for nothing that is there received is left behind on your returning to the world. And <u>being</u> blessed you will bring blessing. Life is given you to give the dying world. And suffering eyes no longer will accuse, but shine in thanks to you who blessing gave. The holy instant's radiance will light <u>your</u> eyes, and give them sight to see beyond <u>all</u> suffering and see Christ's face <u>instead</u>. Healing <u>replaces</u> suffering. Who looks on one cannot <u>perceive</u> the other, for they <u>cannot</u> both be there. And what <u>you</u> see the world will witness, and will witness <u>to</u>.

We've been seeing the same sequence repeated in different ways in this section. First, in that brief moment of love without attack, we experience a holy instant and receive a miracle of healing. Then we return to the world and bring the blessing we have received. As a result, the accusing eyes of those to whom we formerly *didn't* give healing will now shine upon us in gratitude for the healing we *did* give. The face of reproach will become the face of Christ. Those we heal will see what we see. And both the miraculous physical changes our miracles bring and the gratitude of those we have blessed will prove our own healing to us.

7. Thus is <u>your</u> healing everything the world requires, that it may be healed. It needs <u>one</u> lesson that has perfectly been learned. And then, when <u>you</u> forget it, will the world remind you gently of what you have taught. No reinforcement will its thanks withhold from you who let

yourself be healed that it might live. It will call forth its witnesses to show the face of Christ to you who brought the sight to <u>them</u>, by which <u>they</u> witnessed it. The world of accusation is replaced by one in which all eyes look lovingly upon the Friend who brought them their release. And happily your brother will perceive the many friends he thought were enemies.

Here again, we see the final step of this process: The world reinforces our healing. First, we learn the lesson of love without attack perfectly, and we are healed. This healing then extends from us to the world. Finally, when we forget the lesson (I assume that learning it "perfectly" means that we have a *temporary* perfect awareness of it, since Jesus speaks here of forgetting it), the world we healed will remind us of our own healing through its release and its gratitude for that release. We showed the face of Christ to the world; now the world shows the face of Christ to us. And as the brothers we healed look upon the Christ in us, their healing too will be reinforced. They will see the Friend Who brought them healing not only in us, but everywhere they look.

> 8. Problems are not specific but they take specific forms, and these specific shapes make up the world. And no one understands the nature of his problem. If he <u>did,</u> it would be there no more for him to see. Its very <u>nature</u> is that it is *not*. And thus, <u>while</u> he perceives it he can <u>not</u> perceive it as it is. But <u>healing</u> is apparent in specific instances, and generalizes to include them all. This is because they really <u>are</u> the same, <u>despite</u> their different forms. All learning aims at transfer, which becomes complete within two situations that are seen as one, for <u>only</u> common elements are there. Yet this can only be attained by One Who does not see the <u>differences</u> you see. The total transfer of your learning is <u>not</u> made by you. But that it <u>has</u> been made <u>in spite</u> of all the differences you see, convinces <u>you</u> that they could not be real.

Now we shift to a discussion of problems, which reminds me very much of the "transfer of training" discussion in the introduction to the Workbook (W-In.4-7). The true nature of our problems, which the Holy Spirit sees, is that they are all the same and that they are really nothing— they are all equally nothing. We, of course, don't see it this way: We see lots of different problems, and they sure don't look like nothing. So, there's a huge gap between the Holy Spirit's understanding and ours. How does He bridge it?

42

He could just tell us that our problems are all equally nothing, but we with our myriad and seemingly intractable problems would never be convinced by that. So, what He does instead is meet us where we're at: He heals the specific problems we think we see, and then *generalizes* the healing to include all problems. This is why the Workbook asks us to practice with "great specificity" (W-In.6:1). If we just do that, we'll see all of our problems disappear, because "if true perception has been achieved in connection with any person, situation or event, total transfer to everyone and everything is certain" (W-In.5:2). This amazing transfer convinces us as nothing else could that our problems are all equally nothing—they *must* be if they are all solved.

> 9. Your healing <u>will</u> extend, and <u>will</u> be brought to problems that you thought were <u>not</u> your own. And it will <u>also</u> be apparent that your many <u>different</u> problems will be solved as any <u>one</u> of them has been escaped. It <u>cannot</u> be their differences which made this possible, for learning does not jump from situations to their opposites and bring the <u>same</u> results [Ur: effects]. All healing <u>must</u> proceed in lawful manner, in accord with laws that have been properly perceived but <u>never</u> violated. Fear you not the way that <u>you</u> perceive them. You <u>are</u> wrong, but there is One within you Who is <u>right</u>.

Now Jesus applies the previous paragraph's discussion to healing. We experience a healing—escape from some specific problem we've been dealing with. Then, in accord with the law of generalization, the Holy Spirit extends our healing to encompass all problems—not just what we regard as "our" problems, but other people's problems as well. And as we see all of those supposedly different problems vanish one by one, it dawns on us that if they all disappear as a result of the healing of one specific problem, they must be all the same and equally insubstantial.

> 10. Leave, then, the transfer of your learning to the One Who <u>really</u> understands its laws, and Who will <u>guarantee</u> that they remain unviolated and unlimited. Your part is merely to apply what He has taught you <u>to yourself</u>, and He will do the rest. And it is thus the power of your learning will be <u>proved</u> to you by all the many <u>different</u> witnesses it finds. Your brother <u>first</u> among them will be seen, but thousands stand behind him, and beyond each one of them there are a thousand more. Each one may <u>seem</u> to have a problem that is <u>different</u>

from the rest. Yet they are solved <u>together</u>. And their common answer shows the <u>questions</u> could not have been separate.

What an amazing paragraph! If we will just let the Holy Spirit heal us, He will take care of transferring that healing to everyone and everything. Just imagine what that would look like! As we see this transfer taking place—not only to the brother standing in front of us but to thousands of brothers all over the world—we will be fully convinced of the healing that has taken place within us. How could we *not* be convinced with effects like these? What more evidence could we need that all problems are truly the same, vaporous illusions that fade before the infinite power of the miracle like mists in the sun?

> 11. Peace be to you to whom is healing offered. And you will learn that peace is given you when you accept the healing for yourself. Its <u>total</u> value need not be appraised by <u>you</u> to let you understand that you have benefited from it. What occurred within the instant that love entered in <u>without</u> attack will stay with you forever. <u>Your</u> healing will be <u>one</u> of its effects, as will your brother's. Everywhere you go, will you behold its multiplied effects. Yet all the witnesses that you behold will be <u>far</u> less than all there really <u>are</u>. Infinity cannot be understood by merely counting up its separate parts. God thanks you for your healing, for He knows it is a gift of love unto His Son, and therefore is it given unto Him.

These last couple of paragraphs remind me again of Helen and Bill. They accepted the healing of a single specific problem: the conflict in their department that led them to seek a better way. Yet through the Course, the solution to that single problem reached thousands of people, far more than they could ever have been personally aware of. The Course solved and continues to solve all sorts of problems all over the world. I wonder what kind of impact the extension of the Course to so many people had on Helen and Bill. Whether they were consciously aware of it or not, that extension was a powerful witness to the healing that happened when Bill made that impassioned speech and Helen agreed to join him. And I can easily imagine how grateful God must be for the gift of love they gave when their healing led to the scribing of the Course.

Application: Think of a person you're having difficulty getting along with, one that arouses attack thoughts in you. Now, with this person in mind, go through the following visualization:

First, realize that you want healing, and for that to happen, you must—
however briefly—love this person without attack.
Say to the Holy Spirit: "Help me to love this person without attack."
Feel your anger fade away.
Feel your heart fill with love for this person, as a shaft of light comes
down from Heaven and shines upon you.
You feel that you now are healed.

Now, you see this same light shining forth from *you*.
First it touches the brother you were having trouble getting along
with, and he is healed.
Then it radiates farther, streaming out from you in all directions.
Everywhere it extends, healing happens.
Nature is restored.
Couples stop fighting.
Addicts lay down their drugs.
Armies all over the world lay down their weapons.
Suicide bombers unstrap their explosives.
The suffering find comfort.
The hungry find sustenance.
Sickness vanishes.
The dead rise up.

Now you look upon the brother you were having trouble getting along
with.
His eyes are shining on you in holy thanks.
But he is not alone.
A thousand people stand behind him,
and behind each one of them a thousand more.
All eyes are shining upon you in gratitude for the healing you brought
them.
Now you *know* you are healed.
You *must* be, if your healing could have effects like this.

Finally, you realize that your healing has extended much farther than
just to the people you can see.

In fact, it has extended everywhere.

It has reached to infinity.

Your healing has healed the entire Sonship, and thus God Himself is grateful to you for what you have done.

Hear God thank you for your healing.

He knows it is a gift of love unto His Son, and therefore is it given unto Him.

VI. The Witnesses to Sin
Commentary by Greg Mackie

1. Pain demonstrates the body must be real. It is a loud, obscuring voice whose shrieks would silence what the Holy Spirit says, and keep His words from your awareness. Pain compels attention, drawing it away from Him and focusing upon itself. Its purpose is the same as pleasure, for they both are means <u>to make the body real</u>. What shares a common purpose <u>is</u> the same. This is the law of purpose, which unites all those who share in it within itself. Pleasure and pain are <u>equally</u> unreal, because their purpose [to make the body real] <u>cannot</u> be achieved. Thus are they means for nothing, for they have a goal without a meaning. And they share the lack of meaning which their <u>purpose</u> has.

Pain's purpose is to make the body real. This is especially evident with physical pain. Think about it: When you are in pain, doesn't the body seem *incredibly* real? Doesn't it compel attention? And have you ever tried to meditate or ask for guidance while in pain? In my experience, it doesn't work too well.

At this point, we're nodding and saying, "Yeah, pain keeps me from hearing the Holy Spirit's Voice. I'd love to get rid of it." But then Jesus tells us something that's probably much less welcome: *Pleasure is the same thing.* It too compels attention. It too distracts us from hearing the Holy Spirit's Voice. It too has the purpose of making the body real, and because "what shares a common purpose is the same," pleasure and pain are really the same. What a shocking idea! Are we as eager to let go of great sex as we are to let go of our chronic backache?

We might as well let them both go, because they can't really accomplish the goal we've given them. In the end, both are unreal because the body they prop up is itself unreal. Their purpose is therefore akin to trying to make the tooth fairy real. It simply can't be done, so pain and pleasure alike are "means for nothing."

2. Sin shifts from pain to pleasure, and again to pain. For <u>either</u> witness is the same, and carries but one message: "You are here, <u>within</u> this body, and you <u>can</u> be hurt. You can have pleasure, too, but <u>only</u> at the

cost of pain." These witnesses are joined by many more. Each one <u>seems</u> different because it has a different <u>name</u>, and so it seems to answer to a different <u>sound</u>. Except for this, the witnesses of sin are all alike. Call pleasure pain, and it will hurt. Call pain a pleasure, and the pain <u>behind</u> the pleasure will be felt no more. Sin's witnesses but shift from name to name, as one steps forward and another back. Yet which is foremost makes <u>no</u> difference. Sin's witnesses hear but the call of death.

Both pain and pleasure are witnesses to sin—evidence that we are sinners. Why? Because they both affirm that we are imprisoned in bodies that are prey to pain. If this is so, what can we conclude but that we are sinners being *punished* through pain? Indeed, notice that though this paragraph talks about both pain and pleasure, what you always end up with is pain, no matter what you call it. Sin shifts from pain to pleasure to pain. Any pleasure you get is at the cost of pain. If you call pleasure pain you get pain, and if you call pain pleasure you *also* get pain, though it is hidden. And all the witnesses to sin, all the ways we try to establish the body as real, end up delivering the ultimate pain of death. If everything we do leads to death, we must be sinful creatures indeed!

Application: Bring to mind some pain you're currently experiencing. Now, repeat the following words, with the recognition that this is the message your pain is delivering:

> *"You are here, **within** this body, and you **can** be hurt. You can have pleasure, too, but **only** at the cost of pain."*

Now, bring to mind some pleasure you're currently experiencing and repeat these same words. Can you see how your pleasure is delivering the exact same message as your pain? And if this is true, can you see that both deliver the message that you are a sinner encased in a frail body, doomed to pain and death? Is this a message you *want* to hear?

3. This body, purposeless within itself, holds all your memories and all your hopes. You use its eyes to see, its ears to hear, and let it <u>tell</u> you what it is it feels. *It does not know.* It tells you but the <u>names</u> you gave to it to use, when <u>you</u> call forth the witnesses to its reality. You cannot choose <u>among</u> them which are real, for any one you choose is like the

48

rest. This name or that, but nothing more, you choose. You do not <u>make</u> a witness true because you called him by truth's <u>name</u>. The truth is found in him <u>if it is truth he represents</u>. And otherwise he lies, if you should call him by the holy Name of God Himself.

Isn't it interesting how we let the body define our reality? We define our past by the past activities of our body (documented in our photo albums and home movies), and our future by what we hope our body will experience. We use its senses to establish the parameters of our world. We let its sensations tell us how it feels: "That hurts!" "Oooo, yes, that feels good!" This thing we call pain, that thing we call pleasure, and both things are thus made real in our eyes. But things aren't made real just by giving them names; no matter how fond I may be of hobbits named Bilbo, Frodo, and Sam, they're still pure fiction. In like manner, no matter how many times I tell myself that pain and pleasure are real— even if I see them as coming from God—they are no more real than Bilbo, Frodo, and Sam.

> 4. God's Witness sees no witnesses <u>against</u> the body. Neither does He harken to the witnesses by <u>other</u> names that speak in <u>other</u> ways for its reality. He <u>knows</u> it is not real. For <u>nothing</u> could contain what you believe it holds within. Nor <u>could</u> it tell a part of God Himself what it should feel and what its function is. Yet must He love whatever <u>you</u> hold dear. And for each witness to the body's death He sends a witness to your life in Him Who knows no death. Each miracle He brings is witness that the body is <u>not</u> real. Its pains and pleasures does He heal alike, for <u>all</u> sin's witnesses do His replace.

The Holy Spirit needs no witnesses to tell him what the body is, for He *knows* it is unreal. He knows that our reality is limitless spirit, far too great to be encased within a wall of flesh. Yet though He sees the body as unreal, He does not curse it or think it evil—that would actually reinforce its apparent reality. Rather, He *loves* it simply because *we* love it. Therefore, rather than scorning it, He simply reinterprets it. He replaces each witness to sin and death with His star witness to innocence and life: the miracle.

The miracle is the most powerful witness we have of the body's unreality. Think, for instance, of Jesus healing the sick and raising the dead. Think of his resurrection. His entire earthly ministry was a witness to the unreality of the body. Are we willing to witness to the unreality of the body ourselves? Are we willing to let the Holy Spirit heal not only our pains, but our *pleasures* as well? Are we willing to let Him replace *all* of sin's witnesses?

> 5. The miracle makes <u>no</u> distinctions in the names by which sin's witnesses are called. It merely proves that what they <u>represent</u> has no effects. And this it proves <u>because</u> its own effects have come to take their place. It matters not the name by which you called your suffering. <u>It is no longer there</u>. The One Who brings the miracle perceives [Ur: perceived] them all as one, and called by name of fear. As fear is witness unto death, so is the miracle the witness unto life. It is a witness no one can deny, for it is the <u>effects</u> of life it brings. The dying live, the dead arise, and pain has vanished. Yet a miracle speaks not but for itself, but what it <u>represents</u>.

Whether sin's witnesses are called "pain," "pleasure," or something else, the Holy Spirit sees that they all really have only one name: *fear,* the fear of the suffering and death that is the "just" punishment for our sins. But He also knows that fear with its many aliases is totally unreal. The miracles He brings prove this to us; they overturn the testimony of sin's witnesses by replacing sin's effects with *their* effects. Those effects are effects not of death, but of life: "The dying live, the dead arise, and pain has vanished." I think Jesus means quite literally that these things can happen physically when a miracle has come—again, think of Jesus' earthly ministry. The miracle's amazing effects are powerful testimony to the reality of eternal life.

> 6. Love, too, has symbols in a world of sin. The miracle forgives <u>because</u> it stands for what is <u>past</u> forgiveness and is <u>true</u>. How foolish and insane it is to think a miracle is <u>bound</u> by laws that it came solely to <u>undo</u>! The laws of <u>sin</u> have different witnesses with different strengths. And <u>they</u> attest to different sufferings [Ur: suffering]. Yet to the One Who sends forth miracles to bless the world, a tiny stab of pain, a little worldly pleasure, and the throes of death itself are but a single sound; a call for healing, and a plaintive cry for help within a world of misery. It is their <u>sameness</u> that the miracle attests. It is their <u>sameness</u> that it <u>proves</u>. The laws that call them <u>different</u> are dissolved, and <u>shown</u> as powerless. The <u>purpose</u> of a miracle is to accomplish this. And God

Himself has <u>guaranteed</u> the strength of miracles for what they witness <u>to</u>. 7. Be you then witness to the miracle [Ur: Be witnesses unto the miracle], and <u>not</u> the laws of sin. There is no <u>need</u> to suffer any more. But there *is* need that you be healed, because the suffering and sorrow of the world have made it deaf to its salvation and deliverance.

The witnesses to sin have lots of different names—for example, "a tiny stab of pain, a little worldly pleasure, and the throes of death itself." (Notice how, again, pain and pleasure are really the same thing.) They all seem to have different strengths, as in our examples: a tiny stab of pain seems a lot weaker than the throes of death.

But the Holy Spirit throws all of those witnesses for sin, whatever their name and whatever their strength, into one category: They are all "a call for healing, and a plaintive cry for help within a world of misery." He answers this call with miracles, which undo all of the witnesses to sin with equal ease. This proves that they are the same: equally calls for help and equally unreal, powerless against the strength of the miracle to overcome them.

Application:

Think of some of the "witnesses to sin" in your own life:
Those times you've felt a tiny stab of pain (think of specific examples), all the worldly pleasures you've pursued (again, think of specific examples).
Perhaps you've even felt like you were in the throes of death, either literally or psychologically—an event so painful you felt your life was essentially over.

You have used all of these as witnesses to demonstrate that you are a sinner, doomed to pain and death.
But the Holy Spirit hears in all of them but a single sound: a call for healing, and a plaintive cry for help within a world of misery.
Make that call conscious now, by saying to the Holy Spirit:

Holy Spirit, undo everything that witnesses to sin in me,
my stabs of pain, my worldly pleasures, my dedication to death.
There is no need for me to suffer any more.

Let me experience the miracle of forgiveness that witnesses to eternal life.

Let me be witness unto the miracle, and not the laws of sin.

Let me be healed, so that I may proclaim the good news of salvation to a world that, without my healing, is deaf to its salvation and deliverance.

8. The resurrection of the world awaits <u>your</u> healing and <u>your</u> happiness, that you may <u>demonstrate</u> the healing of the world. The holy instant will replace <u>all</u> sin if you but carry its effects with you. And no one will <u>elect</u> to suffer more. What better function <u>could</u> you serve than this? Be healed that you may heal, and suffer not the laws of sin to be applied to <u>you</u>. And truth <u>will</u> be revealed to you who chose to let love's symbols <u>take the place</u> of sin.

This conclusion is very similar to the last section: We let ourselves be healed in the holy instant; then we extend our healing to the world. When others see our suffering replaced with joy, others will choose joy as well. As we refuse to let sin inflict its suffering and death upon us, others will see our demonstration and be moved to do the same. Thus will the world that bears witness to sin be replaced with a world that bears witness to love. What better function could we serve than this?

VII. The Dreamer of the Dream
Commentary by Greg Mackie

1. Suffering is an emphasis upon all that the world has done to injure you. Here is the world's demented version of salvation clearly shown. Like to a dream of punishment, in which the dreamer is unconscious of what brought on the attack against himself, he sees himself attacked unjustly and by something not himself. He is the victim of this "something else," a thing outside himself, for which he has no reason to be held responsible. He must be innocent because he knows not what he does, but what is done to him. Yet is his own attack upon himself apparent still, for it is he who bears the suffering. And he cannot escape because its source is seen outside himself.

Imagine that you felt horribly guilty about something you did, and then went to bed. What would you dream about? Might you not have a "dream of punishment," a nightmare in which you were on the run from the authorities, or on trial for murder, or thrown in a dungeon, or tortured by the Grand Inquisitor? And if in this dream you were completely unconscious of the thing you did in the waking world (a safe assumption, since most of the time we're not aware of the waking world when we dream), wouldn't this all feel like *unjust* punishment? Even though it is all caused by the guilt in your own mind, you wouldn't be aware of that. In your eyes, you would be an innocent victim of attackers outside of you.

According to the Course, this is our literal situation in this world *right now*. It seems that we are constantly at the mercy of a world that is sticking it to us, but what's really happening is that our own guilt is causing us to dream attackers into our lives who punish us for our many "crimes." We're really suffering from our attack on ourselves, but we project it outward because doing so seems to "save" us by preserving our innocence. Rather than saving us, though, this projection keeps us in the nightmare. How can we end our suffering when we think it is caused by something outside us?

2. Now you are being shown you *can* escape. All that is needed is you look upon the problem as it is, and not the way that you have set it

up. How <u>could</u> there be another way to solve a problem that is <u>very</u> simple, but has been obscured by heavy clouds of complication, which were <u>made</u> to keep the problem unresolved? <u>Without</u> the clouds the problem will emerge in all its primitive simplicity. The choice will <u>not</u> be difficult, because the problem is absurd when clearly seen. No one has difficulty making up his mind to let a simple problem be resolved if it is <u>seen</u> as hurting him, and also very easily removed.

Through our projection, we've hidden the problem of our suffering in a dense fog that obscures its true nature. We've placed the cause outside ourselves, where we are powerless to do anything about it. But if we see that all of our suffering is self-inflicted, how simple the situation becomes. Imagine that you're throwing a boomerang on a day when pea-soup fog keeps you from seeing more than a few feet in front of you. You're mystified because you keep getting hit in the back of the head with a boomerang. But once the fog clears up and you see that it's your own boomerang coming around to hit you, the solution to the lumps on your head becomes apparent: Stop throwing the dang boomerang!

> 3. The "reasoning" by which the world is made, on which it rests, by which it is maintained, is simply this: "*You* are the cause of what I do. Your presence <u>justifies</u> my wrath, and you exist and think <u>apart</u> from me. While <u>you</u> attack I <u>must</u> be innocent. And what I suffer from <u>is</u> your attack." No one who looks upon this "reasoning" <u>exactly</u> as it is could fail to see it does <u>not</u> follow and it makes <u>no</u> sense. Yet it <u>seems</u> sensible, because it <u>looks</u> as if the world <u>were</u> hurting you. And so it seems as if there is no <u>need</u> to go beyond the obvious in terms of cause.

If you set aside your knowledge of the Course and think about how you actually live your life day to day, doesn't the reasoning presented here look patently obvious? "*Of course* I suffer from the attacks of people who are separate from me. *Of course* those attacks make me angry and force me to defend myself, as much as I don't want to. *Of course* my defense is a perfectly innocent and wholly justified response to an unjust attack. Duh!"

But if you think about it, does this really make sense? We're saying that somehow, someone or something outside of me has absolute power to determine what I do, what I feel (wrath, suffering), and even where I stand according to the scales of justice (innocence). Is it really plausible to believe that the world has this kind of power over us?

Application: Think of someone in your life that seems to have such power over you and ask yourself: *"Can [name] really be the cause of my actions? of my wrath? of my suffering? of my innocence or guilt?"* Really reflect on these questions. What happens in your mind when you do that?

> 4. There is indeed a need [to go beyond the obvious in terms of cause]. The world's escape from condemnation is a need which those within the world are joined in sharing. Yet they do not recognize their common need. For each one thinks that if he does his part, the condemnation of the world will rest on him. And it is this that he perceives to *be* his part in its deliverance. Vengeance must have a focus. Otherwise is the avenger's knife in his own hand, and pointed to himself. And he must see it in another's hand, if he would be a victim of attack he did not choose. And thus he suffers from the wounds a knife he does not hold has made upon himself.

We need to recognize that the world is wholly innocent of attacking us; *our* attacks, rooted in our guilt, cause our suffering. The entire world shares this need, but it is unrecognized. Why? Because we think that delivering the world from guilt means becoming the world's scapegoat. If we are the attacker, then *we* are so horribly guilty that the entire world will take its perfectly justified vengeance on us. In fact, our sense of guilt will be so intense that we ourselves will slit our own throats. I'm reminded of this line from the Workbook: "You think if what is true about you were revealed to you, you would be struck with horror so intense that you would rush to death by your own hand, living on after seeing this being impossible" (W-pI.93.1:3).

The Course tells us that deep down, we're actually feeling this self-loathing this very moment. This is exactly why we project our attack outward: to make the world *our* scapegoat. It's so horrifying to contemplate the idea that we are vicious attackers that we put the knife in another's hand and blame him. This seems to purchase the innocence we yearn for.

> 5. This is the purpose of the world he sees. And looked at thus, the world provides the means by which this purpose seems to be fulfilled. The means attest the purpose, but are not themselves a cause. Nor will the

<u>cause</u> be changed by seeing it <u>apart</u> from its effects. The cause <u>produces</u> the effects, which then bear witness to the <u>cause,</u> and <u>not</u> themselves. Look, then, <u>beyond</u> effects. It is <u>not</u> here the <u>cause</u> of suffering and sin must lie. And dwell not on the suffering and sin, for they are but <u>reflections</u> of their cause.

The entire world of apparent external attackers has been set up for the purpose of purchasing this false "innocence." It seems to work very well, does it not? This world certainly seems to be the cause of our suffering, and we certainly seem to be innocent of what the world is doing to us.

But the real cause of both our suffering and the external world that seems to inflict it is our own sense of guilt, and none of our attempts to obscure this can change this simple fact. This merciless world is an effect of our guilt; it is evidence of the guilt in our minds, but not the cause of anything in itself. If we really want to find the cause of our suffering, then, we must look beyond both the world and the suffering itself. We must look beyond the reflections if we want to see that which they reflect.

> 6. The part you play in <u>salvaging</u> the world from condemnation <u>is</u> your own escape. Forget not that the witness to the world of evil cannot speak <u>except</u> for what has seen a <u>need</u> for evil in the world. And this is where <u>your</u> guilt was first beheld. In separation from your brother was the first attack upon yourself begun. And it is <u>this</u> the world bears witness to. Seek not another cause, nor look among the mighty legions of its witnesses for its undoing. They <u>support</u> its claim on your allegiance. What <u>conceals</u> the truth is not where you should look to *find* the truth.

It all comes down to our own guilt. This guilt was born when we separated from our brothers in the very beginning, an act which was an attack upon ourselves. Our feeling of guilt for this apparent crime was so terrible that we needed to project it onto the brothers we separated from, in order to see ourselves as "innocent." That projection is still in force today: We see an evil world that inflicts suffering upon us because we still have this need to cover up our guilt by seeing it in someone else. Therefore, the entire world we see—all of the pain and suffering we experience, even unto death—points to our own guilt.

We need to recognize that our guilt is the cause of it all, because only then can we learn the good news: *We are not really guilty.* Only our own self-condemnation is hurting us, so we have the power to escape from our own condemnation simply by stopping our attack on ourselves and accepting our eternal innocence. This, rather than being the world's scapegoat, is our role in setting the world free from condemnation, for if we see ourselves as innocent, we no longer have any need to see an evil world.

> 7. The witnesses to sin all stand within <u>one</u> little space. And it is <u>here</u> you find the <u>cause</u> of your perspective on the world. Once you were unaware of what the cause of everything the world appeared to thrust upon you, uninvited and unasked, must <u>really</u> be. Of one thing you were sure: Of all the many causes you perceived as bringing pain and suffering to you, your guilt was <u>not</u> among them. Nor did you in <u>any</u> way <u>request</u> them for yourself. This is how <u>all</u> illusions came about. The one who makes them does <u>not</u> see himself as making them, and their reality does <u>not</u> depend on him. Whatever cause they have is something quite <u>apart</u> from him, and what he sees is <u>separate</u> from his mind. He <u>cannot</u> doubt his dreams' reality, <u>because</u> he does not see the part he plays in <u>making</u> them and <u>making</u> them seem real.

This entire game of projecting our guilt outward is a "perfect storm" for the ego. It simultaneously hides our guilt from our awareness *and* provides a world that is a perfect punishment device *for* that guilt. Both of these aspects keep that guilt in place: Hiding our guilt from our awareness keeps us from doing anything about it, and getting our guilt punished by the world seems to confirm its reality. Just like that "dream of punishment" in the first paragraph, where our guilt produced a dream of unjust attack on us, we now wander through a dream world caused by our guilt, thinking that the dream is sticking it to *us*.

Application: How well has this dream worked? The proof is in the third through fifth sentences. Ask yourself the following questions:

Before you started studying the Course, where did "my guilt" rank on the list of things you thought caused your suffering? Does a number come to mind, or was it even on the list?

Now that you are a Course student, what is your answer to this same question—not based on Course theory, but on your actual day-to-day experience?

Before you started studying the Course, how many times did you think some suffering you experienced was something you requested? Did you ever think this?

Now that you are a Course student, what is your answer to this same question—again, not based on Course theory, but on your actual day-to-day experience?

Are you willing to seriously consider the idea that *all* of your suffering, without exception, is caused by your guilt—that guilt is actually the only thing on the list?

Are you willing to seriously consider the idea that *all* the suffering you've ever experienced was something you requested?

Are you willing to seriously consider the idea that, just as your guilt can cause a nighttime dream in which you unconsciously punish yourself through a seemingly external world, your "waking" life right now is a version of that very dream?

> 8. No one can waken from a dream the world is dreaming <u>for</u> him. He becomes a part of someone <u>else's</u> dream. He <u>cannot</u> choose to waken from a dream he did not make. Helpless he stands, a victim to a dream conceived and cherished by a <u>separate</u> mind. Careless indeed of him this mind must be, as thoughtless of his peace and happiness as is the weather or the time of day. It loves him not, but casts him as it will in any role that satisfies its dream. So little is his worth that he is but a dancing shadow, leaping up and down according to a senseless plot conceived within the idle dreaming of the world.

The previous paragraphs talked about how we don't doubt the reality of the world we see because we don't realize we're dreaming it—we think it has an objective reality outside of us. And what a crazy world it is. We all have our hopes and dreams for what we would like to happen in our lives, but it seems that we're puppets manipulated by a mad puppet master who couldn't care less about our hopes and dreams.

Have you ever felt like you were simply playing a role in a madman's senseless dream? This paragraph has always reminded me of a famous passage from Shakespeare's *Macbeth*:

> Life's but a walking shadow, a poor player
> That struts and frets his hour upon the stage

And then is heard no more: it is a tale
Told by an idiot, full of sound and fury,
Signifying nothing.

We'll never wake up from this dream until we realize that we're the "idiot."

> 9. This is the <u>only</u> picture you can see; the <u>one</u> alternative that you can choose, the <u>other</u> possibility of cause, if you be <u>not</u> the dreamer of your dreams. And this <u>is</u> what you choose if you deny the cause of suffering is in <u>your</u> mind. Be glad indeed it is, for thus are <u>you</u> the <u>one</u> decider of your destiny in time. The choice <u>is</u> yours to make between a sleeping death and dreams of evil or a happy wakening and joy of life.

The choice is very simple: Either we're dreaming up our own suffering, or our suffering is imposed on us from without. In my experience, the idea that we're causing our own suffering can arouse resistance and even anger in people. In their eyes, it amounts to cruelly "blaming the victim" for his or her suffering, adding guilt to what is already a painful burden.

But what's really cruel is the idea that we're at the mercy of a cruel world that we're powerless to do anything about. We should be glad we're causing our own suffering, for only if we are can we escape from it. By acknowledging our responsibility for our suffering—recognizing it is merely a mistake that calls for correction, not a sin that calls for guilt—we can awaken from our sleeping death to everlasting life.

> 10. What <u>could</u> you choose between but life or death, waking or sleeping, peace or war, your dreams or your reality? There is a risk of thinking death is peace, because the world equates the body with the Self Which God created. Yet a thing can never be its opposite. And death is opposite to peace, because it is the opposite of life. And life is peace. Awaken and forget all thoughts of death, and you will find you have the peace of God. Yet if the choice is <u>really</u> given you, then you must see the causes of the things you choose <u>between</u> exactly <u>as</u> they are and <u>where</u> they are.

The sentences between the first and last sentences of this paragraph are not in the Urtext, and don't seem to be part of the discussion of this section. The sentences that *are* in the Urtext (the first and the last) make a simple point: We have the power to choose between our evil dream of death or a happy awakening to life, but to make that choice, we have to see it exactly as it is. We will learn more about that later.

The sentences between the first and the last are a fascinating aside that addresses a pervasive view about death: We often think death is *peace*. We put "Rest in Peace" on tombstones and tell ourselves that the dearly departed has left this vale of tears for a better place. Our belief that death is peace is rooted in our belief that we are bodies: When our bodies die, we tell ourselves, we are freed from our suffering and find peace, either in an afterlife or in oblivion.

Yet Jesus uses logic to show us that death cannot be peace. The logic goes like this:

Death is opposite to life.
Life is peace.
Therefore, death is opposite to peace. A thing can never be its opposite.
Therefore, death cannot be peace.

11. What choices can be made between two states, but <u>one</u> of which is clearly recognized? Who could be free to choose <u>between</u> effects, when only <u>one</u> is seen as up to him? An honest choice could <u>never</u> be perceived as one in which the choice is split between a tiny you and an enormous world, with <u>different</u> dreams about the truth in you. The gap between reality and dreams lies not between the dreaming of the world and what you dream in secret. <u>They</u> are one. The dreaming of the world is but a part of your own dream you gave away, and saw as if it were its start and ending, both. Yet was it started by your <u>secret</u> dream, which you do <u>not</u> perceive although it <u>caused</u> the part you see and do not doubt is real. How <u>could</u> you doubt it while you lie asleep, and dream in secret that its <u>cause</u> is real?

The third sentence perfectly describes how we see life in this world: as a constant struggle between a "tiny you" with a very limited range of choices and an "enormous world" with far more power and an agenda that runs entirely counter to ours. We have our hopes and dreams for a happy, secure, and successful life, but that "tale told by an idiot" keeps crushing our hopes and dreams into dust.

How can we make an honest choice for a happy awakening when

all we recognize is this battle between the dreaming of the world and the hopes and dreams of little ol' me, in which so little seems up to us? To make that honest choice, we have to recognize the real cause of the dreaming of the world: our "secret dream" (this dream will be described in the next paragraph), a dream that we projected onto the world and then conveniently forgot, so that the dreaming of the world now appears to have a reality independent of us. This secret dream is *totally* up to us, and once we see this, we can choose to undo the dreaming of the world entirely. Yet we won't do this as long as we think that the secret dream is itself real.

> 12. A brother <u>separated</u> from yourself, an ancient enemy, a murderer who stalks you in the night and plots your death, yet plans that it be lingering and slow; of this you dream. Yet <u>underneath</u> this dream is yet another, in which <u>you</u> become the murderer, the secret enemy, the scavenger and the destroyer of your brother and the world alike [Ur: the brother and the world you fear alike]. Here is the <u>cause</u> of suffering, the space <u>between</u> your little ["little" appears to have been added by the editors] dreams and your reality. The little gap you do not even see, the birthplace of illusions and of fear, the time of terror and of ancient hate, the instant of disaster, all are here. Here is the <u>cause</u> of unreality. And it is here that it will be undone.

Earlier, this section said that the cause of all our suffering is not the world, but our own guilt. Now, in this description of our "secret dream," we see clearly *why* we are guilty. Deep down, underneath our complaint that the world is sticking it to us, we're dreaming that *we* are sticking it to the *world*. We're dreaming that we have become ruthless murderers, malevolent parasites bent on destroying everyone and everything that gets in the way of what we want. How would you feel about yourself if you were aware of this and believed it was the truth about you? Profoundly guilty, of course. This guilt is the cause of all our suffering. The desire to avoid facing this guilt is the cause of the dream of the world that *seems* to cause our suffering. And facing this guilt honestly is the way it will finally be undone.

> 13. *You* are the dreamer of the world of dreams. No <u>other</u> cause it has, nor ever will. Nothing more fearful than an idle dream has terrified God's Son, and made him think that he has lost his innocence, denied his

Father, and made war upon himself. So fearful is the dream, so seeming real, he could not waken to reality without the sweat of terror and a scream of mortal fear, unless a gentler dream preceded his awaking, and allowed his calmer mind to welcome, <u>not</u> to fear, the Voice That calls with love to waken him; a gentler dream, in which his suffering was healed and where his brother was his friend. God willed he waken gently and with joy, and <u>gave</u> him means to waken <u>without</u> fear.

This is the punch line of this entire section: "*You* are the dreamer of the world of dreams." We are the ones dreaming that we have become vicious attackers, and thus irredeemably guilty. We are the ones who have projected our guilt onto the world, so that it seems the *world* is attacking *us* and causing all our suffering.

Fortunately, this nightmare of guilt and all its effects is just an "idle dream." We have not lost our innocence, and God wants nothing more than to wake us up to our reality. Yet how can He do this while we're in the middle of the nightmare? We've convinced ourselves that He is out to punish us for our sins. In fact, we see the punishing world as His *means* of punishing us. Because of this, we think that hearing His Voice means it's time to get our comeuppance. Therefore, instead of trying to wake us up from our nightmare directly, God begins the process by giving each terrified dreamer "a gentler dream, in which his suffering was healed and where his brother was his friend." This way, we can welcome the Voice of God and awaken with joy instead of terror.

You may have noticed that this section talks about a lot of different "dreams." Now that all of them have been introduced, here is a summary of them:

1. Our hopes and dreams: This was only briefly alluded to. On the surface, we all dream of finding "peace and happiness," but our hopes for happiness seem to be constantly crushed by an "enormous world" that has an entirely different agenda for us.
2. The dreaming of the world: This is the attacking world that seems to do the crushing.
3. Our secret dream: This is our dream that we are the attacker, and therefore profoundly guilty. This dream is the cause of the first two dreams.
4. The gentler dream: This is God's way of gently waking us up from all our dreams.

14. Accept the dream He gave <u>instead</u> of yours. It is <u>not</u> difficult to change a dream when once the dreamer has been recognized. Rest in the Holy Spirit, and allow His gentle dreams to take the place of those you dreamed in terror and in fear of death. He brings <u>forgiving</u> dreams, in which the choice is <u>not</u> who is the murderer and who shall be the victim. In the dreams <u>He</u> brings there <u>is</u> no murder and there <u>is</u> no death. The dream of guilt is fading from your sight, although your eyes are closed. A smile has come to lighten up your sleeping face. The sleep is peaceful now, for these are happy dreams.

Why is it so important to see the problem as it really is, to recognize that *our* "dream of guilt" is the cause of all our suffering? Because only when we see that we are the dreamer can we choose a different dream. Until then, the only choice seems to be between the second and third dreams above: Do I confess that I'm a guilty murderer, or do I put the knife in the world's hand and scream bloody murder for its apparent victimization of me? But when I realize that all the bloody murder is an idle dream in my own mind, I am now free to accept a dream in which there is *no* murder. I can have a dream of forgiveness, a happy dream.

15. Dream softly of your sinless brother, who unites with you in holy innocence. And from <u>this</u> dream the Lord of Heaven will Himself awaken His beloved Son. Dream of your brother's kindnesses <u>instead</u> of dwelling in your dreams on his mistakes. Select his thoughtfulness to dream about <u>instead</u> of counting up the hurts he gave. Forgive him his illusions, and give thanks to him for all the helpfulness he gave. And do not brush aside his many gifts because he is not perfect in your dreams. He represents his Father, Whom you see as offering both life <u>and</u> death to you.
16. Brother, He gives <u>but</u> life. Yet [Ur: And] what you see as gifts your brother offers <u>represent</u> the gifts you dream your Father gives to you. Let all your brother's gifts be seen in light of charity and kindness offered you. And let no pain disturb your dream of deep appreciation for his gifts to you.

Jesus now brings everything this section has taught down to earth. How do we choose the gentler dream in daily life? It is really very simple: Choose to focus on your brother's love instead of his attacks.

This simple decision undoes everything. It undoes our secret dream that we are an attacker, because it is the decision to *stop attacking*, to love our brothers instead of condemning them. It undoes the dreaming of the world, because with the secret dream gone, there is no more need to project our guilt onto an apparently attacking world. It even gives us a new set of hopes and dreams: Instead of dreaming of getting "peace and happiness" in worldly terms, which usually amounts to triumph over our rivals in that "enormous world" that's trying to dash our dreams, our hopes and dreams are now to help *everyone* find peace and happiness together.

Application: Bring to mind someone who is close to you, someone with whom you have had difficulties.

What, in your eyes, are some of the mistakes this person has made?
What are some of the hurts you think this person has given you?
In what other ways has this person been less than perfect in your eyes?
Now, say the following:

> *This person is my dream symbol for God, so the gifts I see this person giving me are the gifts I see my Father giving me.*

> *Therefore:*
> *I will dream of my brother's kindnesses instead of dwelling in my dreams on his mistakes.*

(Think of some of this person's specific acts of kindness.)

> *I will select his thoughtfulness to dream about instead of counting up the hurts he gave.*

(Think of some of this person's specific acts of thoughtfulness.)

> *And I will not brush aside his many gifts because he is not perfect in my dreams.*

(Think of some of this person's many gifts.)

Now that you have given the gifts of charity and kindness to this person, how do you feel about him or her?
How do you feel about *yourself?*
What gifts do you now think you Father is giving to you?

VIII. The "Hero" of the Dream
Commentary by Greg Mackie

1. The body is the central figure in the dreaming of the world. There is no dream without it, nor does it exist without the dream in which it acts as if it were a person to be seen and be believed. It takes the central place in every dream, which tells the story of how it was made by other bodies, born into the world outside the body, lives a little while and dies, to be united in the dust with other bodies dying like itself. In the brief time allotted it to live, it seeks for other bodies as its friends and enemies. Its safety is its main concern. Its comfort is its guiding rule. It tries to look for pleasure, and avoid the things that would be hurtful. Above all, it tries to teach itself its pains and joys are different and can be told apart.

The last section described our lives using the language of theater, saying that we seem to live "according to a senseless plot conceived within the idle dreaming of the world" (T-27.VII.8:7). Now we are introduced to the star of this little theatrical production: the body. In these paragraphs, Jesus describes the world of bodies we all identify with as if he were an anthropologist observing and describing a strange culture no one has ever seen before. It's hard to argue with his description if we step back and look at our lives. Is it not true that our life story is predominantly about the life and times of our body?

2. The dreaming of the world takes many forms, because the body seeks in many ways to prove it is autonomous and real. It puts things on itself that it has bought with little metal discs or paper strips the world proclaims as valuable and real. It works to get them, doing senseless things, and tosses them away for senseless things it does not need and does not even want. It hires other bodies, that they may protect it and collect more senseless things that it can call its own. It looks about for special bodies that can share its dream. Sometimes it dreams it is a conqueror of bodies weaker than itself. But in some phases of the dream, it is the slave of bodies that would hurt and torture it.

The whole point of this play is to prove that the body is "autonomous and real." Indeed, in these very descriptions, you see no reference to any sort of mind animating the body. *It* puts things on itself, *it* buys things, *it* works to get them, etc. Notice too the emphasis on the dream being "senseless"; there are three references to "senseless things." This follows directly from the absence of mind, since only a mind can make sense of things.

The overall impression of this description is that the story of our lives is the story of a meaningless object (our body) interacting with other meaningless objects. This may sound like a harsh description, but many people have lamented the meaninglessness of earthly life, from the teacher in the biblical book of Ecclesiastes who said "Everything is meaningless" (Eccl. 1:2, NIV) to the existentialists of the last century. Can we relate?

Application: Robert created an excellent paraphrase of these first two paragraphs. Read through it and see if it doesn't more or less describe your life.

"My body was born into this world on the date: _____,
the product of two other bodies called _____.

It lives now for a while, until one day when it will die and be buried in the ground, next to other dead bodies. That will be the end of my life story.

Over the course of its life my body has sought for other bodies that could be its companions in life.

Some have become its friends, such as _____,
some its enemies, such as _____.

Every day it works to keep itself safe, to feed itself, stay healthy, and keep a roof over its head.

It continually seeks for comfort, looks for pleasure, and tries to avoid pain.

Every day it also dresses itself with clothing that it buys with its money.

It goes out and works to get this money, doing things like _____, things which often make little or no sense.

Yet after working so hard for this money, my body often throws it away on things it doesn't really need or want, such as _____.

At times my body has been the victim of other bodies, such as when
_____.

At times, however, the roles have been reversed and my body has been
the victor, the one that commands other bodies, such as when _____."

> 3. The body's serial adventures, from the time of birth to dying are the
> theme of every dream the world has ever had. The "hero" of this dream
> will never change, nor will its purpose. Though the dream itself takes
> many forms, and <u>seems</u> to show a great variety of places and events
> wherein its "hero" finds itself, the dream has but <u>one</u> purpose, taught in
> many ways. This single lesson does it try to teach again, and still again,
> and yet once more; that it is <u>cause</u> and <u>not</u> effect. And <u>you</u> are <u>its</u> effect,
> and <u>cannot</u> be its cause.

That first sentence makes me think of Flash Gordon or the Lone Ranger:
"Tune in next week for the next thrilling episode of *The Adventures of
My Body.*" This exciting show is full of cliffhangers, narrow escapes,
heroic feats of derring-do, and (sadly) the eventual defeat and death of
its mighty "hero." But unbeknownst to us, it is really an educational
program. Underneath all those entertaining adventures is a single lesson
taught in each and every episode: "The body *is* autonomous and real. It's
the only game in town. Therefore, *it* is cause, and *you* are its effect. You
are nothing *but* this body, so don't go thinking that you actually have the
power to change the story."

> 4. Thus are you <u>not</u> the dreamer, but the <u>dream</u>. And so you wander
> idly in and out of places and events that <u>it</u> contrives. That this is all the
> <u>body</u> does is true, for it <u>is</u> but a figure in a dream. But who <u>reacts</u> to
> figures in a dream <u>unless</u> he sees them as if they were real? The <u>instant</u>
> that he sees them as they are they <u>have</u> no more effects on him, <u>because</u>
> he understands he <u>gave</u> them their effects <u>by causing them</u> and <u>making</u>
> them seem real.

The body is just a dream figure; so as long as we believe that it is our
cause, we believe *we* are a dream figure. As the body goes through its
serial adventures, we will have a huge emotional investment in each one:
We will cringe when the mustache-twirling villain ties fair Polly to the
railroad tracks, and exult as our hero rescues her in a nick of time. (Fill

in your own life adventures here.) But what if we realized that all this is simply a fictional story, one that *we're* writing? What if we saw that we are the dreamer, not the dream figure? We would no more be distressed or elated at what's happening in this dream than George Lucas would be distressed or elated at an event in *Star Wars*.

> 5. How willing are you to <u>escape</u> effects of all the dreams the world has ever had? Is it your wish to let <u>no</u> dream appear to be the cause of what it is <u>you</u> do? Then let us merely look upon the dream's beginning, for the part you see is but the <u>second</u> part, whose <u>cause</u> lies in the first. No one asleep and dreaming in the world remembers his attack upon himself. No one believes there really was a time when he knew nothing of a body, and could never have conceived this world as real. He would have seen at once that these ideas are one illusion, too ridiculous for anything but to be laughed away. How serious they now appear to be! And no one can remember when they would have met with laughter and with disbelief. We <u>can</u> remember this, if we but look directly at their <u>cause</u>. And we will see the grounds for laughter, <u>not</u> a cause for fear.

Application: Let's really ask the questions this paragraph is instructing us to ask. With as much heartfelt desire as you can muster, ask:

> *How willing am I to escape effects of all the dreams the world has ever had?*
> *Is it my wish to let no dream appear to be the cause of what it is I do?*

If we really are willing to escape the dreaming of the world, what we must do is look past the dreaming of the world (the "second part") to its underlying cause: the "secret dream" (T-27.VII.11:7) described in the last section. This is our dream of guilt, in which we are vicious attackers destroying everything in our path—a dream which is really an attack upon ourselves. If we really look at this dream and see it for the nonsense that it is, we will see just how equally nonsensical is its effect: this strange idea of being a body at the mercy of an attacking world. And what do we naturally do when we see something totally ridiculous and nonsensical? We *laugh*.

6. Let us return the dream he gave away unto the dreamer, who perceives the dream as <u>separate</u> from himself and done to <u>him</u>. Into eternity, where all is one, there crept a tiny, mad idea, at which the Son of God remembered not to laugh. In his forgetting did the thought become a serious idea, and possible of both accomplishment and real effects. Together, we can laugh them <u>both</u> away, and understand that time can<u>not</u> intrude upon eternity. It <u>is</u> a joke to think that time can come to circumvent eternity, which *means* there is no time.

Now Jesus tells us more about the nature of that secret dream, in one of the most well-known passages in the Course. We had this "tiny, mad idea" of time. What we should have done when this happened was to laugh it away, because again, that is the natural response to the ridiculous. When someone says something that's both trivial ("tiny") and crazy ("mad"), like "The true cause of 9/11 was me *dialing* 911 on my magic terrorist telephone," we can't help but laugh. And what could be more trivial and crazy than the idea that time can circumvent eternity, when eternity by definition means that time cannot even *exist*? What a joke!

However, we forgot to laugh at the joke. We didn't get it. We thought we had really accomplished the impossible. It's as if instead of laughing it off, we sent in the Homeland Security agents to arrest the guy with the magic terrorist telephone. And that's how this whole mess got started.

7. A timelessness in which is time made real; a part of God that can attack itself; a separate brother as an enemy; a mind <u>within</u> a body all are forms of circularity whose ending starts at its beginning, ending at its cause. The world you see depicts <u>exactly</u> what you thought <u>you</u> did. Except that <u>now</u> you think that what you did is being done to <u>you</u>. The guilt for what <u>you</u> thought is being placed <u>outside</u> yourself, and on a guilty world that dreams your dreams and thinks your thoughts <u>instead</u> of you. It brings <u>its</u> vengeance, <u>not</u> your own. <u>It</u> keeps you narrowly confined within a body, which it punishes because of all the sinful things the body does within <u>its</u> dream. You have <u>no</u> power to make the body stop its evil deeds because you did <u>not</u> make it, and can<u>not</u> control its actions nor its purpose nor its fate.

Here are a few more versions of that joke: We actually think that a part of God's seamless oneness attacked itself, our beloved brother somehow became our enemy, and we managed to cram our limitless mind into a little hunk of meat. How ridiculous! But we thought we really did all this, and our guilt for this imagined "crime" was so immense that we dreamed up a world and projected our guilt onto that world.

This led to two effects, one that we experience on the surface of our minds and another that is usually below the surface. First, on the surface, our attacks on others are now seen as *their* attacks on *us*. This is our conventional view of ourselves as innocent victims of a cruel world. Second, underneath the surface, we see these external attacks as *punishment* for our attacks, because we secretly want to punish ourselves for what we think we have done. This is the implication of the fifth and sixth sentences, which speak of the world bringing vengeance on us and punishing us for the acts of our sinful bodies.

Thus, the world we see is simultaneously a dumping ground for the guilt we want to get rid of *and* a punishing device for the guilt we didn't really get rid of. You have to give the ego credit for devising an ingenious system: It seems to give us the innocence *we* want while it actually collects the guilt the *ego* wants.

> 8. The world but demonstrates an ancient truth; you <u>will</u> believe that others do to you <u>exactly</u> what you think you did to them. But once deluded into blaming <u>them</u> you will not see the <u>cause</u> of what they do, <u>because</u> you *want* the guilt to rest on them. How childish is the petulant device to keep your innocence by pushing guilt <u>outside</u> yourself, but <u>never</u> letting go! It is not easy to perceive the jest when all around you do your eyes behold its heavy consequences, but <u>without</u> their trifling cause. Without the cause do its effects seem serious and sad indeed. Yet they but follow. And it is their <u>cause</u> that follows nothing and is but a jest.

Our projection of our guilt onto the world keeps us from seeing the true cause of the world in ourselves, and thus keeps us from seeing how ridiculous that cause really is. It is as if we were living in terror of a huge shadow that looked like a fearsome monster, never realizing that the shadow was actually cast by a two-inch *Lord of the Rings* action figure that came from a cereal box. As long as our eyes are focused on the murder and mayhem all around us, we cannot help but feel weighted down by the grim seriousness of it all. How can we turn our eyes away from this depressing world and "perceive the jest" that is its cause?

9. In gentle laughter does the Holy Spirit perceive the cause, and looks <u>not</u> to effects. How else could He correct <u>your</u> error, who have <u>overlooked</u> the cause entirely? He bids you bring each terrible effect to Him that you may look <u>together</u> on its foolish cause and laugh with Him a while. *You* judge effects, but *He* has judged their <u>cause</u>. And by <u>His</u> judgment are effects removed. Perhaps you come in tears. But hear Him say, "My brother, holy Son of God, behold your idle dream, in which this could occur." And you will leave the holy instant with your laughter and your brother's <u>joined</u> with His.

Here is how we turn away from the depressing world and perceive the jest that is its cause: by doing the practice outlined in this paragraph. Before doing that, though, I want to point out that what we're supposed to laugh at here is not the *effects*, but their *cause*. The fact that we actually believe in the cause and thus experience incredibly painful effects is indeed an unfortunate thing; the Course even says that "God weeps" (T-5.VII.4:5) over this.

Thus, this section isn't suggesting that we become like the schoolyard bully in *The Simpsons*, who points at another person's misfortune and lets out a derisive "Ha ha!" It isn't asking us to say, "Look at all those people dying in Darfur—what a joke!" Rather, it's asking us to say to ourselves: "Let us see and laugh at the ridiculous cause at the root of this terrible effect. If we really see this cause as the Holy Spirit sees it, we will *end* the suffering in Darfur and everywhere else, for 'by His judgment are effects removed.'"

Application: In that spirit, let's do the exercise this paragraph lays out. (Thanks to Robert for creating this application.)

Firstly, think of some "terrible effect," some outer circumstance in your life that you perceive as pressing suffering onto you. Describe this circumstance to the Holy Spirit.

Secondly, look upon the situation with the Holy Spirit. You have been gazing in anguish on the outer appearance, but He looks straight past that appearance to the idea that underlies it. He reduces the outer appearance to the view of reality that it seems to express. Perhaps the view is "Time can come to circumvent eternity," or "My tiny body actually contains my limitless mind," or "I, God's Own Son, can be rendered homeless and lacking." Whatever this view is, it is the actual cause of the outer appearance. The appearance has no reality in itself. It is just the outer picture of this idea. Try to see through the Holy Spirit's eyes, so that you too can see the idea behind the outer form. What view of reality does the outer situation imply? What statement about reality does it make? The Holy Spirit sees it clearly. Try to join with Him so that you, too, can see what this idea is.

Finally, hear the Holy Spirit say to you, "My dear brother, behold your silly dream. Only in a dream could such a ridiculous thing occur." Try to see the idea behind your dream as He sees it. Try to join with His perception and see just how preposterous the idea looks, how laughable it is. Try to realize that such a crazy idea could never produce reality, only dreams, only illusions. Can you see it from His perspective? Can you see how it all looks so silly and so trivial? Can you see how completely ridiculous it appears? Hear Him laughing in your mind, gently and lovingly. Perhaps at first you don't see the humor in this situation, but His laughter is infectious, and as you hear Him continue to laugh, you feel yourself being drawn into laughing with Him. Now you have brought your "terrible effect to Him that you may look together on its foolish cause and laugh with Him a while." So do just that. Laugh with Him a while.

> 10. The secret of salvation is but this: That <u>you</u> are doing this <u>unto yourself</u>. No matter what the form of the attack, this <u>still</u> is true. Whoever takes the role of enemy and of attacker, <u>still</u> is this the truth. Whatever seems to be the cause of any pain and suffering you feel, this is <u>still</u> true. For you would not react at all to figures in a dream you knew that <u>you</u> were dreaming. Let them be as hateful and as vicious as they may, they <u>could</u> have no effect on you unless you failed to recognize it is <u>your</u> dream.

We really need to get the idea that we are causing all of our suffering, for it is nothing less than "the secret of salvation." We have an incredible amount of resistance to this idea, and you can really see Jesus anticipating the exceptions that inevitably come up in our minds as we try to squirm out of it. You can hear him saying, "Yes, even *that* attack you just thought of couldn't have hurt you if you didn't *want* to suffer. Yes, even that time when so-and-so attacked you, you still caused your own suffering. Yes, even *that* apparent cause of your pain and suffering was not the real cause."

All of this follows logically from the idea that this is our dream. If we *really* knew, deep down, that all the forms we see are figures in our own dream, would we be upset if something bad happened to them, or if they did something terrible to our dream-figure body? No, we would be like Jesus, who saw the crucifixion of his own body as nothing to get upset about.

> 11. This single lesson learned will set you free from suffering, <u>whatever</u> form it takes. The Holy Spirit will repeat this <u>one</u> inclusive lesson of deliverance until it has been learned, <u>regardless</u> of the form of suffering that brings you pain. Whatever hurt you bring to Him He will make answer with this very simple truth. For this one answer <u>takes away</u> the cause of every form of sorrow and of pain. The form affects His answer not at all, for He would teach you but the <u>single</u> cause of all of them, no matter <u>what</u> their form. And you will understand that miracles reflect the simple statement, "*I* have done this thing, and it is this I would undo."

Application: Jesus *really* wants us to get this. So, let's take another "terrible effect" that seems to be bringing suffering to us and apply the secret of salvation to it:

> *Holy Spirit, I bring this suffering to you.*
> *In this situation, let me learn the secret of salvation, Your lesson*
> *of deliverance, the birthplace of all miracles, the lesson that*
> *sets me free from all suffering, whatever form it takes:*
>
> *"I am doing this unto myself.*
> *I have done this thing, and it is this I would undo."*

> 12. Bring, then, all forms of suffering to Him Who knows that every one is like the rest. He sees <u>no</u> differences where none exists, and He will teach you how each one is <u>caused</u>. None has a <u>different</u> cause from all the rest, and <u>all</u> of them are easily undone by but a <u>single</u> lesson truly learned. Salvation is a secret you have kept but from yourself.

> The universe proclaims it so. Yet to its witnesses you pay no heed at all. For they attest the thing you do not <u>want</u> to know. They seem to keep it secret <u>from</u> you. Yet you need but learn you chose but <u>not</u> to listen, <u>not</u> to see.

Jesus has called the idea that we cause all of our suffering the "secret of salvation," but it isn't a secret that God is keeping from us. Rather, "Salvation is a secret you have kept but from yourself." In truth, the evidence for this great liberating truth is everywhere we look, if we will only open our eyes. The only reason this truth *seems* like a secret to us is that we're dead set against learning it.

> 13. How differently will you perceive the world when this is recognized! When you forgive the world <u>your</u> guilt, <u>you</u> will be free of it. Its innocence does <u>not</u> demand your guilt, nor does your guiltlessness rest on <u>its</u> sins. This is the obvious; a secret kept from no one but yourself. And it is this that has maintained you <u>separate</u> from the world, and kept your brother <u>separate</u> from you. Now need you but to learn that <u>both</u> of you are innocent <u>or</u> guilty. The one thing that is impossible is that you be <u>unlike</u> each other; that they <u>both</u> be true. This is the only secret yet to learn. And it will be <u>no</u> secret you are healed.

This paragraph reminds me of the fourth paragraph of the previous section. There, we read that each person thinks his part in the world's deliverance is for the world's condemnation to rest on him. In other words, there are apparently two choices: Either the world is guilty and I'm innocent (in which case I am saved) or I'm guilty and the world is innocent (in which case the world is saved). Given those two choices, which one will we choose? That's a real no-brainer: Let's save our own skin by blaming the world for our suffering!

This choice, however, is a false choice. The truth is that because the world is our dream projection, what we see in it and what we see in ourselves must be the same. As long as we use the world as a projection screen for our guilt, we will see the world and ourselves as guilty. But when we forgive the world, we will at last recognize our own innocence. It is through forgiveness that all those witnesses to guilt out there will be transformed into witnesses to the innocence that is the world's and our salvation alike. And this will bring about healing effects so obvious that it will no longer be a secret to anyone.

Commentaries on Chapter 28

THE UNDOING
OF FEAR

I. The Present Memory
Commentary by Robert Perry

1. <u>The miracle does nothing</u>. All it does is to <u>un</u>do. And thus it cancels out the interference to what <u>has been</u> done. It does not add, but merely takes away. And what it takes away is long since gone, but being kept in memory <u>appears</u> to have immediate effects. This world was over long ago. The thoughts that made it are no longer in the mind that thought of them and loved them for a little while. The miracle but shows the past is gone, and what has truly gone <u>has</u> no effects. <u>Remembering</u> a cause can but produce <u>illusions</u> of its presence, <u>not</u> effects.

We think of a miracle as the overturning of the way things are. A miracle reverses the status quo, doing some new and dramatic thing. Jesus, however, says that we have got it all backwards. Heaven is the way things really are; it is the true status quo, you might say. Therefore, the situation in front of us now, the one that is so in need of miracles, is the reversal of the way things are. The miracle simply undoes this reversal, restoring what always was.

"And what it takes away is long since gone." This is a reference to "The Little Hindrance" (T-26.V), where we were taught that this world is already over. It only seems to be here, because we are holding onto it in memory. The scene before our eyes right now is not reality. It is an extremely vivid memory.

As an aside, I had to pause in the writing of this commentary to go to the dentist for a cleaning, during which I found much comfort in the Course's teaching that all of this was over long ago.

2. <u>All</u> the effects of guilt are here no more. For guilt is over. In its passing went its consequences, left without a cause. Why would you cling to it [guilt] in memory if you did not <u>desire</u> its effects? Remembering is as selective as perception, being its past tense. It is perception of the past as if it were occurring <u>now</u>, and still were there to see. Memory, like perception, is a skill made up by you to take the place of what God <u>gave</u> in your creation. And like all the things you made, it can be used to serve <u>another</u> purpose, and to be the means for something <u>else</u>. It can be used to heal and <u>not</u> to hurt, if you so wish it be.

The fact that the world is over is the reason why the miracle can heal. It is not undoing a real, solid problem. It is merely clearing away old memories of something already gone. In particular, it clears away guilt. All of our problems are just the results of us clinging to the memory of guilt. That guilt is over; it has been cleansed from our minds. Yet we still cling to it. And while we do, its punishing effects—which are also gone—seem to hold us in their grip.

We are like an old man who, as a boy, accidentally killed a pet. The boy felt so guilty that it translated into a psychosomatic condition—hysterical blindness. Eventually, though, he healed from his guilt and regained his sight. But now, as an old man, he is living in his memories; particularly, in the memories of this incident. He therefore believes he cannot see, even though he can. He could be remembering all sorts of things, but he has chosen to remember *this* incident. He is remembering selectively. For, as Jesus says in an unforgettable line, "Remembering is as selective as perception, being its past tense." Just as we decide what to focus on in the present, so we decide which memories to focus on. Research into human memory is showing just how selective, subjective, and pliable memory is.

> 3. Nothing employed for healing represents an effort to do anything at all. It is a recognition that you <u>have</u> no needs which mean that something must be <u>done</u>. It is an unselective memory, that is <u>not</u> used to <u>interfere</u> with truth. All things the Holy Spirit can employ for healing have been given Him, <u>without</u> the content and the purposes for which they have been made. They are but skills <u>without</u> an application. They <u>await</u> their use. They have <u>no</u> dedication and <u>no</u> aim.

Healing is based on the recognition that you have no real needs, nothing requiring real doing. It is the recognition that in reality all is well; nothing needs healing. Given this, *you* don't need to do anything. You don't need to wrestle reality into a more pleasing shape.

Because of the nature of healing, the skills that are used for healing are used in a very different way than normal. They are not selectively applied by you in order to further your specific agenda. You stand back from them. You withdraw your agendas from them, and instead offer them to the Holy Spirit to use as He sees fit.

The challenge in this paragraph is to apply all this to *memory*. Can we decide to withdraw our agendas from our use of memory, and let the Holy Spirit use memory only as He sees fit?

> 4. The Holy Spirit can indeed make use of memory, for God Himself is there. Yet this is not a memory of past events, but only of a present state. You are so long accustomed to believe that memory holds only what is past, that it is hard for you to realize it is a skill that can remember *now*. The limitations on remembering the world imposes on it are as vast as those you let the world impose on you. There is no link of memory to the past. If you would have it there, then there it is. But only your desire made the link, and only you have held it to a part of time where guilt appears to linger still.

When we think of the Holy Spirit making use of memory, we think of Him guiding us only to remember certain things from the past (e.g., T-17.III.1). But here, the idea is completely different. We are the ones who think memory is for remembering the past. Jesus said that, used properly, "it is a skill that can remember *now*." Think for a moment about remembering *the present*. What does it mean to remember the present? It must mean that the present, like any memory, was once in your awareness, still exists somewhere in your mind, and can be brought *back* into awareness. Yet surely, remembering a present state rather than past events is not the usual meaning of the word "remember." Jesus acknowledges this in an earlier comment in the Urtext:

> What man perceives as [truth's] attack is his own recognition of the fact that it can always be *remembered*, because it has never been destroyed. This is not a literal remembering as much as a re-membering. (Urtext)

Truth, in other words, is not a past event that is stored in memory and can be accessed. It is like an arm that has been detached from you and can be reattached. That arm, that member, is not a past thing. It exists in the present. It just needs to be re-membered.

> 5. The Holy Spirit's use of memory is quite apart from time. He does not seek to use it as a means to keep the past, but rather as a way to let it go. Memory holds the message it receives, and does what it is given it to do. It does not write the message, nor appoint what it is for. Like to the body, it is purposeless within itself. And if it seems to serve to

cherish ancient hate, and gives you pictures of injustices and hurts that you were saving, this is what you asked its message <u>be</u> and that it is [Ur: and this is what it *is*]. Committed to its vaults, the history of all the body's past is hidden there. All of the strange associations made to keep the past alive, the present dead, are stored within it, waiting your command that they be brought to you, and lived again. And thus do their effects appear to be <u>increased</u> by time, which <u>took away</u> their cause.

Memory is just a tool, totally neutral in itself, just like the body. Therefore, if our memory haunts us by serving up pictures of past "injustices and hurts," if it justifies our "ancient hate," that is not memory's fault. We are the ones making it do that. We are playing memory like a fiddle, making it sing our tune. We are using it to keep the past alive and to forget the present, to dis-member *now* from our awareness.

6. Yet time is but another phase of what <u>does nothing</u>. It works hand in hand with all the other attributes with which you seek to keep concealed the truth about yourself. Time neither takes away nor can restore. And yet you make strange use of it, as if the past had <u>caused</u> the present, which is [therefore] but a <u>consequence</u> in which no change can be made possible because its cause has <u>gone</u>. Yet change must have a cause that will endure, or else it [change] will not last. No change can be made in the present if its cause is <u>past</u>. <u>Only</u> the past is held in memory as you make use of it, and so it [memory] is a way to hold the past <u>against</u> the now.

The passage of time seems to change all things. Yet time doesn't really do anything. Nothing really passes away, just as nothing really is restored. Everything real is timelessly present. Yet we use time to obscure the timelessly present. We draw it like a curtain in front of reality, and then project motion pictures on this curtain. Then we remember the earlier moments of those movies and tell ourselves that they are the cause of what happens now. And since the cause of the present is past, and no one can go back and change the past, we can't really change the present, either. This sounds insane, but if you have ever felt that you are living in the aftermath of some life-shattering event, you know exactly what I mean.

There is a great line in Eugene O'Neill's *Long Day's Journey into*

Night, in which the mother of the family explains why she can't escape the past: "The past is the present, isn't it? It's the future, too. We all try to lie out of that but life won't let us."

> 7. Remember <u>nothing</u> that you taught yourself, for you were badly taught. And who would keep a senseless lesson in his mind, when he can learn and can preserve a <u>better</u> one? When ancient memories of hate appear, remember that their cause is gone. And so you <u>cannot</u> understand what they are <u>for</u>. Let not the cause that you would give them [the memories] <u>now</u> be what it was that made them what they were, or seemed to be. Be <u>glad</u> that it [the cause that made them what they were] is gone, for this is what you would be pardoned <u>from</u>. And see, instead, the <u>new</u> effects of cause accepted *now*, with consequences *here*. They will surprise you with their loveliness. The ancient <u>new</u> ideas they bring will be the happy consequences of a Cause so ancient that it <u>far</u> exceeds the span of memory which your perception sees.

We need to learn how to use memory in a whole new way. When memories of old injustices come to mind, we need to tell ourselves that what caused those memories is over. What caused them is not so much the past events as "the thoughts that made" the events. Rather than clinging to that ancient past, we need to remember the present. In the present lies "a Cause so ancient that it far exceeds the span of memory which your perception sees." And from this Cause will proceed new effects, "ancient new ideas" that will surprise us with their loveliness. Rather than staring in sorrow at a tragic past, we will gaze in wonder on the world that God's Love reveals to us now.

Application: Think of one of your most painful memories. Realize how this memory seems to be a significant cause of your present situation in life.

Now realize that you are engaging in selective memory. Indeed, any memory of the past is selective memory, for it shuts out the present. And that is the whole point of remembering the past, to keep you in a state of forgetfulness of the present.

Now take a few moments and try to reverse this. Say:

I have used memory to forget the present.

But I want to remember the present.
The present is buried in my mind.
But I can call it back to mind.
I can re-member it.
Holy Spirit, help me remember now.
For God Himself is there.

Then just spend some time with those last two lines, opening your mind to the memory of now.

> 8. This is the Cause the Holy Spirit has remembered <u>for</u> you, when you would forget. It is <u>not</u> past because He let It not be unremembered. It has never changed, because there never was a time in which He did not keep It safely in your mind. Its consequences will indeed <u>seem</u> new, because you thought that you remembered not their Cause. Yet was It <u>never</u> absent from your mind, for it was <u>not</u> your Father's Will that He be unremembered by His [Ur: only] Son.

When we remember God and experience the effects of God, it will all seem very new. But that is only an appearance. In fact, the memory and its effects have always been there. All the while that we forgot God, the Holy Spirit kept God's memory fresh in our mind, waiting for us to merely draw aside the veil and see it. After all, God could not abide being forgotten by His only Son.

> 9. What *you* remember never <u>was</u>. It came from causelessness which you <u>confused</u> with cause. It <u>can</u> deserve but laughter, when you learn you have remembered consequences that were causeless and could never <u>be</u> effects. The miracle reminds you of a Cause forever present, perfectly untouched by time and interference. <u>Never</u> changed from what It <u>is</u>. And <u>you</u> are Its effect, as changeless and as perfect as Itself. Its memory does <u>not</u> lie in the past, nor waits the future. It is <u>not</u> revealed in miracles. They but remind you that It has not gone [and only if It had gone would It need to be revealed]. When you forgive It [the Cause— God] for <u>your</u> sins, It will no longer <u>be</u> denied.

Jesus is contrasting the two different memories here. Our memory remembers a long sequence of senseless events—so senseless that they can't have any real cause. They must be a dream. We remember a story that never happened, because it had no real cause. Our reaction to it should be not grief, but laughter.

In contrast, the miracle reminds us of a Cause that has always been right here. This Cause has never been hidden. The only curtain that has to be drawn aside is the curtain of our own denial. And what are the effects of this Cause? We are.

This, then, is our choice. We can remember the crazy effects of a vacuous cause (the tiny, mad idea), or we can remember that we are the perfect Effects of the perfect Cause.

> 10. You who have sought to lay a judgment on your own Creator <u>cannot</u> understand it is <u>not</u> He Who laid a judgment on His Son. You would <u>deny</u> Him His Effects, yet have They never <u>been</u> denied. There <u>was</u> no time in which His Son could be condemned for what was causeless and <u>against</u> His [God's] Will. What <u>your</u> remembering would witness to is but the fear of God. He has not <u>done</u> the thing you fear. No more have <u>you</u>. And so your innocence has <u>not</u> been lost. You need <u>no</u> healing to be healed. In quietness, see in the miracle a lesson in allowing Cause to have Its <u>Own</u> Effects, and doing <u>nothing</u> that would interfere.

What I get from this puzzling paragraph is this: We think that the separation was a colossal sin on our part, which caused God to condemn us. And we think that all the injustice and tragedy we see around us is God settling the score. The world we see, therefore, is a constant testimony to the fear of God.

But all of this represents a misunderstanding of cause. We didn't do what we thought we did. The separation was not really done. It was the unreal effect of an unreal cause (the tiny, mad idea). Further, God didn't do what we thought He did. His supposed vengeance on us is just the fabric of our own crazy dream.

The miracle allows us to let go of this false account of causation. Through it, we acknowledge the real Cause and return to our rightful place as His Effects.

> 11. The miracle comes quietly into the mind that stops an instant and is still. It reaches gently from that quiet time, and from the mind it healed in quiet then, to other minds to <u>share</u> its quietness. And they will

join in doing nothing to prevent its [the miracle's] radiant extension back into the Mind Which caused <u>all</u> minds to be. Born out of sharing, there can <u>be</u> no pause in time to cause the miracle delay in hastening to all unquiet minds, and bringing them an instant's stillness, when the memory of God returns to them. Their <u>own</u> remembering is quiet now, and what has come to take its place will not be wholly unremembered afterwards.

This is such a lovely paragraph. Let me lay it out in iambic pentameter (which, as you may recall, is a form of meter in which each line has five pairs of syllables, with the accent on the second syllable of each pair). Please read it again, this time feeling the beauty in each line and the quietness that pervades the whole:

The miracle comes quietly into
the mind that stops an instant and is still.
It reaches gently from that quiet time,
and from the mind it healed in quiet then,
to other minds to share its quietness.
And they will join in doing nothing to
prevent its radiant extension back
into the Mind Which caused all minds to be.
Born out of sharing, there can be no pause
in time to cause the miracle delay
in hastening to all unquiet minds,
and bringing them an instant's stillness, when
the memory of God returns to them.
Their own remembering is quiet now,
and what has come to take its place will not
be wholly unremembered afterwards.

Here, then, is the formula for forgetting what we remember and remembering God: We must be still for just an instant. This will allow the miracle into our mind, and from there it will reach out and draw everyone into the memory that we now enjoy, the memory of God.

12. He [the Holy Spirit] to Whom time is given offers thanks for every quiet instant given Him. For in that instant is God's [Ur: His {the Holy

Spirit's}] memory allowed to offer all its treasures to the Son of God, for whom they have been kept. How gladly does He [the Holy Spirit] offer them unto the one [God's Son, us] for whom He has been given them! And His Creator <u>shares</u> His thanks, because He would not be deprived of His Effects. The instant's silence that His Son accepts gives welcome to eternity and Him [God], and lets Them enter where They would abide. For in that instant does the Son of God do <u>nothing</u> that would make himself afraid.

In that holy instant, in which the mind is still, the Holy Spirit has a chance to give us the gift that was placed in His trust when it all began: the memory of God. How would you feel if you had waited to give a gift for thirteen billion years, and finally someone had given you the chance to give it? This is why the Holy Spirit is grateful when we sit down for an instant to still our mind. And why God, as the original Giver of the gift, is grateful, too. We should remember Their gratitude the next time we sit down to do our practice.

A theoretical aside: It is a commonly accepted teaching among many Course students that the Holy Spirit is the memory of God. This implies that the Holy Spirit is not really a Person Who does things, but just our own memory of being with God, onto which we project an illusion of personhood. I have searched for twenty years for a passage that identified the Holy Spirit with the memory of God. I found one that came close—this one. In the second sentence, God's memory offers all its treasures to the Son. And in the third sentence, the Holy Spirit offers these same treasures to the Son. So both God's memory and the Holy Spirit are doing the same thing. This does not unambiguously say they *are* the same thing, but it does carry that implication.

This was very strange, for it would go against the clear teaching throughout the Course that frames the Holy Spirit and the memory of God as two distinct and different things (though related—see, for instance, W-pII.352.1:7). I was pleased, therefore, to discover that this apparent identification of the two was a product of the editing. What originally read "His memory" meaning "the Holy Spirit's memory" (the memory He has been given for us) was changed by the editors to "God's memory." This discovery undoes the one hint in the entire Course that the Holy Spirit and the memory of God are the same thing. And *this* preserves the idea that the Holy Spirit is an active, loving, intentional Agent.

13. How instantly the memory of God arises in the mind that has no fear to keep the memory away! Its own remembering has gone. There is no past to keep its fearful image in the way of glad awakening to present peace. The trumpets of eternity resound throughout the stillness, yet disturb it not. And what is <u>now</u> remembered is not fear, but rather is the Cause that fear was made to render unremembered and undone. The stillness speaks in gentle sounds of love the Son of God remembers from <u>before</u> his own remembering came <u>in between</u> the present and the past, to shut them [the gentle sounds of love] out.

The memory of God arises in our mind the instant we stop fearing it. And we stop fearing it the instant we stop remembering the world. The world, as we saw in paragraph 10, is a constant reminder that God should be feared. It is the "proof" that we sinned and that He is out to get us. When we realize that this is a false memory, then the one true memory comes streaming in. When it does, we enter a stillness that, paradoxically, is filled with sound. The trumpets of eternity are resounding throughout it. The gentle sounds of God's Love for us fill the silence. And yet the silence remains perfectly silent. A stillness full of trumpets that do not disturb the stillness. A silence full of the sounds of love that do not break the silence. Clearly, this is beyond our current understanding.

14. Now is the Son of God at last aware of <u>present</u> Cause and Its benign Effects. Now does he understand what he has made is causeless, having [Ur: making] <u>no</u> effects at all. He <u>has</u> done nothing. And in seeing <u>this</u>, he understands he never had a <u>need</u> for doing <u>anything</u>, and never did. His Cause <u>is</u> Its Effects. There never <u>was</u> a cause beside It that could generate a <u>different</u> past or future. <u>Its</u> Effects are changelessly eternal, <u>beyond</u> fear, and <u>past</u> the world of sin entirely.

When the memory of God (the final awakening to reality) dawns on us, then we will at last "get it." We will realize that everything we caused apart from God—including the entire universe and its long history—was never really caused. We never committed the sin we thought we did. And so we never needed to do anything to redeem ourselves. Now we have at last accepted the one true Cause—our Father—and that Cause's changeless Effects—ourselves.

15. What has been lost, to see the causeless <u>not</u>? And where is sacrifice, when memory of God has come to <u>take the place</u> of loss? What better

way to close the little gap between illusions and reality than to allow the memory of God to flow <u>across</u> it, making it [the gap] a bridge an instant will suffice to reach beyond? For God has closed it with Himself. His memory has <u>not</u> gone by, and left a stranded Son forever on a shore where he can glimpse <u>another</u> shore that he can never reach. His Father wills that he be lifted up and gently carried over. <u>He</u> has built the bridge, and it is He Who will transport His Son across it. Have no fear that He will fail in what He wills. Nor that you be excluded from the Will that <u>is</u> for you.

We are afraid to lose the world we made, but can it be a loss to stop seeing what never was? The world is where all the loss came from, but now the world has been replaced by the memory of God. So loss itself has disappeared.

Will this ever happen to us, personally? Will we ever experience that final, permanent remembering of God? It seems that we have stood upon the shore of this world forever, faintly glimpsing the distant shore of Heaven, yet unable to swim across the channel ourselves. Yet would God leave His Son stranded and unable to reach Him? He, therefore, has closed the gap. He has built the bridge. And He will carry us across it. We can let go of our fear that we will never get there. We can let go of it because we are God's Son and He loves His Son.

II. Reversing Effect and Cause
Commentary by Robert Perry

1. Without a cause there can be no effects, and yet without effects there is no <u>cause</u>. The cause a cause is *made* by its effects; the Father *is* a Father by His Son. Effects do not <u>create</u> their cause, but they <u>establish</u> its causation. Thus, the Son gives Fatherhood to his Creator, and <u>receives</u> the gift that he has given Him. It is *because* he is God's Son that he must <u>also</u> be a father, who creates as God created him. The circle of creation has no end. Its starting and its ending are the same. But in itself it holds the universe of all creation, without beginning <u>and</u> without an end.

The section begins by making an obvious point: Unless a cause has effects, it is not a cause. This means that the effects, in a sense, grant the status of "cause" *to* their cause. And this means that we, in a sense, grant the status of Cause to our Father. We give Him Fatherhood. And since giving is receiving, by giving Him Fatherhood, we receive it. We become fathers ourselves. We become creators. And thus creation continues without end.

2. Fatherhood *is* creation. Love <u>must</u> be extended. Purity is not confined. It is the <u>nature</u> of the innocent to be forever uncontained, without a barrier or limitation. Thus is purity <u>not</u> of the body [which is contained, limited]. Nor can it be <u>found</u> where limitation is. The body <u>can</u> be healed by its <u>effects</u>, which are as limitless as is itself. Yet must all healing come about because the mind is recognized as <u>not</u> within the body, and its innocence is quite <u>apart</u> from it [the body], and where all healing <u>is</u>. Where, then, is healing? <u>Only</u> where its cause is <u>given</u> its effects. For sickness is a meaningless attempt to give effects to causelessness, and <u>make</u> it be a cause.

For creation to have an endpoint goes against the nature of creation. For love to be contained goes against the nature of love. It is the same with purity. Purity (or innocence), to be itself, must be "forever uncontained, without a barrier or limitation." How, then, can we even speak of a pure

88

body? For there is no such thing as a body that is uncontained, "without a barrier or limitation."

The body can be healed by purity, for being unlimited, its effects extend to everything. But purity is not about doing a Master Cleanse diet or having a colonic. It is about the mind realizing it is not even inside the body, but is instead part of limitless purity. From this limitless condition, the *mind's* purity will be brought back to the body, and heal it.

> 3. Always in sickness does the Son of God attempt to make himself his cause, and <u>not</u> allow himself to be his Father's Son. For this impossible desire, he does not believe that he is Love's effect [Ur: *effects*], and must be cause <u>because</u> of what he is. The cause of healing is the <u>only</u> Cause of everything. It has but *one* effect. And in that recognition, causelessness is <u>given</u> no effects and none is <u>seen</u>. A mind within a body and a world of other bodies, each with <u>separate</u> minds, are your "creations," you the "other" mind, creating with effects <u>unlike</u> yourself. And <u>as</u> their "father," you must be like them.

As you can see, this is a very philosophical section. Continuing the theme of the end of the last paragraph, this paragraph links sickness with the confusion of cause and effect. True causation is where God, the First Cause, causes us, His Son, and then we turn around and cause our effects, our creations. Everything in this causal line is pure spirit.

False causation is where we separate off from our Cause, denying that we are His Son. Then we have our own separate effects, which are totally unlike our Father's Effects (us) and totally unlike our true effects (our creations). Our separate effects consist of the sick world of bodies, each with a little piece of mind locked up inside. The whole thing is plagued by sickness, simply because a sick thought gave rise to it and pervades it like a fogbank of germs. And since we caused this world, we figure we must be like it. We must be a mind inside a body.

Healing comes when we reverse all this and once again acknowledge the one true Cause.

> 4. Nothing at all has happened but that you have put yourself to sleep, and dreamed a dream in which you were an alien to yourself, and but a part of someone <u>else's</u> dream. The miracle does not awaken you, but merely shows you who the <u>dreamer</u> is. It teaches you there <u>is</u> a choice

of dreams while you are still asleep, depending on the <u>purpose</u> of your dreaming. Do you wish for dreams of healing, or for dreams of death? A dream is like a memory in that it pictures what you <u>wanted</u> shown to you.

We have not actually left our Cause. We have merely put ourselves to sleep, and had a dream in which someone else (the world, our parents, our boss, our kids) seemed to be dreaming us. The miracle corrects this, not by waking us up; its aim is more modest than that. It just shows us that we, in fact, are the dreamer. And thus we can choose to dream a dream that reflects our reality as God's Effect. This will be a dream of healing, rather than the dream of death that seems thrust on us by the world. Yet whichever dream we have, the fact remains that it is *our* dream.

5. An empty storehouse, with an open door, holds <u>all</u> your shreds of memories and dreams. Yet if you are the <u>dreamer</u>, you perceive this much at least: That <u>you</u> have caused the dream, and can accept <u>another</u> dream as well. But for this change in content of the dream, it <u>must</u> be realized that it is <u>you</u> who dreamed the dreaming that you do not like. It is but an effect that *you* have caused, and you would not <u>be</u> cause of this effect. In dreams of murder and attack are <u>you</u> the victim in a dying body slain. But in forgiving dreams is <u>no one</u> asked to be the victim and the sufferer. These are the happy dreams the miracle exchanges for your own. It does <u>not</u> ask you make another; <u>only</u> that you see you made the one you would <u>exchange</u> for this.

The memories and dreams of which this world is made are gone from the storehouse of our mind. They left a long time ago. This is another way of saying that this world is over. Yet even if our dream is in reality nothing, we remain the dreamer who causes it. It is crucial that we accept our role as cause, as dreamer, as counterintuitive as this may be. For only then can we accept another dream. We don't have to make that new dream ourselves; we just take responsibility for the old one. We merely need to say, "I don't want the dream in which my body is attacked and slain. I don't want the dream of victimhood. I want the forgiving dream in which no one is a victim." When we at last say that and mean it, the miracle will give the forgiving dream to us in exchange for our dream.

6. This world is <u>causeless</u>, as is every dream that anyone has dreamed within the world. No plans are possible, and no design exists that could

be found and understood. What else could be <u>expected</u> from a thing that has no cause? Yet if it <u>has</u> no cause, <u>it has no purpose</u>. You may cause a dream, but never will you give it real <u>effects</u>. For that would change its <u>cause</u>, and it is this you <u>cannot</u> do. The dreamer of a dream is <u>not</u> awake, but does <u>not</u> know he sleeps. He sees <u>illusions</u> of himself as sick or well, depressed or happy, but without a stable cause with <u>guaranteed</u> effects.

We try so hard to make our way through the world. We try to figure out how the world works, how it is designed, so that we can craft effective plans. We try to understand the purpose of the world, what larger aim it is meant to fulfill. How strange, then, to hear from Jesus that all of these questions miss the point. How can the world have a design or a purpose or an aim that it will fulfill, if it was never caused in the first place? We are like the dreamer who sees a world in front of him and does not realize he is asleep, does not realize this place he sees does not exist. We are like the dreamer who sees himself shifting from health to sickness, not realizing that things change so erratically because his dream is the outpicturing of an unstable cause.

> 7. The miracle establishes you dream a dream, and that its content is not true. This is a crucial step in dealing with illusions. No one is <u>afraid</u> of them when he perceives <u>he made them up</u>. The fear was held in place <u>because</u> he did not see that he was <u>author</u> of the dream, and not a figure <u>in</u> the dream. He gives <u>himself</u> the consequences that he dreams he gave his brother. And it is but this the dream has put together and has offered him, to show him that his wishes have been done. Thus does he fear his <u>own</u> attack, but sees it at another's hands. As victim, he is suffering from its effects, but [apparently] <u>not</u> their cause. He authored <u>not</u> his own attack, and he is innocent of what he caused. The miracle does nothing but to show him that <u>he</u> has done nothing. What he fears is cause <u>without</u> the consequences that would <u>make</u> it cause. And so it never was.

How would it feel to look around you at your world and say, "This is not real; I am dreaming this, and it is not true"? If you really believed this, the immediate effect would be that the world would no longer make you afraid. It can only cause you fear when you think that you are just a figure in the dream, not the dreamer pulling all the strings.

Here is what is really going on. All the things the world is doing to you are just pictures of what you think *you* did to *it*. Its attacks on you are pictures of your attacks on the world. To put this differently, every time you see a hand raised against you, you are looking in a kind of time-lag mirror, in which you are really seeing a hand that *you* raised against someone else. The time lag between the hand you raised against another and the hand raised against you keeps you from realizing that you are merely looking in a mirror.

Superficially, the mirror seems to show you that you are the innocent victim of an unjust attack. But on a deeper level, it seems to show you that you are getting your just deserts. It seems to prove that you really did attack the world in the first place, or else why would it be attacking you back? How could your attack have produced such real effects unless it had been a real cause?

This is where the miracle comes in. By making the effects disappear, it shows you that your attack couldn't have been a real cause, because its supposed effects have just vanished. If all the raised hands you see in the mirror suddenly lower and drop their rocks, isn't it fair to conclude that you must have never committed the crime they were going to punish you for?

Application: Think of a recent attack on you that genuinely hurt. Then say to yourself,

> *This is a mirror image of what I think I did to others.*
> *I show myself this image to prove that I really did it, that I really sinned.*
> *The miracle will change this image to a benign one.*
> *And thus it will show me that I never sinned.*

8. The separation started with the dream the Father was deprived of His Effects, and powerless to keep them since He was no longer their Creator. In the dream, the dreamer made <u>himself</u>. But what he made has turned <u>against</u> him, taking on the role of its creator, as the dreamer had. And as he hated <u>his</u> Creator, so the figures in the dream have hated <u>him</u>. His body is their slave, which they abuse because the motives <u>he</u> has given it have <u>they</u> adopted as their own. And hate it for the vengeance

it would offer <u>them</u>. It is <u>their</u> vengeance on the body which appears to prove the dreamer <u>could</u> not be the maker of the dream. Effect and cause are first split off, and then <u>reversed,</u> so that effect becomes a cause; the cause, effect.

I have always found this paragraph fascinating. It details a two-step process to explain why the world is so attacking. First, we turned against our Creator. We split off from Him and proclaimed ourselves a self-caused effect. Out of this, we made this dream world. This means that the world was made from the idea of "cause hated by its effect." If the template for the world was "cause hated by its effect," and *we* are the cause with the *world* being our effect, how is the world going to feel toward us?

The second step starts with us giving our body abusive motives. We order it to abuse the other dream figures. Those dream figures then turn around and abuse our body. Why? Because first, they were made of the same cloth as our body. If we made our body out of attack, then the rest of the dream figures were made of that, too. But more to the point, they aim their attacks on our body in particular because they have been abused *by* it and are now taking revenge *on* it.

The dream, in other words, is again a time-lag mirror. The mirror pictures our attack on God and our attack on the world. Those are the attacks we are really seeing whenever we see others attacking us. A sobering thought, isn't it?

But we have forgotten all this. We have covered over the tracks of our causation. All we see now is a bunch of dream figures taking vengeance on us. How, we wonder, could that be coming from us? Why on earth would we cause a dream that treats us so poorly? Look what the dream is doing to us. Surely we are its effect, not its cause.

> 9. This is the separation's final step, with which salvation, which proceeds to go the <u>other</u> way, begins. This final step is an effect of what has gone before, <u>appearing</u> as a cause. The miracle is the first step in giving <u>back</u> to cause the function of causation, <u>not</u> effect. For <u>this</u> confusion has produced the dream, and while it lasts will wakening be feared. Nor will the call to wakening be heard, because it <u>seems</u> to be the call to fear.

As we just saw, the separation went through several steps to reach the final step in which we seem to be utterly at the mercy of the world we made. At this final step, cause and effect are hopelessly reversed, so that our trivial effect (the world) seems to be our all-powerful cause, to which we are totally subservient. Here, at this lowest point, is where salvation begins, and increasingly gives causation back to where it belongs. It gives it back to us, as maker of the world. And it gives it back to God, as Creator of reality. As long as we think that we stole causation from God and made a world apart from Him, we will understandably be afraid of waking up to Him. That would be like coming home after impersonating our father at the bank and draining his bank accounts.

> 10. Like <u>every</u> lesson that the Holy Spirit requests you learn, the miracle is clear. It <u>demonstrates</u> what He would have you learn, and <u>shows</u> you its effects are what you <u>want</u>. In His forgiving dreams are the <u>effects</u> of yours undone, and hated enemies perceived as friends with merciful intent. Their enmity is seen as causeless now, <u>because</u> they did not make it [you did]. And you can accept the role of maker of their hate, <u>because</u> you see that it has no effects. Now are you freed from this much of the dream; the world is neutral, and the bodies that still seem to move about as separate things <u>need not be feared</u>. And so they are <u>not sick</u>.

We have been told that the miracle brings us the forgiving dream, but how does it do that? Does everyone suddenly turn nice? The way this paragraph talks, the miracle shows us a different *meaning* in the same attacking bodies. The miracle will show us that the hate we saw driving those bodies was really projected onto them by us. The red glow we saw in their eyes was really the devil within ourselves. Their power to hurt us was really granted them by us. This is not to say that the minds directing those bodies were free of hate. Yet when we peel off *our* hate from them, we will see beneath *their* hate, and see that, deep down, they are really "friends with merciful intent."

In seeing this, we will also realize that, when we made those hateful figures, we didn't really make anything. We made a mirage. Our cause didn't produce real effects, and so it wasn't a real cause—which means we didn't sin.

All of this will show us that the bodies out there are simply neutral.

They don't wield the power of hate, the power of hurt. And so they "need not be feared." And being free of this sinful power, they can't really be sick.

> 11. The miracle returns the <u>cause</u> of fear to you who made it. But it <u>also</u> shows that, <u>having</u> no effects, it is <u>not</u> cause, because the function of causation is to <u>have</u> effects. And where effects are gone, there <u>is</u> no cause. Thus is the body healed by miracles <u>because</u> they show the mind <u>made</u> sickness, and employed the body to be victim, or <u>effect,</u> of what it made. Yet <u>half</u> the lesson will not teach the whole. The miracle is useless if you learn but that the <u>body</u> can be healed, for this is <u>not</u> the lesson it was sent to teach. The lesson is the *mind* was sick that thought the body <u>could</u> be sick; projecting <u>out</u> its guilt caused <u>nothing</u>, and had <u>no</u> effects.

I think this paragraph is one of the Course's most important statements of the relationship between the miracle and physical healing. It openly says, "Thus is the body healed by miracles." Miracles *can* heal the body because illness is caused by the mind projecting guilt onto the body. Being of the mind, miracles can undo what the mind has done. Yet the idea that bodies can be healed is not the lesson that miracles are sent to teach. They are sent to us to teach a much deeper lesson: that when the mind projected its guilt and caused illness, it really caused *nothing*. It caused only a dream. And that is why the supposed illness can be so quickly and easily dispelled, because it was just vapor.

Application: Think of an illness (either yours or someone else's) that you believe was miraculously healed. Then say,

> *This miracle was sent to teach that when the mind projected its guilt and made this illness, it really made **nothing**.*

> 12. This world is full of miracles. They stand in shining silence next to every dream of pain and suffering, of sin and guilt. They are the dream's <u>alternative</u>, the choice to be the dreamer, rather than deny the active role in making up the dream. They are the glad effects of taking <u>back</u> the consequence of sickness to its cause. The body is released because

the mind acknowledges "this is not <u>done to</u> me, but *I* am doing this." And thus the mind is free to make another choice instead. Beginning here, salvation will proceed to change the course of every step in the descent to separation, until all the steps have been retraced, the ladder gone, and <u>all</u> the dreaming of the world undone.

Miracles are always there, standing off to the side unseen, waiting for us. They are the pivot on which the whole journey turns. We have been descending the ladder of separation for eons. It is the ladder of causation confusion. As we descend, we are increasingly convinced that what we caused, caused us. Yet one day, in the iron grip of our effects, we see the miracle, standing "in shining silence" next to our dream of pain and sickness. We accept the miracle, and realize that the affliction in our body is not being done to us, but that, rather, we are doing this. Thus the miracle gives us back the role of causation. And thus we start back up that same ladder, undoing our causation confusion step by step, until all the steps have been retraced, the ladder itself disappears, and we fully and finally acknowledge our Cause.

III. The Agreement to Join
Commentary by Robert Perry

1. What waits in perfect certainty <u>beyond</u> salvation is not our concern [in this course]. For you have barely started to allow your first, uncertain steps to be directed up the ladder separation led you down. The miracle alone is your concern at present. Here is where we [in this course] must <u>begin</u>. And having started, will the way be made serene and simple in the rising up to waking and the ending of the dream.

Yes, heavenly knowledge is our final goal. And yes, such knowledge towers far above the miracle. Yet the miracle is what we need *now*. It is where the Course puts its focus. For we have barely started up that long ladder we climbed down. We are just a few steps from the bottom. Putting our main focus on knowledge, on having experiences of Heaven, will most likely lead to one of two things: feeling occasionally inspired while we stay stuck at our current step, or training our mind to have mystical experiences while our character remains unregenerate, safely insulated from the miracle.

When you accept a miracle, you do not <u>add</u> your dream of fear to one that is <u>already</u> being dreamed. Without <u>support</u>, the dream will fade away without effects. For it is your <u>support</u> that strengthens it.
2. No mind is sick until another mind <u>agrees</u> that they are separate. And thus it is their <u>joint</u> decision to be sick. If you <u>withhold</u> agreement and accept the part <u>you</u> play in making sickness real, the other mind cannot project its guilt without your aid in <u>letting</u> it perceive itself as separate and apart from <u>you</u>. Thus is the body <u>not</u> perceived as sick by <u>both</u> your minds from <u>separate</u> points of view. <u>Uniting</u> with a brother's mind prevents the <u>cause</u> of sickness and perceived effects. Healing is the effect of minds that join, as sickness comes from minds that separate.

These sentences rest on an interesting claim: Sickness comes out of a belief, but this belief, to be held, requires others to agree with it. We are, after all, social creatures. It is extremely difficult for us to hold onto a belief in total isolation. We need the agreement of others. Before we give something our full assent, we need to see them nodding.

In the case of sickness, this is ironic, for sickness comes from the belief in separation. This means that we need others to *join* with us in agreeing that we are *separate*. Sickness depends on this strange contradiction. What, then, happens if they don't agree? What happens if someone, especially someone we respect and value, refuses to believe that we are, in fact, separate? According to Jesus, we will not be able to maintain our sickness.

> 3. The miracle does nothing just *because* the minds <u>are</u> joined, and <u>cannot</u> separate. Yet in the dreaming has this been reversed, and separate minds are seen as bodies, which <u>are</u> separated and which cannot <u>join</u>. Do not allow your brother to be sick, for if he is, have <u>you</u> abandoned him to his own dream by <u>sharing</u> it with him. He has not seen the cause of sickness where it is [in the gap between you], and <u>you</u> have overlooked [in the usual sense of denial] the gap between you, where the sickness has been bred [by your agreement]. Thus are you <u>joined</u> in sickness, to preserve the little gap unhealed, where sickness is kept carefully protected, cherished, and upheld by firm belief, lest God should come to bridge the little gap that leads to Him. Fight not His coming with illusions, for it is His coming that you <u>want</u> above all things that seem to glisten in the dream.

The miracle doesn't do some new thing, it simply reveals that minds are already joined. This is how it brings healing. In this world, it certainly appears that we are all separate. Yet that is the illusion, and anything that leaves that illusion unchallenged is allowing sickness to be. Hence, Jesus' injunction: "Do not allow your brother to be sick." When we see a loved one that is sick, a dozen things go through our mind about how we might be able to help: visiting, helping with their care or daily tasks, or offering medical advice, or spiritual counsel. What we usually don't think is, "I need to withdraw my agreement that we are separate." As long as we don't withdraw that agreement, then both of us are ignoring the real cause of the sickness, the little gap between us. Jesus says, "Thus are you joined in sickness, to preserve the little gap unhealed."

> 4. The end of dreaming is the end of <u>fear</u>, and love was <u>never</u> in the world of dreams. The gap *is* little. Yet it holds the seeds of pestilence

and every form of ill, because it is a <u>wish</u> to keep apart and <u>not</u> to join. And thus it seems to give a <u>cause</u> to sickness which is <u>not</u> its cause. The <u>purpose</u> of the gap is all the cause that sickness has. For it was made to keep you separated, in a body which you see as if it were the <u>cause</u> of pain.

The body, of course, seems to be the cause of pain and sickness. When we get sick we think it is due to germs or genes or some other biological cause. We don't think that it's because there is a gap between us and others. This gap (which becomes an important theme beginning in this section) is not a physical gap. "It is a *wish* to keep apart and *not* to join." In this single, simple wish lie the seeds of every form of sickness.

5. The cause of pain is separation, <u>not</u> the body, which is only its <u>effect</u>. Yet separation is but empty space, enclosing nothing, doing nothing, and as unsubstantial as the empty place between the ripples that a ship has made in passing by. And covered just as fast, as water rushes in to close the gap, and as the waves in joining cover it. Where is the gap <u>between</u> the waves when they have joined, and covered up the space which seemed to keep them separate for a little while? Where are the grounds for sickness when the minds have joined to close the little gap <u>between</u> them, where the seeds of sickness seemed to grow?

Application: Think of some physical ailment of yours, either an illness or some other kind of impaired functioning.

This seems to have a biological cause.
But its real cause is separation between me and others,
particularly between me and [name a few people you feel especially separate from].
Yet separation is just empty space.
It is nothing.

Then visualize the separation between you and these people as "the empty place between the ripples that a ship has made in passing by."
That is how insubstantial this separation is.

Then watch as the "water rushes in to close the gap, and as the waves in joining cover it."

Realize this represents you and these people closing the gap between you.

Then hear Jesus ask you, "Where is the gap between the waves when they have joined, and covered up the space which seemed to keep them separate for a little while?

Where are the grounds for sickness when the minds have joined to close the little gap between them, where the seeds of sickness seemed to grow?"

> 6. God builds the bridge [across the gap], but only in the space left clean and vacant by the miracle. The seeds [Ur: weeds] of sickness and the shame of guilt [Ur: sin] He <u>cannot</u> bridge, for He can not destroy the alien will that He created not. Let its effects be gone and clutch them not with eager hands, to keep them for yourself. The miracle will brush them all aside, and thus make room for Him Who wills to come and bridge His Son's returning to Himself.

God will build the bridge that carries us across the gap between us and our brothers. This bridging refers to our final awakening, when there is no longer even the tiniest gap remaining between the Sons of God. However, God cannot bridge it as long as the gap remains our wish. He cannot bridge it while it is choked with "the weeds of sickness and the shame of sin" (Urtext version). We, then, need to engage in some weed clearing, for which we use (please excuse the lame metaphor) the miracle brush: "The miracle will brush them all aside, and thus make room for Him."

> 7. Count, then, the silver miracles and golden dreams of happiness as all the treasures you would keep within the storehouse of the world. The door is open, <u>not</u> to thieves, but to your starving brothers, who mistook for gold the shining of a pebble, and who stored a heap of snow that shone like silver. They have nothing left behind the open door. What is the world except a little gap perceived to tear eternity apart, and break it into days and months and years? And what are <u>you</u> who live within the world except a picture of the Son of God in broken pieces, each concealed within a separate and uncertain bit of clay?

What a poignant paragraph! Our brothers have spent their lives storing "things that seem to glisten in the dream." They have valued these shiny things above unity with one another. Yet in the process, they stored a gleaming pebble they mistook for gold and "a heap of snow that shone like silver." Now they look inside their treasure house, expecting to gloat on the sight of their hoard, and all they see is a worthless pebble in a puddle of water. Maybe they see what would normally be called real gold and silver, yet the truth is still that it is just a pebble in a puddle. After all their hoarding, they have nothing, nothing real. They are starving for the bread of life, and thirsting for living water.

Our job is to have a different storehouse, where we store a different kind of silver and gold. What we store are "silver miracles and golden dreams of happiness [referring to the happy dream]." These are the precious gifts that wipe away the space between us. These are the true riches that restore the unity of the Son who seemed to splinter into a billion fragments, leaving each fragment lonely and deprived. These are *real* treasures. Let us, then, leave the door of our treasure house open so that our starving brothers can come in from the cold and share in our trove of miracles, which will release all of us from the ancient soul sickness of being alone.

> 8. Be not afraid, my child, but let your world be gently lit by miracles. And where the little gap was seen to stand <u>between</u> you and your brother, join him there. And so sickness will now be seen <u>without</u> a cause. The dream of healing in forgiveness lies, and gently shows you that you [Ur: shows you *you* have] never sinned. The miracle would leave <u>no</u> proof of guilt to bring you witness to what never <u>was</u>. And in your storehouse it will make a place of welcome for your Father and your Self. The door is open, that all those may come who would no longer starve, and would enjoy the feast of plenty set before them there. And they will meet with your invited Guests the miracle has asked to come to you.

It is time to invite our starving brothers into our storehouse, to join us for a joyous feast, a feast of miracles. We have stood apart from them. There has been a gap between us, out of which has sprung sickness and sin. Now it is time to dispense with this gap. Right where the gap has been we set up our feast. And the miracles we partake in together wipe away what remains of that dreadful and unnecessary gap. The years of icy separation fall away and we are reconciled. And as the gap between us passes away, all of our sins that produced the gap pass away, too. The healing that we experience demonstrates that our sins had no real effect, that we never really sinned.

This feast of miracles is so holy that it invites the most holy Guests there are: our Father and our Self. And They never refuse an invitation. Can you imagine what a feast would be like at which God and Christ suddenly showed up? They will attend our feast, but not as special guests Who keep Themselves apart. Our brothers will meet with Them. There will be nothing but reconciliation and unity between all of our guests.

> 9. This is a feast unlike indeed to those the dreaming of the world has shown. For here, the more that anyone receives, the more is left for all the rest to share. The Guests have brought unlimited supply with Them. And no one is deprived or can deprive. Here is a feast the Father lays before His Son, and shares it equally with him. And in Their sharing there can <u>be</u> no gap in which abundance falters and grows thin. Here can the lean years enter not, for time waits not upon this feast, which <u>has</u> no end. For Love has set its table in the space that seemed to keep your Guests <u>apart</u> from you.

The Guests (God and Christ) are not just showing up, They are bringing the food—the miracles. They are the Ones laying the feast before us. And what a feast! "The Guests have brought unlimited supply with Them." This food is totally unlike normal food, "For here, the more that anyone receives, the more is left for all the rest to share." Just imagine that. There is no way for this feast to ever run out. Our brothers' condition of starvation has been *permanently* reversed. Indeed, this is a feast that will never end. The moment it started, it ended everything that came before it. For that is what happens when Love sets its table in the gap that used to keep us and our brothers apart.

Application: A visualization:

Think about someone you feel painfully separate from.
Feel the gap between you.
This gap is not really one of space.

It is a mutual wish that you be separate and apart.

Now see that this person is starving, starving for real sustenance, starving for the bread of life.

Have compassion on this person.

Invite a miracle to come into the space between you, and cleanse it of that alien wish to be separate.

Picture this as Love setting a table between you, and laying out a sumptuous feast for the two of you.

This is not a feast of physical food.

It is a feast of miracles.

Imagine what it would be like for the two of you to partake in miracles together, miracles that would wipe away the gap that separates you.

See the joy on this person's face as starvation is replaced with completion.

Now see the table lengthen in both directions.

Invite all of your starving brothers to join you in this feast of miracles.

See them enter one by one to sit at your table.

Notice that the food has miraculous properties, for the more that anyone receives, the more there is left for all the rest to share.

Finally, see the holy Guests arrive; see God and Christ join the feast.

And see Them lovingly greet each person who is there.

This is a symbolic picture of what your life can literally become: a feast of miracles, shared by you and everyone you meet, replacing the hunger of loneliness with the fullness of joining; a feast in which the Presence of God and Christ is constantly felt, a feast in which the abundance of miracles never falters, and indeed only grows greater with time, for this is a feast that has no end.

IV. The Greater Joining
Commentary by Robert Perry

1. Accepting the Atonement for yourself means <u>not</u> to give support to someone's dream of sickness and of death. It means that you share <u>not</u> his wish to separate, and let him turn illusions on himself. Nor do you wish that they be turned, instead, on <u>you</u>. Thus have they <u>no</u> effects. And <u>you</u> are free of dreams of pain because you let <u>him</u> be. <u>Unless</u> you help him, you will suffer pain with him because that is your wish. And you become a figure in <u>his</u> dream of pain, as he in <u>yours</u>. So do you and your brother <u>both</u> become illusions, and without identity. You could be anyone or anything, depending on whose evil dream you share. You can be sure of just <u>one</u> thing; that you are evil, for you share in dreams of fear.

"The sole responsibility of the miracle worker is to accept the Atonement for himself" (T-2.V.5:1). This well-known line can easily seem like the perfect Course justification for the idea that I just need to attend to me; your Atonement is your business. Yet here Jesus says that accepting the Atonement for myself means acknowledging my oneness with another, which then sets *both* of us free. It means getting outside the notion that anything is just about me.

If, on the other hand, you agree with someone's belief that the two of you are separate, several things flow from that. First, you are actually supporting that person's belief in separateness, and thus strengthening the sickness that stems from it. Second, you suffer with him, because you share in the belief that is the source of suffering. Third, you lose identity. Why? Because you have let your brother's belief in separateness dictate who you are—dictate that you are separate. Thus, you become a figure in his dream, a puppet on his string. And puppets don't have an identity of their own.

Thus, when it comes to the belief in separation, you must refuse to be a conformist.

2. There is a way of finding certainty <u>right here and now</u>. Refuse to be a part of fearful dreams <u>whatever</u> form they take, for you will lose

identity in them. You <u>find</u> yourself by <u>not</u> accepting them as causing you, and <u>giving</u> you effects. You stand apart from them, but <u>not</u> apart from him who dreams them. Thus you separate the dreamer from the dream, and join in <u>one</u>, but let the <u>other</u> go. The dream is but illusion in the mind. And with the <u>mind</u> you <u>would</u> unite, but <u>never</u> with the dream. It is the <u>dream</u> you fear, and <u>not</u> the mind. You see them as the same, because you think that *you* are but a dream. And what is real and what is but illusion <u>in yourself</u> you do not know and cannot tell apart.

If everyone around you thinks they are separate, do you have to go along with that? If everyone thinks that there is reason for fear, do you have to agree? If you let their dream dictate who you are, then, in your eyes, you will no longer have an identity of your own. You will become a ghost, "a dancing shadow" (T-27.VII.8:7).

The thing to do is to refuse to agree with their dream—not so much in your speech, but in your *mind*. Stand apart from the dream (again, in your mind), as you would mentally stand apart from some crazy primitive ritual that you don't understand. But while separating from the dream, join with the dreamer. If your dearest love suddenly thought she was Amelia Earhart, you would stand apart from this mistaken identity, yet wouldn't you still feel joined with her?

We, however, think it is all or nothing: either join with both dream and dreamer or separate from both. That is because we have confused ourselves with a dream. The trick is to make a razor-sharp distinction, to "join in one, but let the other go."

> 3. Like you, your brother thinks <u>he</u> is a dream. Share not in his illusion of himself, for <u>your</u> identity depends on his reality. Think, rather, of him as a mind in which illusions still persist, but as a mind which brother is to you. He is not brother made by what he <u>dreams</u>, nor is his body, "hero" of the dream, your brother. It is his <u>reality</u> that is your brother, as is yours to him. Your mind and his <u>are</u> joined in brotherhood. His body and his dreams but <u>seem</u> to make a little gap, where yours have joined with his.

Application: Choose the first person that comes to mind and say:

You are the dreamer, not the dream.
I will not share in your illusions of yourself as a separate being.

Rather, I think of you as a mind in which illusions still persist, but
 as a mind which is my brother.
Your dreams about yourself are not what make you my brother.
Nor is your body, "hero" of the dream, my brother.
*Your **reality** is my brother.*
Our minds are joined in brotherhood.

4. And yet, between your <u>minds</u> there <u>is</u> no gap. To join his dreams is thus to meet him <u>not</u>, because his dreams would <u>separate</u> from you. Therefore release him, merely by your claim on brotherhood, and <u>not</u> on dreams of fear. Let him acknowledge who he <u>is</u>, by not supporting his illusions by your faith, for if you do, you will have faith in <u>yours</u>. With faith in yours, <u>he</u> will not be released, and <u>you</u> are kept in bondage to his dreams. And dreams of fear will haunt the little gap, inhabited but by illusions which you have <u>supported</u> in your brother's [Ur: each other's] mind.

Let's bring this talk about joining someone's dreams down to earth. The particular situation Jesus has in mind here is this: Someone is experiencing sickness, which has ultimately come from her belief in separateness. You are observing this person. Do you identify her with her sickness? Do you feel sympathy for her? Do you pity her because she and her sickness are bound together? This is what Jesus is talking about. If your answer to these questions is "yes," then you are joining in her dream. And since the dream lies in the gap between you, you are reinforcing that gap, reinforcing your separateness. Instead, refuse to believe in the gap, or any dream that populates the gap, and join with her *mind*, for "between your *minds* there *is* no gap" (Urtext version).

5. Be certain, if you do <u>your</u> part, he will do his, for he will <u>join</u> you where <u>you</u> stand. Call not to him to meet you in the gap <u>between</u> you, or you <u>must</u> believe that it is <u>your</u> reality as well as his. You <u>cannot</u> do his part, but this you *do* when you become a passive figure in his dreams, <u>instead</u> of dreamer of your own. Identity in dreams is meaningless <u>because</u> the dreamer and the dream are one. Who shares a dream must <u>be</u> the dream he shares, because <u>by</u> sharing is a cause produced.

So often we do try to join in the gap. We say, "I agree that you have been so victimized, and you agree that I am your greatest supporter." Instead of joining in the gap, we need to acknowledge that there is no gap. This is our part, and "If you do your part, he will do his…he will join you where you stand." We can't do his part, but we can trust *him* to do his part if we do *ours*. In other words, if there is someone in your life that you are feeling separate from, stand in the place of joining, and trust him or her to join you there.

The third sentence speaks of us trying to "do his part." How? We let his part dictate what we do. We let his belief in separateness dictate our beliefs. He reads his lines, and then we repeat those same lines word for word. In essence, then, his part "does" us.

> 6. You share confusion and you <u>are</u> confused, for in the gap no stable self exists. What is the same [your dreams and his?] seems different, because what <u>is</u> the same [you and your brother?] appears to be unlike. His dreams are yours because you <u>let</u> them be. But if you took your <u>own</u> away would he be free of them, and of his own as well. Your dreams are witnesses to his, and his attest the truth of yours. Yet if you see there <u>is</u> no truth in yours, his dreams will go, and he will understand what <u>made</u> the dream.

If you agree with your brother's confused and unstable illusions of what he is, they will determine your perception of yourself. You will be confused about yourself. You will feel like an unstable self. Yet his dreams only dictate your self-perception when you let them. If you withdrew *your* dreams, if you believed that you are different from what he thinks he is, everything would change. Without the support of your dreams, his dreams would evaporate. And then he would finally understand that his own mind, not you, not the world, made this supposed identity of his.

> 7. The Holy Spirit is in <u>both</u> your minds, and He <u>is</u> One because there is no gap that separates His Oneness from Itself. The gap between your bodies matters not, for what is joined in Him is <u>always</u> one. No one is sick if someone <u>else</u> accepts his union <u>with</u> him. His desire to be a sick and separated mind can <u>not</u> remain without a witness or a cause. And both <u>are</u> gone if someone wills to be united with him. He has dreams that he was separated from his brother who, by sharing <u>not</u> his dream,

has left the space between them vacant. And the Father comes to join His Son the Holy Spirit joined.

Application: Think of someone you know who is sick, and repeat these words to him or her:

The Holy Spirit is in both of our minds.
And He is One because there is no gap that separates His Oneness from Itself.
The gap between our bodies matters not, for what is joined in Him is always one.
I accept my union with you.
And because I do, you cannot be sick.
Your desire to be a sick and separated mind cannot remain without a witness and without a cause.
And both are gone if I will to unite with you.
I will to unite with you.

8. The Holy Spirit's function is to take the broken picture of the Son of God and put the pieces into place again. This holy picture, healed entirely, does He hold out to every separate piece that thinks it is a picture in itself. To each He offers his Identity, Which the whole picture represents, instead of just a little, broken bit that he insisted was himself. And when he sees this picture he will recognize himself. If you share not your brother's evil dream, this is the picture that the miracle will place within the little gap, left clean of all the seeds of sickness and of sin. And here the Father will receive His Son, because His Son was gracious to himself.

In the previous section, Jesus mentions that all of us together are "a picture of the Son of God in broken pieces, each concealed within a separate and uncertain bit of clay" (T-28.III.7:5). Now he says that the Holy Spirit's job is to put all the pieces back together, to reassemble the whole picture. Then the Holy Spirit presents this whole picture to each one of us and tells us that this is who we are. We think we are just one small broken piece, one little shard. But He says no, each one of us is the whole thing.

All we need to do to accept the whole picture as who we are is refuse to agree with our brother's dreams. If we will just leave the little gap clean and open, free of the dreams that occupied it, the Holy Spirit will lay this picture in the gap, and we will look upon it and recognize our own true face.

> 9. I thank You, Father, knowing You will come to close each little gap that lies between the broken pieces of Your holy Son. Your holiness, complete and perfect, lies in every one of them. And they <u>are</u> joined because what is in one <u>is</u> in them all. How holy is the smallest grain of sand, when it is recognized as being part of the completed picture of God's Son! The forms the broken pieces seem to take mean nothing. For the whole is in each one. And every aspect of the Son of God is just the same as every other part.

Jesus rarely breaks into prayer in the Course, but he does a few times. (See the final paragraphs of the Text, for instance.) This prayer is a song of gratitude for the fact that all of us seemingly broken pieces will one day be reunited. Think about that for a moment. What more glorious news could there be than that? It is also a song of praise to the holiness and perfection of each of the broken pieces, each of the Sons of God. It literally doesn't matter if a Son takes the form of a human body or takes the form of *a grain of sand* (!). "The forms the broken pieces seem to take mean nothing. For the whole is in each one. And every aspect of the Son of God is just the same as every other part."

Application: Let's go ahead and pray this prayer ourselves and make it our own.

> *I thank You, Father, knowing You will come to close each little*
> *gap that lies between the broken pieces of Your holy Son.*
> *Your holiness, complete and perfect, lies in every one of them.*
> *And they are joined because what is in one is in them all.*
> *How holy is the smallest grain of sand, when it is recognized as*
> *being part of the completed picture of God's Son!*
> *The forms the broken pieces seem to take mean nothing.*
> *For the whole is in each one.*
> *And every aspect of the Son of God is just the same as every other*
> *part.*

10. Join not your brother's dreams but join with <u>him,</u> and where you join His Son the Father <u>is</u>. Who seeks for substitutes when he perceives <u>he has lost nothing</u>? Who would <u>want</u> to have the "benefits" of sickness when he has received the simple happiness of health? What God has given cannot <u>be</u> a loss, and what is not of Him has <u>no</u> effects. What, then, would you perceive within the gap? The seeds of sickness come from the belief that there is <u>joy</u> in separation, and its giving up <u>would be a sacrifice</u>. But miracles are the result when you do not insist on seeing in the gap what is not there. Your willingness to <u>let</u> illusions go is all the Healer of God's Son requires. He will place the miracle of healing where the seeds of sickness were. And there will be <u>no</u> loss, but <u>only</u> gain.

For some reason, we are actually *attached* to the gap that separates us from our brother. We are actually attached to the seeds of sickness that lie in that gap, because somehow we *want* the "benefits" of sin. And so we reach for a substitute joining; we join our brother's dreams, rather than joining with him. Yet in place of this pseudo-joining, we could have the real thing. We could have real union. Isn't that what we all want? All we need to do is not insist on seeing those Technicolor dreams in the gap. We need simply see the gap as what it is: empty and without substance. Then the Holy Spirit "will place the miracle of healing where the seeds of sickness were. And there will be *no* loss, but *only* gain" (Urtext version).

V. The Alternate to Dreams of Fear
Commentary by Robert Perry

1. What is a sense of sickness but a sense of limitation? Of a splitting *off* and separating *from*? A gap that is perceived between you and your brother, and what is now seen as health? [Ur: A gap perceived *between* ourselves and what is seen as health?] And so the good is seen to be [Ur: The good is seen] <u>outside</u>; the evil, <u>in</u>. And thus is sickness separating <u>off</u> the self from good, and <u>keeping</u> evil in [Ur: there]. God is the <u>Alternate</u> to dreams of fear. Who shares in them can <u>never</u> share in Him. But who <u>withdraws</u> his mind from sharing them *is* sharing Him. There <u>is</u> no other choice. Except you share it, <u>nothing</u> can exist. And <u>you</u> exist because God shared His Will with you, that His creation might create.

When we are sick, don't we feel like what Jesus describes here—by ourselves in our own little corner, split off from health and wholeness? We sometimes feel like a pus-filled boil, while all things good seem to lie outside of us. Jesus implies here that this feeling is not just the product of sickness; it is the *source* of sickness. He implies that sickness comes from a deep-seated sense that the good is outside and evil inside. This is why it is so crucial that we not support someone's dream of sickness. We must share in God instead of sharing in dreams. If we share in them, we *can't* share in Him.

2. It is the <u>sharing</u> of the evil dreams of hate and malice, bitterness and death, of sin and suffering and pain and loss, that makes them real. <u>Unshared</u>, they are perceived as meaningless. The fear is gone from them <u>because you did not give them your support</u>. Where fear has gone there love <u>must</u> come, because there <u>are</u> but these alternatives. Where one appears, the other <u>disappears</u>. And which you <u>share</u> becomes the only one you <u>have</u>. You <u>have</u> the one that you accept, because it is the only one you wish to have [Ur: you *want*].

Application: Think of someone you know who is sick, and silently speak these words to this person:

111

Your sickness seems to separate you from health and wholeness.
It is the product of a deep-seated belief that you are separated off
from goodness.
If I shared this belief, I would make it real.
Thus, I refuse to share it, so that you can see it as meaningless.
I will only share in the reality of love, not the dream of fear.
I see you as one with goodness, always and forever.

3. You share <u>no</u> evil dreams if you forgive the dreamer, and perceive that he is <u>not</u> the dream he made. And so he <u>cannot</u> be a part of <u>yours</u>, from which you <u>both</u> are free. Forgiveness <u>separates</u> the dreamer from the evil dream, and thus releases him. Remember [from the previous section] if you <u>share</u> an evil dream, you will believe you <u>are</u> the dream you share. And fearing it, you will not <u>want</u> to know your own Identity, because you think that <u>It</u> is fearful. And you <u>will</u> deny your Self, and walk upon an alien ground which your Creator did not make, and where you seem to be a something you are not. You <u>will</u> make war upon your Self, Which <u>seems</u> to be your enemy; and <u>will</u> attack your brother, as a part of what you hate. There is no compromise. You are your Self or an illusion. What <u>can</u> be between illusion and the truth? A middle ground, where you can be a thing that is <u>not</u> you, <u>must</u> be a dream and <u>cannot</u> be the truth.

Again and again Jesus returns to this theme of not sharing our brother's evil dreams, not agreeing with them. Forgiveness doesn't find a way to *approve* of the evil dreams. Rather, "Forgiveness *separates* the dreamer from the evil dream, and thus releases him" (Urtext version).

Application: Think of someone you are holding resentments about, and say,

I separate you from your evil dream.
I thus forgive you.
And I thus release you.

If, on the other hand, you keep the dreamer and the dream joined together, then you are giving that dream power to dictate who you are. If you share a fearful dream, you will think you *are* the dream. And thinking you are something fearful, you will recoil from knowing who you are. You will not want to know your Identity. You will thus deny It and make war upon It (and on your brothers who are part of It). You will walk in a place God created not (called planet Earth), where you are someone else (called a human being). If you deny your Self, this is what you get. There is no in-between. What lies in between truth and illusion is only more illusion.

Application: Think of someone you know whom you see as terribly sick, in one way or another. Now ask yourself, "If this person is at one with his or her sickness, what does that say about me and my illusions?" Can you sense that, because you see this person as being united with his or her sickness, then you see yourself as united with yours—your illnesses, your problems, and your unhealthy beliefs? Being at one with these things, you must be a creature of the earth. You must walk on an alien ground that your Creator did not create. You must live in a place where you cannot be His Son. See how all of this flows from the single decision to *not* separate this person from his or her evil dreams.

> 4. You have conceived a little gap between illusions and the truth to be the place where all your safety lies, and where your Self is safely hidden by what you have made. Here [in the gap] is a world established that is sick, and this the world the body's eyes perceive. Here are the sounds it hears; the voices that its ears were made to hear. Yet sights and sounds the body can perceive are meaningless. It cannot see nor hear. It does not know what seeing *is*; what listening is *for*. It is as little able to perceive as it can judge or understand or know. Its eyes are blind; its ears are deaf. It can not think, and so it cannot have effects.

Imagine that you are a brilliant inventor who has come to hate himself. He doesn't want to know himself. And so he creates a clear plastic sphere, about three inches across. And in this sphere he makes a miniature world, where the people and the animals are so tiny that they cannot be seen with the human eye. And so he designs a tiny robot, the same size as they are, to travel around in this microscopic environment. The tiny robot has an even tinier camera for eyes and an infinitesimal microphone for ears. As a final step, the inventor dons headgear so that now he sees what the robot's eyes see and he hears what the robot's ears hear. Finally, he gets completely absorbed in the microscopic world he placed in the little plastic bubble, and forgets entirely about the self that he hates.

This, of course, is a metaphor for what we have done. The plastic bubble is the little gap. The robot is our body, and we are the inventor.

> 5. What is there God created to be sick? And what that He created not can <u>be</u>? Let not your eyes behold a dream; your ears bear witness to illusion. They were made to look upon a world that is not there; to hear the voices that can make no sound. Yet are there other sounds and other sights that *can* be seen and heard and <u>understood</u>. For eyes and ears are senses without sense, and what they see and hear they but report. It is not <u>they</u> that hear and see, but <u>you</u>, who <u>put together</u> every jagged piece, each senseless scrap and shred of evidence, and <u>make</u> a witness to the world you want. Let not the body's ears and eyes perceive these countless fragments seen within the gap that <u>you</u> imagined, and let <u>them</u> persuade their maker his imaginings are real.

The world we have built inside the little gap is a world of sickness. Everything is sick to one degree or another. Everything is fighting off invading germs and pests and the inexorable march of time. How can God have created a world like this? Yet if He didn't create it, how can it be there at all? The rest of the paragraph says, in essence, that since the world's not there, don't treat the testimony of your eyes and ears as evidence of anything.

I have put these sentences in the first person. Please go ahead and read them again, slowly, treating them as true:

> *I will not let my eyes behold a dream;*
> *my ears bear witness to illusion.*
> *My eyes and ears were made to look upon a world that is not there;*
> *to hear the voices that can make no sound.*
> *Yet are there other sounds and other sights that can be seen and*
> *heard and understood.*
> *For my eyes and ears are senses without sense,*
> *and what they see and hear they but report.*

V. The Alternate to Dreams of Fear

It is not they that hear and see, but I.
It is I who put together every jagged piece, each senseless scrap
and shred of evidence,
and make a witness to the world I want to be the truth.
I will not let my body's ears and eyes perceive these countless
fragments seen within the gap that I imagined,
and let them persuade me that my imaginings are real.

6. Creation proves reality because it <u>shares</u> the function <u>all</u> creation shares. It is not made of little bits of glass, a piece of wood, a thread or two, perhaps, all put together to <u>attest</u> its truth. Reality does not depend on <u>this</u>. There <u>is</u> no gap that separates the truth from dreams and from illusions. Truth has left no room for them in <u>any</u> place or time. For it fills every place and every time, and makes them wholly indivisible.

We are constantly scanning our visual environment in an attempt to understand each situation. We are like crime scene investigators, who connect a drop of blood and a human hair and a thread of clothing, and make a whole story out of it. On the surface, we do this in order to understand what is going on. On a deeper level, though, we do this in order to convince ourselves that something really *is* going on, to convince ourselves that this world is real.

This process of putting together scraps of sense data is such a precarious one, isn't it? It is so flimsy and subjective. Reality, thank goodness, does not depend on this precarious process. Indeed, reality has filled every place and time with itself, making all places one place and all time one time. It has left no room for the gap. Therefore, the gap in which we see this world is not even there.

7. You who believe there is a little gap between you and your brother [Ur: between you], do not see [Ur: understand] that it is <u>here</u> you are [Ur: kept] as prisoners in a world perceived to be <u>existing</u> here. The world you see does not exist, <u>because</u> the place where you perceive it is not real. The gap is carefully concealed in fog, and misty pictures rise to cover it with vague uncertain forms and changing shapes, forever unsubstantial and unsure. Yet in the gap is <u>nothing</u>. And there <u>are</u> no awesome secrets and no darkened tombs where terror rises from the

bones of death. Look at the little gap, and you behold the innocence and emptiness of sin that you will see within yourself, when you have lost the fear of recognizing love.

Think of the gap that you feel between you and another person. Now realize that that gap is actually the "space" in which the whole world exists, a world that is not there.

Actually, the world (in this paragraph) is not really *inside* the gap. Rather, the gap is covered in fog, and the world is projected onto the outside of the fog. Thus, everything we see before us is just a motion picture projected onto mist. Given all the action we see on the fog, we assume that the fog must conceal something of real substance. Since the movie we see is a story of sickness, we suspect that the fog conceals something really dark and evil, a darkened tomb with awesome secrets, "where terror rises from the bones of death." This suspicion manifests in all the conspiracy theories that claim to reveal the dark secret behind what goes on in our world.

Yet, if we could actually clear the fog away and really look on the gap, unadorned, we would see that it's actually empty. There's nothing in there. There is no dark secret that explains all the sickness in the world. The gap is completely empty of sin, empty of any substance at all. And this emptiness of sin is what we will see in ourselves "when you have lost the fear of recognizing love."

VI. The Secret Vows
Commentary by Robert Perry

1. Who punishes the body is insane. For here the little gap is <u>seen</u>, and yet it is <u>not</u> here. It [the body] has not judged <u>itself</u>, nor made itself to be what it is not. <u>It</u> does not seek to make of pain a joy and look for lasting pleasure in the dust. It does not <u>tell</u> you what its purpose is and <u>cannot</u> understand what it is for. <u>It does not victimize</u>, because it has no will, no preferences and <u>no doubts</u>. It does not wonder what it is. And so it has no <u>need</u> to be competitive. It <u>can</u> be victimized, but <u>cannot</u> feel itself as victim. It accepts no role, but does what it is told, <u>without</u> attack.

Application: Look at your body and say (try to keep glancing at it, after glancing at each line to say):

It is insane to punish my body.
*It has not judged **itself**, nor made itself to be what it is not.*
***It** does not seek to make of pain a joy and look for lasting pleasure in the dust.*
*It does not **tell** me what its purpose is and **cannot** understand what it is for.*
***It does not victimize**, because it has no will, no preferences and **no doubts**.*
It does not wonder what it is.
*And so it has no **need** to be competitive.*
*It **can** be victimized, but **cannot** feel itself as victim.*
*It accepts no role, but does what it is told, **without** attack.*

2. It is indeed a senseless point of view to hold responsible for sight a thing that cannot see, and blame it for the sounds you do not like, although it cannot hear. It suffers not the punishment you give because it has no feeling. It behaves in ways you want, but never makes the choice. It is not born and does not die. It can but follow aimlessly the

117

path on which it has been set. And if that path is changed, it walks as easily another way. It takes no sides and judges not the road it travels. It perceives no gap, because it does not hate. It can be used for hate, but it cannot be hateful made thereby.

Application: Look at your body again, and then repeat these words (again, try to glance back and forth between these words and your body),

> *It is senseless to hold this body responsible for sight when it cannot see,*
> *and blame it for the sounds I do not like, although it cannot hear.*
> *It suffers not the punishment I give because it **has** no feeling.*
> *It behaves in ways I want, but **never** makes the choice.*
> *It is not born and does not die.*
> *It can but follow aimlessly the path on which it has been set.*
> *And if that path is changed, it walks as easily another way.*
> *It takes no sides and judges not the road it travels.*
> *It perceives no gap, because **it does not hate**.*
> *It can be **used** for hate, but it cannot be hateful **made** thereby.*

How did it feel to do these two exercises? For me, it had the effect of draining a sense of autonomy and meaning from my body. Rather than seeming to have a will of its own, my body seemed more like a neutral instrument—which puts the spotlight on how my mind is choosing to *use* my body.

3. The thing you hate and fear and loathe and <u>want</u> [i.e., the body], the body does not know. You send it forth to <u>seek</u> for separation and <u>be</u> separate. And <u>then</u> you hate it, <u>not</u> for what it is, but for the uses you have <u>made</u> of it. You shrink from what <u>it</u> sees and what <u>it</u> hears, and hate its frailty and littleness. And you despise its acts, but <u>not</u> your own. It sees and acts for *you*. It hears <u>your</u> voice. And it is frail and little by <u>your</u> wish. It <u>seems</u> to punish you, and thus <u>deserve</u> your hatred for the limitations that it brings to you. Yet you have made of it a symbol for the limitations that you want your <u>mind</u> to have and see and <u>keep</u>.

A question that may have arisen with the first two paragraphs was "What is all this talk about punishing my body and holding it responsible?" That theme is drawn out in this third paragraph. According to Jesus, we all hate our bodies, not so much for their appearance and their abilities (or lack thereof), but for deeper reasons. We hate them for the selfish and hateful things they do. We hate them for making us separate from others. We hate them for the superficial pleasures they seek. We hate them for their frailty and littleness. And we hate them for the miserable world they show us with their eyes and ears. We hate them, in other words, not as humans wanting a *better* body, but as Sons of God feeling dragged down by *having* a body. We hold the body responsible for our lowly estate, and our hatred of it (given how powerful our minds are) punishes it and makes it sick.

Application: Try to get in touch with your hatred of your body. Try to feel yourself as a Son of God who dimly remembers being holy, limitless, and all-powerful. As this Son of God, you now watch your body do unholy things, and you feel dragged down. You experience yourself as cooped up in a tiny vessel, and you feel belittled. You see how easily this vessel breaks, and you feel fragile. Try to get in touch with the feeling "This is not right! This body has turned me into something I'm not. It has turned me into a lowly worm. Because of it, I'm no longer a Son of God."

Then realize that it hasn't done anything to you at all. It has simply followed your orders. It has done what you directed it to do. You have used it to convince yourself that you are no longer a Son of God.

> 4. The body <u>represents</u> the gap between the little bit of mind you call your own and all the rest of what is <u>really</u> yours. You hate it, yet you think it <u>is</u> your self, and that, <u>without</u> it, would your self be lost. This is the secret vow that you have made with every brother who would walk apart. This is the secret oath you take again, whenever you perceive yourself attacked. No one can suffer if he does <u>not</u> see himself attacked, <u>and losing by attack</u>. Unstated and unheard in consciousness is every pledge to sickness. Yet it is a promise to another to be hurt by him, and to attack him in return.

The body is just a symbol, a dream symbol. It is a visual picture of an ancient, secret vow we made. We made this vow to each other. The two of us stood before the ego's altar and pledged, "I promise to be separate from you. I promise to be hurt by you. And I promise to hurt you in return." The body is nothing more than the visual illustration of that vow.

Whenever we see ourselves as attacked, we take this oath once again. Whenever we agree that a brother is separate from us (as the previous three sections talked about), we renew our unholy vows. And at the end we add, "And I promise to be sick, and to agree that you are sick."

Society, of course, rests on a vast network of agreements, and different societies have different ones. Most of these agreements are unconscious. We act by them, but don't know they are there. What Jesus is talking about here is the mother of all social agreements. This is the bedrock of the social contract. This is the matrix from which it all springs—the agreement to be separate.

> 5. Sickness is anger taken out upon the body, so that <u>it</u> will suffer pain. It is the obvious effect of what was made in secret, <u>in agreement</u> with another's secret wish to be apart from you, as you would be apart from him. Unless you <u>both</u> agree that is your wish, it <u>can</u> have no effects. Whoever says, "There <u>is</u> no gap between my mind and yours" has kept <u>God's</u> promise, <u>not</u> his tiny oath to be forever faithful unto death. And by his healing <u>is</u> his brother healed.

We made our ancient oath, and poof! The body appeared. Then we forgot our oath, and were aware only of the body. We then blamed all of the effects of our vows on the body. We became angry at it, and this made it sick.

Our job is to withdraw the vow we made with our brother, to not uphold our end of the agreement. Our job is to keep the promise we made to God, not the unholy promise we made in secret with each other.

Application: Think of someone you see as separate from you, and suffering in his or her separateness. Then say:

*There **is** no gap between my mind and yours [name].*

Say it again and again. Try to feel that it is true. Realize that you are undoing that secret vow you took to be separate.

> 6. Let this be your agreement with each one; that you be one with him and not apart. And he will keep the promise that you make with him, because it is the one that he has made to God, as God has made to him. God keeps His promises; His Son keeps his. In his creation did his Father say, "You are beloved of Me and I of you forever. Be you perfect as Myself, for you can never be apart from Me." His Son remembers not that he replied "I will," though in that promise he was born. Yet God reminds him of it every time he does not share a promise to be sick, but lets his mind be healed and unified. His secret vows are powerless before the Will of God, Whose promises he shares. And what he substitutes is not his will, who has made promise of himself to God.

What a lovely paragraph! If we change our pledge to our brother to "There is no gap between my mind and yours," then that person will keep the promise that we make with him, because it is the promise he and God made to each other before time was. When God created us, He said, "You are beloved of Me and I of you forever. Be you perfect as Myself, for you can never be apart from Me." And we replied, "I will." That promise on our part somehow completed the act of our creation. Therefore, that promise became stamped on our very being. It is inherent in our nature to say, "I will be perfect as You, God, for I can never be apart from You."

We have forgotten that sublime promise we made in eternity. Yet God reminds us of it every time we refuse to keep our unholy vow to be separate, every time we say to a brother, "There is no gap between my mind and yours." He reminds us of an unbreakable promise we made in the beginning, when we promised ourselves to Him.

VII. The Ark of Safety
Commentary by Robert Perry

1. God asks for nothing, and His Son, like Him, need ask for nothing. For there is no lack in him. An empty space, a little gap, would <u>be</u> a lack. And it is only there that he could want for something he has not. A space where God is not, a gap between the Father and the Son is <u>not</u> the Will of Either, Who have promised to be one. God's promise is a promise to <u>Himself</u>, and there is no one who could <u>be</u> untrue to what He wills as part of what He <u>is</u>. The promise that there <u>is</u> no gap between Himself and what He is cannot <u>be</u> false. What will can come between what <u>must</u> be one, and in Whose Wholeness there can <u>be</u> no gap?

We don't need to ask for anything, simply because we cannot really be lacking. The only way we could be lacking would be if the little gap were real, if there really were an empty space between us and everyone else, including God. Yet how could this gap be real? We and God have promised to be one. God promised this not only to us, but to Himself. How could God—or anyone—break His promise? I just came across this verse from the Bible: "The promises of the Lord are promises that are pure, silver refined in a furnace on the ground, purified seven times" (Psalms 12:6). What, therefore, will we grant reality to, the apparent gap that separates us from all things or the promise of God that there can never be a gap?

2. The beautiful relationship you have with all your brothers is a part of you <u>because</u> it is a part of God Himself. Are you not sick, if you deny yourself your wholeness and your health, the Source of help, the Call to healing and the Call to heal? Your savior waits for healing, and the world waits with him. Nor are <u>you</u> apart from it. For healing will be one or not at all, its oneness being where the healing is [Ur: *lies*]. What could <u>correct</u> for separation but its opposite? There is no middle ground in <u>any</u> aspect of salvation. You accept it wholly or accept it not. What is unseparated must be <u>joined</u>. And what is joined cannot <u>be</u> separate.

It is not as if others can be torn from us while we remain ourselves. The beautiful relationship we have with them (in reality) is part of the fabric of our being, and even part of the fabric of *God's* Being. Our total relationship with them is our wholeness and health. Why, therefore, would we deny it? Why would we want to sever it?

Our savior is waiting for us to again acknowledge this total relationship, so that he can be healed. Indeed, the whole world is waiting for this. And so are we. Healing will come to all of us as one, or will not come at all. Healing comes as one because it comes from oneness. What but oneness could correct for separateness? And this oneness, as the final lines remind us, must be accepted wholly or accepted not.

> 3. Either there <u>is</u> a gap between you and your brother, or you <u>are</u> as one. There is no in between, no other choice, and no allegiance to be split <u>between</u> the two. A split allegiance is but faithlessness to both, and merely sets you spinning round, to grasp uncertainly at any straw that seems to hold some promise of relief. Yet who can build his home upon a straw, and count on it as shelter from the wind?

Application: Think about this either/or statement:

> *Either there is a gap between me and my brother, or we are as one.*
> *There is no in between.*

Logically, this has to be an either/or thing. If we try to split our allegiance between the two, that just makes a mess of everything. At this point, we have no fixed allegiance, no foundation on which to stand. This leaves us grasping at any straw that comes by and seems to promise relief. So now that straw becomes our foundation; we have built our house upon a straw. And since our foundation is one that is blown about by any breeze, now *we* are blown about by any breeze.

If you have ever felt that you had no shelter from the winds of life, did you consider that it was because you hadn't committed yourself to a firm foundation?

> The body can be made a home like this, <u>because</u> it lacks foundation in the truth. And yet, <u>because</u> it does, it can be seen as <u>not</u> your home, but

123

merely as an aid to help you reach the Home where God abides.

4. With *this* as purpose <u>is</u> the body healed. It is <u>not</u> used to witness to the dream of separation and disease. Nor is it idly blamed for what it did not do. It serves to help the <u>healing</u> of God's Son, and for <u>this</u> purpose it cannot <u>be</u> sick. It will not join a purpose not your own, and you have chosen that it <u>not</u> be sick. All miracles are based upon this choice, and <u>given</u> you the instant it is made. No forms of sickness are immune, because the choice cannot be <u>made</u> in terms of form. The choice of <u>sickness</u> seems to be of form, yet it is one [all its forms are one], as is its opposite [healing]. And <u>you</u> are sick or well, accordingly.

Because the body has no real foundation, it too is a house that is blown about by every breeze. Yet because it has no foundation, we can also consider it *not* our home, but instead "merely an aid to help you reach the Home where God abides." And if this is how you see it, then it will be healed, and will be impervious to the winds of germs and weather.

Yet how exactly does this choice heal the body? Think about it. If the body's purpose is to serve the healing of God's Son, how can it truly serve that purpose while being sick? For its sickness would be a powerful witness, a witness to what my brothers have done to me (see T-27.I), a witness to my own secret sins, and a witness to the separation between us. My sick body would be a constant placard I carry that reads, "I sinned. You injured me. We're separate." Thus, the choice to heal God's Son is automatically the choice for a different placard, a different body.

5. But <u>never</u> you alone. This world is but the dream that you can <u>be</u> alone, and think without affecting those apart from you. To be alone <u>must</u> mean you are apart, and if you are, you cannot <u>but</u> be sick. This <u>seems</u> to prove that you must be <u>apart</u>. Yet all it means is that you tried to keep a promise to be true to faithlessness. Yet faithlessness <u>is</u> sickness. It is like the house set upon straw. It <u>seems</u> to be quite solid and substantial <u>in itself</u>. Yet its stability cannot be judged <u>apart</u> from its foundation. If it rests on straw, there is no need to bar the door and lock the windows and make fast the bolts. The wind <u>will</u> topple it, and rain <u>will</u> come and carry it into oblivion [a reference to Matthew 7:27].

We do treat our body like a house. We try to keep it in good repair, in good health. We try to keep harmful agents, like germs or toxins, from barging in the front door or sneaking in through the windows. Yet while we do this, we are ignoring the fact that our house is resting on a flimsy foundation. In extravagant language that reminds us of his famous saying about the log sticking out of our eye, Jesus says that our house's foundation is a piece of straw. And a piece of straw, of course, can be blown about by any wind, and washed away by even a mild rain, taking our house with it. Because of our body's flimsy foundation, no matter how solid the body is in itself, its foundation leaves it open to being toppled by anything.

This foundation is faithlessness. Indeed, it is an ironic "promise to be true [faithful] to faithlessness." In paragraph 3, faithlessness meant splitting our allegiance between separateness and oneness. But here, it seems that faithlessness is faith in separation. If we are all separate, all limited and fallible, all contending with each other across the divide, how can we really have faith in anyone? Thus, faith in separation is really faithlessness, and this is what makes our body sick.

> 6. What is the <u>sense</u> in seeking to be safe in what was <u>made</u> for danger and for fear? Why burden it with further locks and chains and heavy anchors, when its weakness lies, <u>not</u> in itself, but in the frailty of the little gap of nothingness whereon it stands? What <u>can</u> be safe that rests upon a shadow? Would you build your home upon what <u>will</u> collapse beneath a feather's weight?

Why pour all of our efforts into making the house safe, into making the body healthy, "when its weakness lies, not in itself, but in the frailty of the little gap of nothingness whereon it stands"? This house is standing on separation, and separation is empty space. No wonder it is so vulnerable to everything around it.

> 7. Your home is built upon your brother's health, upon his happiness, his sinlessness, and everything his Father promised him. No secret promise you have made <u>instead</u> has shaken the Foundation of his home. The winds will blow upon it and the rain will beat against it, but with <u>no</u> effect. The world will wash away and yet this house will stand forever, for its strength lies <u>not</u> within itself alone. It is an ark of safety, resting on God's promise that His Son is safe forever in Himself. What gap can interpose itself between the safety of this shelter and its Source? From here the body can be seen as what it is, and neither less

nor more in worth than the extent to which it can be used to liberate God's Son unto his home. And with this holy purpose is it made a home of holiness a little while, because it shares your Father's Will with <u>you</u>.

It is so common to see our foundation as being our own two feet, so to speak. But that means that we are standing on separateness. We are standing on the gap between us and everyone else. And that gap is empty space. It is the straw. Instead, we need to see our foundation as being our *brother's* health, happiness, sinlessness, and oneness with us. We made a secret vow that this foundation would no longer be there. But that vow had no effect on it. Nothing can shake this foundation, for God has promised it will remain forever.

What Jesus has done in the paragraph's final lines is combine the image from the gospels of the house built on rock ("and the rain descended, the floods came, and the winds blew and beat on that house; and it did not fall, for it was founded on the rock"—Matthew 7:25) with God's promise after the Great Flood ("I set My rainbow in the cloud, and it shall be for the sign of the covenant between Me and the earth….the waters shall never again become a flood to destroy all flesh"—Genesis 9:13, 15). The message that results I have tried to condense into the following application:

Application: Choose someone you know and repeat these lines:

My house is not this body.
And my house does not stand on the empty space of separation.
My house is [name's] ark, where I dwell in safety with [name].
This house rests securely on [name's] health, happiness, and
    oneness with me.
In this house, I am safe from the storms of the world.
It can withstand the winds and rain.
It will still be there when the world has washed away.
For it rests not on the sea, but on God's promise that His Son is
    safe forever in Himself.
From this ark, I can see my body as what it is, just an instrument
    which can be used to liberate God's Son unto his home.

Commentaries on Chapter 29

THE AWAKENING

I. The Closing of the Gap
Commentary by Robert Perry

1. There is no time, no place, no state where God is absent. There is <u>nothing</u> to be feared. There is no way in which a gap could be conceived of in the Wholeness that is His. The compromise the least and littlest gap would represent in His eternal Love is quite impossible. For it would mean His Love could harbor just a hint of hate, His gentleness turn sometimes to attack, and His eternal patience sometimes fail. All this do you <u>believe</u>, when you perceive a gap between your brother and yourself. How could you trust Him, then? For He must be deceptive in His Love. Be wary, then; let Him not come too close, and leave a gap between you and His Love, through which you can escape if there be need for you to flee.

If we think there is a gap between us and our brother, we must also conclude that there is a gap in God's Love. A God that would create a gap between everyone, a gap that is the source of all loneliness and all war, must have a gap in His Love, as well as a gap in His intelligence! At that point, how can you trust Him? This gap "would mean His Love could harbor just a hint of hate, His gentleness turn sometimes to attack, and His eternal patience sometimes fail." Therefore, you better make sure you keep a safe gap between Him and yourself, so that you have an escape route.

Application: Think of some particular time (maybe one coming up today) or place that you associate with fear right now. Then repeat,

> *There is no time, no place, no state where God is absent.*
> *There is **nothing** to be feared.*

2. Here is the fear of God most plainly seen. For love *is* treacherous to those who fear, since fear and hate can <u>never</u> be apart. No one who hates but is afraid of love, and therefore <u>must</u> he be afraid of God. Certain it is he knows not what love <u>means</u>. He fears to love and loves

129

to hate, and so he thinks that love is fearful; hate is love. This is the consequence the little gap <u>must</u> bring to those who cherish it, and think that it is their salvation and their hope.

The punch line of the first paragraph was that if we see a gap between ourselves and others, we will end up being afraid of God. This paragraph now gives a different explanation for this. It says, as best as I can reconstruct it,

If we cherish the gap between us, then we will be in fear.
If we fear, then we will also hate.
If we hate, we will be afraid of love (presumably because love overturns the emotion we are so attached to).
God is Love.
Therefore, if we hate, we will be afraid of God.

3. The fear of God! The greatest obstacle that peace must flow across has not yet gone. The rest are past, but this one still remains to block your path, and make the way to light seem dark and fearful, perilous and bleak. You had <u>decided</u> that your brother is your enemy. <u>Sometimes</u> a friend, perhaps, provided that your separate interests made your friendship possible a little while. But <u>not</u> without a gap perceived between you and him, lest he turn again into an enemy. Let him come close to you, and you jumped back; as you approached, did he but instantly withdraw. A cautious friendship, and limited in scope and carefully restricted in amount, became the treaty that you had made with him. Thus you and your brother but shared a qualified entente, in which a clause of separation was a point you both agreed to keep intact. And violating this was thought to be a breach of treaty not to be allowed.

The fear of God, that last and greatest obstacle to peace still remains, because we want to keep the gap between us and our brother. The second thing produces the first.

Application: Think of someone with whom you don't want to get overly close, and then say:

I have decided that [name] is my enemy.

Sometimes a friend, perhaps, provided that our separate interests make our friendship possible a little while.

But not without a gap perceived between me and [name], lest [name] turn again into an enemy.

Let [name] come close to me, and I jump back; as I approach, [name] but instantly withdraws.

A cautious friendship, and limited in scope and carefully restricted in amount, has become the treaty that I made with [name].

Thus we share a qualified entente, in which a clause of separation is a point we both agree to keep intact.

And violating this is thought to be a breach of treaty not to be allowed.

Do these words ring true?

4. The gap between you and your brother is <u>not</u> one of space between two separate bodies. And this but <u>seems</u> to be dividing off your separate minds. It is the <u>symbol</u> of a promise made to meet when you prefer, and separate till you and he [Ur: until you both] elect to meet again. And then your bodies seem to get in touch, and thereby signify a meeting place to join. But always is it possible for you and him to go your separate ways. Conditional upon the "right" to separate will you and he agree to meet from time to time, and keep apart in intervals of separation, which do protect you from the "sacrifice" of love. <u>The body saves you</u>, for it gets away from total sacrifice and gives to you the time in which to build again your separate self [Ur: selves], which you truly believe diminishes as you and your brother [Ur: which you believe *diminish* as you] meet.

The gap between us and another is not really one of physical space. That space is just a symbol of the real gap—our secret vow to be separate. We made a promise to each other to be separate entities that could meet when we wanted and be apart when we wanted. Out of this promise came space, to make it all possible. If it weren't for space, how could we come closer and go further apart at will?

Thus, we get together for a meeting, but only on the condition that we have the freedom to separate. Imagine if you were forced to be in close quarters with some batty relative of yours 24/7. Even with someone you love, too much time together causes you to lose track of your own identity. You start to form a joint identity with that person, and lose touch with yourself. That's when you need time apart, to rebuild your separate self.

> 5. The body <u>could</u> not separate your mind from your brother's [Ur: your minds] unless you <u>wanted</u> it to be a cause of separation and of distance seen between you and him. Thus do you <u>endow</u> it with a power that lies <u>not</u> within itself. And herein lies its power over you. For now you think that <u>it</u> determines when your brother and you [Ur: when you] meet, and limits your ability to make communion with your brother's [Ur: each other's] mind. And now it <u>tells</u> you where to go and how to go there, what is feasible for you to undertake, and what you <u>cannot</u> do. It dictates what its health can tolerate, and what will tire it and make it sick. And its "inherent" weaknesses set up the limitations on what <u>you</u> would do, and keep your <u>purpose</u> limited and weak.

The body is one big excuse for separation, isn't it? First, it seems to impose on us the raw fact of separateness. It quarantines each of us off in our tiny vehicles. That means that to be together, we need to arrange for these vehicles to meet. The when and where of these meetings then have to fit within our respective vehicles' schedules—another limitation. These limitations just keep going. Our vehicle tells us if a particular meeting is simply too much for its strength and stamina to tolerate. It tells us if this meeting will put its health at risk. It even tells us that certain tasks—for instance, certain instances of serving our brothers—are too much for it, leaving us to choose only those purposes that are pre-approved by it.

The body, however, is not the cause of separateness. It is just the excuse. We don't *want* to join, and so we make the body into a convenient and constant impediment to joining. This, actually, is what gives it all its power over us. It's as if we bought a pet monkey so that it would be harder to socialize with our in-laws, but then, once we bought the monkey, its needs and messes began to dominate our life.

> 6. The body <u>will</u> accommodate to this, if you would have it so. It <u>will</u> allow but limited indulgences in "love," with intervals of hatred in between. And it <u>will</u> take command of when to "love," and when to

shrink more safely into fear. It will be sick <u>because</u> you do not know what loving means. And so you <u>must</u> misuse each circumstance and everyone you meet, and see in them a purpose <u>not</u> your [Ur: their] own.

The body will put all sorts of limitations on joining, because that is what we hired it to do. Hiring it as our excuse to not join is a misuse of it, but the misuses will not stop there. We will end up misusing "each circumstance and everyone you meet." After all, with what do we participate in each circumstance? And with what do we interact with each person we meet? With our body, of course.

> 7. It is not love that asks a sacrifice. But fear <u>demands</u> the sacrifice of love, for in love's presence fear cannot abide. For hate to be maintained, love <u>must</u> be feared; and only <u>sometimes</u> present, <u>sometimes</u> gone. Thus is love seen as treacherous, because <u>it</u> seems to come and go uncertainly, and offer no stability to you. You do <u>not</u> see how limited and weak is <u>your</u> allegiance, and how frequently you have demanded that love go away, and leave you quietly alone in "peace."

This paragraph, like paragraph 2, traces the effects of hanging on to fear and hate. If we want fear and hate, we will have to sacrifice love. For love would shine them away. We don't need to sacrifice love entirely, we tell ourselves. We just need to make sure it only comes around intermittently.

Then, however, once we see love come and go, we decide that that's what love is like. Like the wind, it can't be relied upon. It comes and lights on our shoulder, and then it flies away. So now love appears to be treacherous. It seems to offer no stability. As a result, we view it with suspicion. We keep our distance. What we do not see is "how frequently you have demanded that love go away, and leave you quietly alone in 'peace.'"

> 8. The body, innocent of goals [Ur: *any* goal], is your excuse for variable goals <u>you</u> hold, and force the body to maintain. You do not fear its weakness, but its lack of strength *or* weakness. Would you know that <u>nothing</u> stands between you and your brother? Would you know there <u>is</u> no gap behind which you can hide? There <u>is</u> a shock that comes to those who learn their savior is their enemy no more. There <u>is</u> a wariness that is aroused by learning that the body is not real. And

there <u>are</u> overtones of seeming fear around the happy message, "God is Love."

The body has no goals, but, as we have seen, we purposefully (though unconsciously) dream a body that has so many needs, vulnerabilities, and limitations that it constantly gets in the way of joining with others. Then we hold it up as our big excuse for not joining. It becomes the shield we conveniently hide behind. Therefore, the last thing we want to hear is that it's nothing, that it's just an image in a dream, and therefore cannot stand between us and our brother at all. We feel naked without our shield. We are afraid to learn that our brother is really our savior, not our enemy. And we are also afraid to hear that there are no gaps in God's Love, that He is only Love and nothing else.

> 9. Yet all that happens when the gap is gone is peace eternal. Nothing <u>more</u> than that, and nothing less. Without the fear of God, what could induce you to abandon Him? What toys or trinkets in the gap could serve to hold you back an instant from His Love? Would you <u>allow</u> the body to say "no" to Heaven's calling, were you not afraid to find a <u>loss</u> of self in finding God? Yet <u>can</u> your self be lost by being found?

We do fear the disappearance of the gap (and its outer symbol, the body). We think the gap keeps us safe from losing ourselves. Too much joining with our brothers signifies the end of the unique identity we have built up over all these years. Too much joining with God signifies the end of our separate identity altogether.

Yet once the gap is actually gone, fear goes with it. We get in touch with what Jesus called (in the Urtext) "the irresistible attraction," next to which the attraction of all worldly things seems like nothing. And as we give in to this overpowering desire to unite with our Father, we find the opposite of what we feared. We expected to lose our self. "Yet," Jesus asks, "*can* your self be lost by being found?"

That last line is the great answer to the fear of losing self, a fear that crops up many times on the spiritual path. Whenever you fear losing your identity, your boundaries, your self, whether during meditation or while trying to forgive, just ask yourself, "*Can* my self be lost by being found?"

II. The Coming of the Guest
Commentary by Robert Perry

1. Why would you not perceive it as <u>release</u> from suffering to learn that you are free? Why would you not <u>acclaim</u> the truth instead of looking on it as an enemy? Why does an <u>easy</u> path, so clearly marked it is impossible to lose the way, seem thorny, rough and far too difficult for you to follow? Is it not because you see it as the road to hell instead of looking on it as a simple way, without a sacrifice or <u>any</u> loss, to find yourself in Heaven and in God? Until you realize you give up <u>nothing</u>, until you understand there <u>is</u> no loss, you will have some regrets about the way that you have chosen. And you will <u>not</u> see the many gains your choice has offered you. Yet though you do not see them, they are there. Their <u>cause</u> has been effected, and they <u>must</u> be present where their cause has entered in.

Let's ask ourselves those three questions that open this section:

*Why would I not perceive it as **release** from suffering to learn that I am free?*

*Why would I not **acclaim** the truth instead of looking on it as an enemy?*

*Why does an **easy** path, so clearly marked it is impossible to lose the way, seem thorny, rough and far too difficult for me to follow?*

Why? Because, says Jesus, we see the path he has laid out for us as the road of sacrifice and thus the road to hell. This is why it is crucial that we realize that the Course entails absolutely no sacrifice or loss. Until then, we will view it with suspicion and keep it at arm's length. And we will be blind to all the gains it holds out to us. These gains, in fact, are already there. We have accepted their Cause and so we must be in possession of Its effects.

2. You have accepted healing's cause [Ur: Cause], and so it must be you are healed. And being healed, the power to heal must also now

135

be yours. The miracle is not a separate thing that happens suddenly, as an effect without a cause. Nor is it, in itself, a cause. But where its cause [Ur: Cause] is must it be. Now is it caused, though not as yet perceived. And its effects are there, though not yet seen. Look inward now, and you will not behold a reason for regret, but cause indeed for glad rejoicing and for hope of peace.

This (as we have seen so often) is talk about what happened in Helen and Bill's decision to join in a better way. When they did that, they accepted the Cause of all healing and all miracles—God. If they would only look within, they would see that God is there, along with the power to work miracles, and all the effects that miracles bring as well. They would see cause for hope and rejoicing, rather than cause for regret.

We should apply this to ourselves. In our own way, we have accepted "healing's Cause" (Urtext version). Therefore, even though we look about our lives and see much cause for regret and hopelessness, if we could only look deep within, we would see reason for hope. We would see cause for rejoicing.

> 3. It <u>has</u> been hopeless to attempt to find the hope of peace upon a battleground. It <u>has</u> been futile to demand escape from sin and pain of what was made to serve the function of <u>retaining</u> sin and pain. For pain and sin are <u>one</u> illusion, as are hate and fear, attack and guilt but one. Where they are causeless their effects <u>are</u> gone, and love <u>must</u> come wherever they are not. Why are you not rejoicing? You <u>are</u> free of pain and sickness, misery and loss, and <u>all</u> effects of hatred and attack. No more is pain your friend and guilt your god, and you should <u>welcome</u> the effects of love.

It is no wonder we have been hopeless, for we have placed our hopes in the wrong places. We have looked for peace on a battleground. We have asked our body to deliver us from sin and pain, even though it was made to generate sin and pain. Thankfully, then, this new hope of ours is not based on the old ways magically working all of a sudden. It is based on the Cause to which we gave a home deep inside us. In that place, this Cause has freed us of all "pain and sickness, misery and loss, and all effects of hatred and attack." "And love must come wherever they are not." Let us take this seriously, and then let Jesus' probing question prompt some real reflection: "Why are you not rejoicing?"

4. Your Guest *has* come. You asked Him, and He came. You did not hear Him enter, for you did not wholly welcome Him. And yet His gifts came with Him. He has laid them at your feet, and asks you now that you will look on them and take them for your own. He <u>needs</u> your help in giving them to all who walk apart, believing they are separate and alone. They <u>will</u> be healed when you accept your gifts, because your Guest will welcome everyone whose feet have touched the holy ground whereon you stand, and where His gifts for them are laid.

What an interesting picture. Think of a time when you made a pivotal choice for God or love or forgiveness. This made the ground on which you stand holy ground. And this invited God in, though not wholeheartedly.

As a symbolic picture of this, imagine that you invited God into your home as your Guest. He then responds to your invitation and comes in. However, you "did not wholly welcome Him." Therefore, you are resistant to His arrival, and so while you sit engrossed in a TV show, you don't even hear Him come in. In a gesture of generosity and tribute, He spreads His gifts out at your feet, but you won't look on them. Once He lays them out, He says, "I need your help. I have a long list of people I want to invite here, to this holy living room. These gifts are for them, too. But first I need you to accept them." It seems obvious what you would do in this situation if you found yourself in it. Is it possible that you are in it right now?

5. You do not see how much you now can <u>give</u>, because of everything you have received. Yet He Who entered in but waits for <u>you</u> to come where you invited <u>Him</u> to be. There is no other place where He can find His host, nor where His host can meet with Him. And nowhere else His gifts of peace and joy, and all the happiness His Presence brings, can be obtained. For they are where He is Who brought them with Him, that they might be yours. You cannot see your Guest, but you <u>can</u> see the gifts He brought. And when you <u>look</u> on them, you will believe His Presence <u>must</u> be there. For what you now can do could not <u>be</u> done without the love and grace His Presence holds.

Most of us don't believe that we have very much to give. Yet that is a denial of the Guest we invited in. If He is in us, how can it be that we have little to give? To give our gifts, however, we need to join with Him. We need to come to that place within us where we invited Him to be. We cannot see Him with our eyes. But if we tap into that deep well within us, and then draw forth its living water and share it with everyone we meet, then this will prove to us that He must be there. "For what you now can do could not *be* done without the love and grace His Presence holds" (Urtext version).

Surely there are certain things we have done for others that would not have been possible if we had been acting truly alone, things that demonstrated that Something greater was working through us. Imagine that happening to you every day, even several times a day. What would that do to your sense that God is distant and elusive?

> 6. Such is the promise of the living God;[:] His Son have life and every living thing be part of him, and nothing else have life. What you have given "life" [i.e., the body] is not alive, and symbolizes but your wish to be alive apart from life, alive in death, with death perceived as life, and [true] living, death. Confusion follows on confusion here, for on confusion has this world been based, and there is nothing else it rests upon. Its basis does not change, although it seems to be in constant change. Yet what is that except the state confusion really means? Stability to those who are confused is meaningless, and shift and change become the law on which they predicate their lives.

God has laid His gifts at our feet to give everyone because His fundamental promise is that His Son have life. The corollary of this is that nothing else can have life. We, however, have turned this on its head. We have given life to something that is not God's Son: the body. This "life," however, is just the functioning of a biological machine. Is that real life? Is that pure, limitless vitality? And if the body is really not alive, doesn't that mean that we are living inside a corpse? Ironically, while we hang onto this condition that we call life, then real life, life without boundaries in Heaven, looks like death to us. It looks like the extinguishment of our very identity.

We have, in other words, totally confused life and death. And when you are confused, your mind constantly jumps all over the place. Yet that constant change means that nothing is really changing—you're still confused. That's what the state of confusion is, a state in which constant change signifies that you are still in the exact same state.

7. The body does not change. It represents the larger dream that change is <u>possible</u>. To change is to attain a state unlike the one in which you found yourself before. There <u>is</u> no change in immortality, and Heaven knows it not. Yet here on earth it has a double purpose, for it can be made to teach opposing things. And they reflect the teacher who is teaching them. The body can appear to change with time, with sickness or with health, and with events that seem to alter it. Yet this but means the mind remains unchanged in its belief of what the <u>purpose</u> of the body is.

Since the body is a product of our confusion of life and death, it makes sense that the state of the body mirrors the state of confusion itself. In the state of confusion, as I said, constant change means that your confusion remains unchanged. Likewise, the body's constant change and instability means that nothing of substance has changed. The body's basis remains unchanged, its basis being the "larger dream." that gave rise to it, the dream that you can change your original state of immortality.

This is how the ego uses change, to show that the more things change, the more they stay the same. But the Holy Spirit has a whole other use for change.

8. Sickness is a demand the body be a thing that it is not. Its [the body's] <u>nothingness</u> is guarantee that it can *not* be sick. In your demand that it be <u>more</u> than this lies the idea of sickness. For it asks that God be <u>less</u> than all He really is. What, then, becomes of <u>you</u>, for it <u>is</u> you [not God] of whom the sacrifice [this lessening] is asked? For He is told that part of Him <u>belongs</u> to Him no longer. He must sacrifice your self, and in His sacrifice are <u>you</u> made more and He is lessened by the loss of you. And what is <u>gone</u> from Him ["what is not in Him" {10:3}—meaning, the body] becomes your god, <u>protecting</u> you from being part of Him.

Sickness is a demand that the body be something. Huh? The reasoning goes like this: When we demand that the body be real, then we give it power to separate our minds from everything else, including God. In this view, the body was the cause of us leaving God. Because of it, He had to sacrifice us. He lost us and was lessened in the process. We, however, seem to gain from this. Our newfound independence seems to exalt us. Thus, we worship the body that walls us off and keeps us separate from Him. Yet we, not God, are the ones who have sacrificed. We have lost everything. And somehow this loss translates into physical sickness. How it does that will be explained in the next paragraph.

> 9. The body that is asked to be a god <u>will</u> be attacked, because its nothingness has not been recognized. And so it seems to be a thing with power <u>in itself</u>. As something, it <u>can</u> be perceived and thought to feel and act, and hold you in its grasp as prisoner to itself. And it <u>can</u> fail to be what you demanded that it be. And you <u>will</u> hate it for its littleness, unmindful that the failure does not lie in that it is not <u>more</u> than it should be, but <u>only</u> in <u>your</u> failure to perceive that it is nothing. Yet its nothingness <u>is</u> your salvation, from which you would flee.

This important statement of how sickness occurs envisions a series of unconscious processes that ultimately give rise to sickness. First, we worship the body, because it has made us separate from God and thereby raised us up as a god in our own right. Second, this worshipping of it gives it power in our eyes, power to feel and act on its own, power to enforce whatever it wants on us. Third, the body seems to wield this power over us in a negative fashion, in several ways, three of which are listed in this paragraph:

- It makes us its prisoner.
- It fails to provide all the rewards that we demand from it.
- It is little and thereby forces us to be little.

Fourth, since we perceive it as wielding negative power over us, we attack it, and this mental attack is what makes it sick. What we don't realize is that the problem does not lie in it, but in us for demanding that it be *something*. If we would just acknowledge that it has no such power, that it is nothing, it couldn't be sick.

> 10. As "something" is the body asked to be God's enemy, replacing what He is with littleness and limit and despair. It is <u>His</u> loss you celebrate when you behold the body as a thing you love, or look upon it as a thing you hate. For if He be the Sum of everything, then what is <u>not</u> in Him does not exist, and His completion <u>is</u> its nothingness. Your savior is <u>not</u> dead, nor does he dwell in what was built as temple unto death. He lives in God, and it is this that makes him savior unto <u>you</u>,

and <u>only</u> this. His body's nothingness releases yours from sickness and from death. For what is yours cannot be more or [Ur: *nor*] less than what is his.

If you regard your body as something, then you will see it as being in a tug o' war with God, tearing you away from Him, and "replacing what He is with littleness and limit and despair." So, do you regard your body as something? Well, yes; we all do. It doesn't matter if you love it or hate it—both amount to regarding it as *something*.

Application: Look down at your body and say:

> *If I regard this as something,*
> *then I will see it as a god in its own right.*
> *I will see it as an idol that tears me away from my Father.*
> *Whether I love it or hate it, I am celebrating His Loss.*
> *Yet if He is the Sum of everything,*
> *what is not in Him does not exist.*

All of this is true of our brother's body as well. His body is nothing. He does not live in "what was built as temple unto death." Rather, he lives in unlimited life, in God. This is what we are meant to see in our brother: that his body is nothing, that he lives in God, not in it. This sight will save us, for it will show us that the same things must be true of us as well.

Application: Choose someone and visualize this person's body. Then say:

> *That body was built as a temple unto death.*
> *But you don't live in that body, for it is nothing.*
> *You don't live in death; you live in unlimited life.*
> *You live in God.*
> *And what is true of you must be true of me as well.*

III. God's Witnesses
Commentary by Robert Perry

This is one of my favorite sections in the Course. It contains a vision of salvation as not a private event in the mind, but as passed back and forth between two brothers. Try to read it with an open mind. Its message that we can't awaken ourselves, that we need a brother to wake us up, is not conventional Course wisdom, to say the least. But conventional or not, it is exceedingly beautiful.

> 1. Condemn your savior not because he thinks he is a body. For [Ur: Far] beyond his dreams is his reality. But he must learn he is a savior first, before he can remember what he is. And he must save who would <u>be</u> saved. On saving <u>you</u> depends his happiness. For who is savior but the one who <u>gives</u> salvation? Thus he learns it must be his to give. <u>Unless</u> he gives he will not know he <u>has</u>, for giving is the proof of having. Only those who think that God is lessened by their strength could fail to understand this must be so. For who <u>could</u> give unless he has, and who could lose by giving what must be <u>increased</u> thereby?

This paragraph contains a very different notion of savior than the standard one among Course students. Rather than someone being my savior because he pushes my buttons and thereby makes me aware of my ego, someone is my savior in a more straightforward sense: by giving me salvation. Indeed, a definition of savior is given: "Who is savior but the one who gives salvation?"

This paragraph, in fact, sketches a whole process. First, my savior thinks he is a body. And how do people act when they think they are a body? They need food, they need sex, they need comfort, they need to feel special. And so they use their bodies to get all these things. This turns everyone else into one of three things: food, an obstacle, or irrelevant. Now we can see why Jesus says, "Condemn your savior not because he thinks he is a body." Normally, of course, this is exactly why we condemn him, because his belief that he is a body causes him to do all those things we don't like.

From here, he goes on a journey. His journey begins when at some point he starts taking up his function of "saving you." He starts giving you the salvation he possesses deep within him. And as he gives, rather than losing what he gave, it increases. For giving salvation proves to him that it's there within him, and this increases his awareness of it. Through giving salvation, he finally learns "he is a savior." And only when he learns that he is a savior can he remember his reality, which lies beyond his dreams and even beyond salvation.

> 2. Think you the Father <u>lost</u> Himself when He created you? Was <u>He</u> made weak because He shared His Love? Was He made incomplete by <u>your</u> perfection? Or are you the proof that He <u>is</u> perfect and complete? Deny Him not His witness in the dream His Son prefers to his reality. He must be savior <u>from</u> the dream he made, that he be free of it. He must see someone <u>else</u> as <u>not</u> a body, one with him without the wall the world has built to keep apart all living things who know not that they live.

When God gave us our being, when He gave us strength and perfection, He did not lose. He was not drained. Rather, His gift of perfection and completion was the *proof* that He was perfect and complete. Beholding that proof, He experienced an increase, not a decrease.

Therefore, each one of us—in our reality as God created us—is the proof of God's perfection. And we are called to reflect that reality here in this world. We are called to be God's witnesses in this world. We do that by giving salvation to our brothers. And when we do, just like God, we will find not loss, but increase.

This is everyone's calling here. Before our brother can be free of the dream he made, he must become a savior. He must become God's witness. "He must see someone else as not a body, one with him without the wall the world has built to keep apart all living things who know not that they live." This is how he saves. He may believe he is a body, but his function is to see *others* as something beyond the body. And by doing this, he eventually awakens to his *own* reality beyond the body.

Is this how we think of the people in our lives? That they are here to free themselves from the dream by seeing beyond our body and awakening us to the spirit we really are? This may be how we think of spiritual masters, but what about our friends, our coworkers, our neighbors?

Finally, we have this puzzling line "Deny Him not His witness in the dream His Son prefers to his reality." Somehow, it is up to us whether or not our brother takes on his role as God's witness in this dream. How can that be? The rest of the section will make that abundantly clear.

> 3. Within the dream of bodies and of death
> is yet one theme of truth; no more, perhaps,
> than just a tiny spark, a space of light
> created in the dark, where God still shines.
> You cannot wake yourself. Yet you can <u>let</u>
> yourself be wakened. You can overlook
> your brother's dreams. So perfectly can you
> forgive him his illusions he becomes
> your savior from <u>your</u> dreams. And as you see
> him shining in the space of light where God
> abides within the darkness, you will see
> that God Himself is where his body is.
> Before this light the body disappears,
> as heavy shadows <u>must</u> give way to light.
> The darkness cannot <u>choose</u> that it remain.
> The coming of the light <u>means</u> it is gone.
> In glory will you see your brother then,
> and understand what <u>really</u> fills the gap
> so long perceived as keeping you apart.
> There, in its place, God's witness has set forth
> the gentle way of kindness to God's Son.
> Whom you forgive is <u>given</u> power to
> forgive you your illusions. By your gift
> of freedom is it given unto <u>you</u>.

I have laid this paragraph out in iambic pentameter because I find it to be one of the most beautiful and poignant paragraphs in the Course. I have many times tried to express what I see in this paragraph, particularly its first half. I'll try again one more time.

This world is such a dark dream, a dream of contending bodies that fight for a while and then die. In the meantime, each one looks out for itself, by taking from its neighbor. Truth seems entirely absent in this gloomy place, trodden underfoot by the chaotic stampede of self-serving bodies. But it is not so. There is "yet one theme of truth." There remains one tiny spark in the night, one small space where the darkness parts and "where God still shines." What is this one last ember of truth?

It is something that passes between me and you. I want to awaken from the dream, yet unlike everything else in the dream, awakening is not something I can grab for myself. Rather, I find it by responding radically differently when *you* try to grab something from *me*. Normally, in this situation, I would defend my territory and condemn you. But now, I do what looks like suicide in the dream: I refuse to protect myself. Instead, I overlook your assault. I decide that your attack was an illusion, and I put all my trust in the hidden holiness in you. This causes that holiness to stir to life. It rises to the surface and finally breaks forth in glory. Before its light, your body vanishes, and I stand transfixed before the holy light that you really are. Standing perfectly still, I let you shine the light of forgiveness on me. I let you, my former attacker, forgive me all of *my* illusions. I let you give me a gift that I could never give myself, the priceless gift of salvation.

This is the one truly beautiful thing that can happen in this dark and senseless world. We cannot wake ourselves. Yet we can let ourselves be wakened. We can overlook our brother's dreams.

> 4. Make way for love, which you did not create, but which you <u>can</u> extend. On earth this means forgive your brother, that the darkness may be lifted from <u>your</u> mind. When light has come to him through your forgiveness, he will not forget his savior, leaving him unsaved. For it was in <u>your</u> face he saw the light that he would keep beside him, as he walks through darkness to the everlasting Light.

When we hear that line "Whom you forgive is given power to forgive you your illusions," our first thought is probably, "But can I trust him? How do I know he won't he just take my gift and run?" This paragraph is meant to answer those concerns. "When light has come to him through your forgiveness, he will not forget his savior, leaving him unsaved." This is pictured in terms of a travel image. It's as if my brother and I are both in chains, unable to move ahead. But then the light of love shines from my face and frees my brother to move on. How can he now forget me and leave me behind, still stuck in my chains? He is going *toward* the everlasting Light, but he's not there yet. The light in my face is his only light for now. My shining face is the little light that reminds him of the greater Light to which he travels. What else, then, would he do but make sure I stay beside him?

> 5. How holy are you, that the Son of God can be your savior in the midst of dreams of desolation and disaster. See how eagerly he comes, and steps aside from heavy shadows that have hidden him, and shines on you in gratitude and love. He is himself, but not himself alone. And as his Father lost not part of him in your creation, so the light in him is brighter still because you gave your light to him, to save him from the dark. And now the light in you must be as bright as shines in him. This is the spark that shines within the dream;[:] that you can help him waken, and be sure his waking eyes will rest on you. And in his glad salvation <u>you</u> are saved.

This paragraph completes the image begun in Paragraph 3, the image of your ecstatic experience of the "space of light where God abides within the dream." You have seen your brother's body shined away, and your brother shining with the glory of God. Now your brother steps forth from the heavy shadows (the body) that have hidden him, "and shines on you in gratitude and love." He shines all the brighter because the light in you has been given him. And now his shining causes you to shine just as brightly as him. And he has saved you. This mutual act of stepping outside your egos, this mutual exchange of salvation—"this is the spark that shines within the dream."

The section concludes with a lovely image. If you wake someone up, you can be sure you will be the first one his waking eyes will rest on. This is literally true, of course, but here it is a metaphor. Now it means: If you wake someone up spiritually, you can be sure that his loving gaze will first rest on you and illumine you.

Application: A visualization:

Begin by asking the Holy Spirit, "Who is the main person You want me to see as my savior right now, my savior who is called to waken me by giving me salvation?"

Choose the first person that comes to mind.

Begin by thinking about the dreams of this person that you have trouble overlooking.

Now realize that those dreams seem so bad because they get in the way of *your* dreams—the things you want from the world.

Yet the only thing that matters in this world is waking up from dreams.

Further, you are simply unable to wake yourself. You'll never do it without his help.

Yet you have "the power to release your savior, that he may give salvation unto you" (T-21.II.3:8).

Now have a sense of overlooking his dreams.

Realize they are just illusions, and forgive them.

See past them to the holiness in him.

Nothing is more important in this world.

"Forgive your brother, that the darkness may be lifted from *your* mind."

"So perfectly can you forgive him his illusions he becomes your savior from *your* dreams."

See him now shining in the space of light where God abides within the darkness, and as you do, you see that God Himself is where his body is.

Before this light his body disappears, as heavy shadows must give way to light.

In glory do you see your brother now, shining with divine radiance.

This glory is what really fills the gap so long perceived as keeping you apart.

Trust that now that light has come to him through your forgiveness, he will not forget you, his savior, leaving you unsaved.

For it was in your face he saw the light that he would keep beside him, as he walks through darkness to the everlasting Light.

Now *let* him be your savior.

Realize that he sees in you a holiness you cannot see,

And that this sight is your salvation.

Give him seniority in this one area.

Let him give you his gift. Take it in.

It is only your ego that would refuse it.

See how eagerly he comes, and steps aside from heavy shadows that

have hidden him,
and shines on you in gratitude and love.
He is himself, but not himself alone.
He is God's witness, shining on you God's evaluation of you.
The light in him is so bright because he carries the light God gave him
and the light you gave him.
And now the light in you must be as bright as shines in him.

Within the dream of bodies and of death is yet one theme of truth;
no more, perhaps, than just a tiny spark, a space of light created in the
dark,
where God still shines.
This is it.
This is the spark that shines within the dream:
that you can help him waken,
and be sure his waking eyes will rest on you.
And in his glad salvation *you* are saved.

IV. Dream Roles
Commentary by Robert Perry

1. Do you believe that truth can be but <u>some</u> illusions? They are dreams *because* they are not true. Their <u>equal</u> lack of truth becomes the basis for the miracle, which <u>means</u> that you have understood that dreams are dreams; and that escape depends, <u>not</u> on the [particular] dream, but <u>only</u> on awaking. <u>Could</u> it be some dreams are <u>kept</u>, and others <u>wakened from</u>? The choice is <u>not</u> between which dreams to keep, but <u>only</u> if you want to live in dreams or to awaken from them. Thus it is the miracle does not select <u>some</u> dreams to leave untouched by its beneficence. You cannot dream some dreams and wake from some, for you are either sleeping <u>or</u> awake. And dreaming goes with only <u>one</u> of these.

The opening paragraph clearly announces the subject of this section: our desire for the miracle to heal some dreams while we keep others for our enjoyment. We want to be saved from our pains but not our pleasures. This implies that we believe some dreams are illusions, while others (the ones we like) are true. Yet the desire to keep *any* dreams means that we want to stay in the dreaming state, which means, of course, that we want to stay asleep. We need, therefore, to invite the miracle to heal *all* dreams. Only this represents a commitment to waking up.

What Jesus means by "dream" here seems to be something like "a scene or a figure within the dream of your life."

2. The dreams you <u>think</u> you like would hold you back as much as those in which the fear is seen. For <u>every</u> dream is but a dream of fear, no matter what the form it seems to take. The fear is seen within, without, or both. Or it can be disguised in pleasant form. But never is it <u>absent</u> from the dream, for fear is the material of dreams, from which they <u>all</u> are made. Their form can change, but they cannot be <u>made</u> of something else. The miracle were treacherous indeed if it allowed you still to be afraid because you did not <u>recognize</u> the fear. You would not then be <u>willing</u> to awake, for which the miracle prepares the way.

In reading the first paragraph, we were probably thinking, "But why would I want to be released from the dreams I *like*?" This paragraph answers: because all dreams (outside of the happy dream, of course, which is a state of mind, not a set of external conditions) are dreams of fear. Fear is the material of which they are made. These dreams fall into two categories: *obvious* dreams of fear and *disguised* dreams of fear.

By wanting to heal them all, therefore, the miracle is actually benevolent. It doesn't want to allow "you still to be afraid [just] because you did not recognize the fear." For then you would stay stuck forever in dreams, thinking you are enjoying the scenes in front of you, not knowing why you are always afraid, and fiercely attached to staying asleep and dreaming.

> 3. In simplest form, it can be said attack is a response to function unfulfilled <u>as you perceive the function</u>. It can be in you or someone else, but where it is perceived it will be there it is attacked. Depression or assault must be the theme of every dream, for they are made of fear. The thin disguise of pleasure and of joy in which they may be wrapped but slightly veils the heavy lump of fear that is their core. And it is <u>this</u> the miracle perceives, and <u>not</u> the wrappings in which it is bound.

That first line is one of those great Course lines: "attack is a response to function unfulfilled as you perceive the function." Isn't this true? When you attack, it's because something or someone (perhaps even yourself) has not fulfilled its proper function—*as you defined that function*.

I love that image of each pleasant dream having a *core* and a *wrapping*. The core is a "heavy lump of fear," while the wrapping is a "thin disguise of pleasure and of joy" that "but slightly veils" the core. When I read this, I picture a dense lump of dough (though to be true to the meaning, I probably should picture it as excrement) wrapped in tissue paper. We just see the tissue paper, and coo over the pretty patterns on it. The miracle, however, mercifully sees, and wants to deliver us from, the core.

> 4. When you are angry, is it not because someone has failed to fill the function <u>you</u> allotted him? And does not <u>this</u> become the "reason" your attack is justified? The dreams you <u>think</u> you like are those in which the functions <u>you</u> have given have been filled; the needs which <u>you</u> ascribe to you are met. It does not matter if they be fulfilled or merely

wanted. It is the idea that they <u>exist</u> from which the fears arise. Dreams are not wanted more or less. They are desired or not. And each one represents some function that you have assigned; some goal which an event, or body, or a thing *should* represent, and *should* achieve for you. If it succeeds you think you <u>like</u> the dream. If it should fail you think the dream is sad. But whether it succeeds or fails is not its core, but just the flimsy covering.

Isn't your automatic answer to this paragraph's opening question "yes"? We get angry and we attack because others aren't fulfilling the function we allotted them. This process begins with us having a need. Then we assign others the role of meeting that need. Then they predictably screw it up. And then we don't like the dream. The irony, I'm sure, does not escape us: We are mad at them because they failed the role that *we* wrote for them.

But this is all about the wrapping. If we like the wrapping, then we think our need has been met. If we hate the wrapping, our need remains unmet. But it's the *existence* of the need that is the crucial thing. The fact that it exists at all makes us deeply afraid, afraid that it won't be fulfilled, even if it might be for now. And that fear is the real core of the dream, whatever its wrapping is.

Application: Think of some person or situation in your life with which you are relatively pleased. Realize you like it because you have a need that you perceive is being met by this person or situation. Now try to get in touch with the fear that this need will stop being met, that something will happen to take away the delicate conditions that meet it. Notice that the pleasing circumstances have confirmed that you really do have this need. Thus, this dream of happiness really carries fear at its core, the fear that, having this need, even if it is being met now, it may not be ten minutes from now.

5. How happy would your dreams become if you were <u>not</u> the one who gave the "proper" role to every figure which the dream contains. No one can fail but your <u>idea</u> of him, and there <u>is</u> no betrayal but of this. The core of dreams the Holy Spirit gives is <u>never</u> one of fear. The coverings may not appear to change, but what they <u>mean</u> has changed

<u>because</u> they cover something else. Perceptions are determined by their purpose, in that they seem to <u>be</u> what they are <u>for</u>. A shadow figure who attacks becomes a brother giving you a chance to help, if this [helping] becomes the <u>function</u> of the dream. And dreams of sadness thus are turned to joy.

We are in constant fear because we assign everything the role of meeting some need of ours, and we are forever afraid that our need won't be met, and feel continually betrayed because it hasn't been met. Yet all that people have done is betray our *idea* of who they were supposed to be. Can we imagine how happy we would be if we didn't go around assigning everyone a role?

This is why the Holy Spirit's dreams are so happy. The purpose of these dreams has been changed. Their outer coverings may stay exactly the same (or may not), but the meaning we see in them is completely different because the purpose we give them has been transformed. Rather than giving others the purpose of filling our needs, we give *ourselves* the purpose of helping *them*.

This changes everything. In one mode, we see the person in front of us as an attacker, because he intentionally failed to fulfill our needs. And we see superimposed on him a long line of shadow figures from the past who likewise failed. In the other mode, we see a brother *giving* us a chance to help. And since our whole purpose is to help, giving us a chance to help is a real gift which inspires real gratitude.

Application: Think of someone who failed to fulfill the function you allotted him or her, and say:

> *You only failed my idea of you.*
> *There is no betrayal but of this.*
> *I set you free from the role I assigned you.*
> *My only purpose now is to help.*

6. What is your brother <u>for</u>? You do not know, because <u>your</u> function is obscure to you. Do <u>not</u> ascribe a role to him that you imagine would bring happiness to you. And do not try to hurt him when he fails to take the part that you assigned to him, in what you dream your life

was meant to be. He asks for help in every dream he has, and you have help to give him if you see the <u>function</u> of the dream as He perceives its function, Who can utilize all dreams as means to serve the function given Him. Because He loves the dreamer, <u>not</u> the dream, each dream becomes an offering of love. For at its center is His Love for you, which lights <u>whatever</u> form it takes with love.

Application: Choose someone whom you have shackled with your expectations, and then read this paragraph again, filling in either this person's name or your name, as specified:

What is your brother [name] for?

You do not know, [fill in your name], because your function [to be truly helpful] is obscure to you.

Do not ascribe a role to [name] that you imagine would bring happiness to you, [your name].

And do not try to hurt him when he fails to take the part that you assigned to him [your name], in what you dream your life was meant to be.

[Name] asks for help in every dream he has, and you have help to give him [your name], if you see the function of the dream as He perceives its function, Who can utilize all dreams to serve the function [of helpfulness] given Him.

Because He loves the dreamer [you and your brother], not the dream, each dream becomes an offering of love.

For at its center is His Love for you, [your name], which lights whatever form it takes with love.

V. The Changeless Dwelling Place
Commentary by Robert Perry

1. There is a place in you where this whole world has been forgotten; where no memory of sin and of illusion lingers still. There is a place in you which time has left, and echoes of eternity are heard. There is a resting place so still no sound except a hymn to Heaven rises up to gladden God the Father and the Son. Where Both abide are They remembered, Both. And where They are is Heaven and is peace.
2. Think not that you can change Their dwelling place. For your Identity abides in Them, and where They are, forever must <u>you</u> be. The changelessness of Heaven is in you, so deep within that nothing in this world but passes by, unnoticed and unseen. The still infinity of endless peace surrounds you gently in its soft embrace, so strong and quiet, tranquil in the might of its Creator, nothing can intrude upon the sacred Son of God within.

Application: Please read these beautiful paragraphs again, this time put in the first person. Try to really imagine that what they say is true:

There is a place in me where this whole world has been forgotten; where no memory of sin and of illusion lingers still.

There is a place in me which time has left, and echoes of eternity are heard.

There is a resting place in me so still no sound except a hymn to Heaven rises up to gladden God the Father and the Son.

Where Both abide are They remembered, Both.

And where They are is Heaven and is peace.

I will not think that I can change Their dwelling place.

For my Identity abides in Them, and where They are, forever must I be.

The changelessness of Heaven is in me, so deep within that nothing in this world but passes by, unnoticed and unseen.

The still infinity of endless peace surrounds me gently in its soft embrace, so strong and quiet, tranquil in the might of its Creator, that nothing can intrude upon the sacred Son of God within me.

3. Here is the role the Holy Spirit gives to you who wait upon the Son of God, and would behold him waken and be glad. He is a part of you and you of him, <u>because</u> he is his Father's Son, and not for <u>any</u> purpose you may see in him. Nothing is asked of you but to <u>accept</u> the changeless and eternal that abide in him, for <u>your</u> Identity is there. The peace in you <u>can</u> but be found in him. And every thought of love you offer him but brings you nearer to your wakening to peace eternal and to endless joy.

The role we are given to play in our brother's salvation is simply to acknowledge that what the first two paragraphs said about *us* is true of *him* as well. We find our peace by acknowledging the eternal peace that abides in him. We find our "wakening to peace eternal and to endless joy" by offering him kindly thoughts of love.

Notice that we have been called to "wait upon" our brother. "Wait upon" means "to attend as a servant" (Merriam-Webster Dictionary). Just as a waiter attends a diner as a servant, and wants to see that diner eat and be content, so we attend our brother, the Son of God, as a servant, and want to "behold him waken and be glad."

4. This sacred Son of God is like yourself; the mirror of his Father's Love for you, the soft reminder of his Father's Love by which he was created and which still abides in him as it abides in you. Be very still and hear God's Voice in him, and let It tell you what his function is. He was created that <u>you</u> might be whole, for only the complete can be a part of God's completion, which created you.

Application: Think of someone whom you have chained to your expectations, and then repeat these lines to this person:

You [name] are a sacred Son of God.
And you are like myself.

155

You are the mirror of my Father's Love for me.
You are the soft reminder of the Love that created you, and which
still abides in you as it abides in me.
*You were created so that **I** might be whole.*
Let me be still and hear God's Voice in you telling me what your
function is.

Then listen quietly to the Holy Spirit speaking to you from this person.
Let Him tell you what this person is really for.

> 5. There is no gift the Father asks of you but that you see in all creation
> but the shining glory of His gift to you. Behold His Son, His perfect
> gift, in whom his Father shines forever, and to whom is all creation
> given as his own. <u>Because</u> he has it is it given you, and where it lies in
> him behold <u>your</u> peace. The quiet that surrounds you dwells in him, and
> <u>from</u> this quiet come the happy dreams in which your hands are joined
> in innocence. These are not hands that grasp in dreams of pain. They
> hold no sword, for they have left their hold on every vain illusion of
> the world. And being empty they receive, instead, a brother's hand in
> which completion lies.

When we hear talk about the gift that God asks of us, we usually get
a little nervous. Just what might He ask? Here we are told. The only gift
He wants is for us to behold the shining glory of His perfect Son, our
brother, and realize that everything this brother has is ours. "*Because*
he has it is it given you, and where it lies behold *your* peace" (Urtext
version).

Seeing the quietness that lives in him is where the happy dreams come
from. In these dreams, our hands are not filled with loot and weapons.
They are not engaged in grabbing and stabbing. Instead, our hands are
empty. And then, being empty, they receive (not grab) the hand of a
brother.

> 6. If you but knew the glorious goal that lies beyond forgiveness, you
> would not keep hold on any [unforgiving] thought, however light the
> touch of evil on it may appear to be. For you would understand how
> great the cost of holding anything God did not give in minds that can

direct the hand to bless, and lead God's Son [your brother] unto his Father's house [a reference to the prodigal son parable]. Would you not <u>want</u> to be a friend to him, created by his Father as His home? If God esteems him worthy of Himself, would <u>you</u> attack him with the hands of hate? Who would lay bloody hands on Heaven itself, and hope to find its peace? Your brother thinks he holds the hand of death. Believe him not. But learn, instead, how blessed are you who can release him, just by offering him yours.

We don't realize what we are doing when we judge a brother. We are holding a thought that God did not give us, and thus alienating ourselves from Him. We are attacking the one whom God created and deemed worthy to be His Own home. How can we reach Heaven this way? That would be like laying bloody hands on Heaven itself, and hoping to find its peace. If only we knew the incomparable glory of the goal of Heaven, we would immediately drop every thought that stood in its way. We would instantly decide to be a friend to our brother, instead of enemy. We would bless him and lead him home, rather than laying bloody hands on him. We would note with compassion that he believes he walks through life holding the hand of the angel of death. But we would prove him wrong, by showing him that he holds our hand instead.

7. A dream is given you in which he is your savior, <u>not</u> your enemy in hate. A dream is given you in which you have forgiven him for all his dreams of death; a dream of hope you <u>share</u> with him, instead of dreaming evil separate dreams of hate. Why does it seem so hard to share this dream? Because unless the Holy Spirit gives the dream its function, it was made for hate, and will continue in death's services. Each form it takes in some way calls for death. And those who serve the lord of death have come to worship in a separated world, each with his tiny spear and rusted sword, to keep his ancient promises to die.

Application: Think of someone you share the journey with, and say to this person,

I want the dream in which you are my savior, not my enemy in hate.
I want the dream in which I have forgiven you for all your dreams

of death.
I want a dream of hope that we share, in which we no longer dream separate dreams of hate.

"Why does it seem so hard to share this dream?" Because we keep wanting to engineer the joining in our way, rather than letting the Holy Spirit do it in His way. As long as we are in charge, the "joining" will just be another variation on our ancient agreement to be separate and to die. That agreement runs so deep that we simply cannot underestimate its pull. It is like a constant undertow, pulling us out to sea even when we seem to be struggling to reach the shore.

The paragraph's final image is so pitiful. We have each made a sacred promise to the lord of death, a promise to worship him and to die. And to keep this promise, we have come to this separated world, carrying a tiny spear and rusted sword that we have held onto for eons. With our pathetic weapons, we are seemingly ready to kill, but we are ultimately determined to die.

> 8. Such is the core of fear in every dream that has been kept apart from use by Him Who sees a different function for a dream. When dreams are <u>shared</u> they lose the function of attack and separation, even though it was for this that every dream was made. Yet nothing in the world of dreams remains without the hope of change and betterment, for here is <u>not</u> where changelessness is found. Let us be glad indeed that this is so, and seek not the eternal in this world. Forgiving dreams are means to step aside from dreaming of a world <u>outside</u> yourself. And leading finally beyond <u>all</u> dreams, unto the peace of everlasting life.

Remember the previous section saying that a heavy lump of fear is the core of every dream? Now Jesus refers back to that, saying that the picture of us from the end of the previous paragraph *is* that core. This explains why we are so afraid. When we take off the thin tissue in which each dream is wrapped, we discover a heavy crystal sphere, at the center of which is a holographic image of us with our tiny spear and rusted sword, determined to die. Sensing that picture is inside the wrappings, we try to keep them on; we try not to look, but we are still afraid.

The answer to this dream of death is a *shared* dream, in which we drop our spear and sword and take our brother's hand instead. This overturns the whole purpose for which the dream was made, the purpose of attack and separation. It overturns what seemed to be unchangeable. It seemed as if the feuding and the dying would go on forever. But nothing in this world is changeless, and the transition from dreams of death to dreams of joining is *the* change we need to make. This is the change that first leads out of the old dreams and then beyond all dreams, as we return to our changeless dwelling place.

VI. Forgiveness and the End of Time
Commentary by Robert Perry

1. How willing are you to forgive your brother? How much do you desire peace instead of endless strife and misery and pain? These questions are the same, in different form. Forgiveness is your peace, for herein lies the end of separation and the dream of danger and destruction, sin and death; of madness and of murder, grief and loss. This is the "sacrifice" salvation asks, and gladly offers peace instead of this.

Application: First, choose the person you probably have the deepest resentment toward. Then ask yourself, on a scale of 1 to 10 (let a number just pop into your mind), "How willing am I to forgive this person?" Now realize that the number that popped into your mind was also your answer to this question: "How much do I desire peace instead of endless strife and misery and pain?"

Does forgiving this person feel like a sacrifice? Realize that the only things you "sacrifice" are separation and the dream of danger, destruction, sin, death, madness, murder, grief, and loss.

2. Swear not to die, you holy Son of God! You make a bargain that you cannot keep. The Son of Life cannot be killed. He is immortal as his Father. What he is cannot be changed. He is the only thing in all the universe that must be one. What seems eternal all will have an end. The stars will disappear, and night and day will be no more. All things that come and go, the tides, the seasons and the lives of men; all things that change with time and bloom and fade will not return. Where time has set an end is not where the eternal is. God's Son can never change by what men made of him. He will be as he was and as he is, for time appointed not his destiny, nor set the hour of his birth and death. Forgiveness will not change him. Yet time waits upon forgiveness that the things of time may disappear because they have no use.

In this paragraph, Jesus pulls all the stops out, trying to get across to us how futile is our ancient promise to die. When we made that pledge—

which was part of our vow to be separate—we made a promise that we cannot keep. We are the Son of Life. How can we be killed? We are like one of those immortals in science fiction movies who, when they are stabbed, double over for a moment, but then stand up again as the wound instantly heals.

We sometimes look around us at the things of nature that seem to last forever—the tides, the seasons, night and day, the stars themselves. Little do we realize that we will outlast all of them.

Application: Repeat these words:

> *The tides will last as long as the ocean lasts.*
> *But I will last longer.*
> *The seasons will last as long as the earth lasts.*
> *But I will last longer.*
> *Day and night will last as long as the solar system lasts.*
> *But I will last longer.*
> *The stars will last as long as the physical universe lasts.*
> *But I will last longer.*
> *They are all things of time, but I am eternal.*
> *Therefore, I give up my ancient promise to die, for it is a promise*
> * I could never keep.*

3. Nothing survives its purpose. If it be conceived to die, then die it must unless it does not take this purpose as its own. Change is the only thing that can be made a blessing here, where purpose is <u>not</u> fixed, however changeless it <u>appears</u> to be. Think not that <u>you</u> can set a goal unlike God's purpose <u>for</u> you, and establish it as changeless and eternal. You <u>can</u> give yourself a purpose that you do not have. But you can <u>not</u> remove the power to change your mind, and see <u>another</u> purpose there.

As long as we assign to this dream the purpose of death, then everything in it, including ourselves, will seem to die. That is the purpose that makes this world such a place of death, where hopes and dreams die more often than bodies do. We do have this ability to set a grim purpose. We can give ourselves the purpose of death, even though it is the opposite of the purpose God gave us. But we cannot make it permanent. No matter what, we are always free to change our minds and opt out of death. And with that change, everything changes.

> 4. Change is the greatest gift God gave to all that <u>you</u> would make eternal, to ensure that <u>only</u> Heaven would not pass away. You were <u>not</u> born to die. You <u>cannot</u> change, because your function <u>has</u> been fixed by God. All other goals are set in time and change that time might be preserved, <u>excepting one</u>. Forgiveness does not aim at <u>keeping</u> time, but at its ending, when it has no use. Its purpose ended, it is gone. And where it once held seeming sway is now restored the function God established for His Son in full awareness. Time can set no end to its fulfillment nor its changelessness. There is no death because the living share the function their Creator gave to them. Life's function <u>cannot</u> be to die. It must be life's <u>extension</u>, that it be as one forever and forever, <u>without</u> end.

In a course that repeatedly says reality is changeless and change is illusion, it is surprising to hear the author sing the praises of change! But it makes sense when you think about it. In this world, change is desperately needed and change can seem impossible. Our underlying promise to die has made a world in which everything seems to crawl inexorably toward death. At age 20, we think we can change it all. By age 60, we have given up. The only thing that is sure is that time will keep rolling on toward death. And that is what we want to believe, that time is permanent, that there's nothing we can do about it. All of our goals are about the things of time in order to reinforce the reality of time.

All of our goals, that is, except one. Forgiveness is the one goal that *ends* time. Its aim is to reestablish our true function. Being the Son of Life, our true function cannot be to die. Our function must be the extension of life, limitless life. This is the endless function of creation in eternity.

> 5. This world will bind your feet and tie your hands and kill your body <u>only</u> if you think that it was made to crucify God's Son. For even though it <u>was</u> a dream of death, you need not let it stand for this to you. Let *this* be changed, and nothing in the world but <u>must</u> be changed as well. For nothing here but is defined as what you see it <u>for</u>.

True, the world was made as a dream of death. It was made to be a place where all change supports the sad conclusion that nothing ever really changes. But we can give the world a new purpose, and then everything will change—*really* change. For the final power here is not what we saw the world as being for in the beginning, but what we see it as being for *now*.

> 6. How lovely is the world whose purpose is forgiveness of God's Son! How free from fear, how filled with blessing and with happiness! And what a joyous thing it is to dwell a little while in such a happy place! Nor <u>can</u> it be forgot, in such a world, it *is* a little while till timelessness comes quietly to take the place of time.

Imagine a world whose purpose is not to kill for the sake of food or dominance. Imagine a world whose purpose is not to catch the killers and bring them to justice (i.e., punishment). Imagine a world whose purpose is to forgive all the Sons of God who thought they were killers. What do you think such a world would be like? What would it be like to live there? How happy do you think you would be?

Thus, we start out in a world whose constant change means that nothing is really changing, that everything is still rolling downhill toward the grave. Then we experience real change. We change the purpose of the world, and we see it transform into a radically different kind of place. Yet in this new world, we never forget that it is preparing us for the coming of true changelessness, the coming of eternity. Thus, we go from *pseudo-changelessness* to *change* to *real changelessness*.

VII. Seek Not Outside Yourself
Commentary by Robert Perry

1. Seek not outside yourself. For it will fail, and you will weep each time an idol falls. Heaven cannot be found where it is not, and there can be no peace <u>excepting</u> there. Each idol that you worship when God calls will never answer in His place. There <u>is</u> no other answer you can substitute, and find the happiness His answer brings. Seek not outside yourself. For all your pain comes simply from a futile search for what you want, insisting <u>where</u> it must be found. What if it is not there? Do you prefer that you be right or happy? Be you glad that you are told where happiness abides, and seek no longer elsewhere. You will fail. But it is given you to know the truth, and <u>not</u> to seek for it outside yourself.

We have spent our lives seeking outside ourselves. And how many times have we wept when an idol has fallen? More times than we can count. We seek the idols when that stirring for something more arises in us. This stirring is actually God calling to us. But then we answer His call by praying to something else—a fat paycheck, a sexy body, a flat screen TV—the list is endless. This is why we never find what we are looking for. We look to idols when we are looking for God.

This paragraph contains the famous "right or happy" passage. We often quote this to mean "If I just stop caring about being right, I will be happy." But notice what it means in its actual context: "If I stop being so attached to being right about where salvation is (outside me), then I can realize that I am wrong. Then I can find out where salvation *really* is (inside me). Then I will be truly right, which will allow me to be truly happy (because now I will look for salvation in the right place)."

The real goal, in other words, is not to stop caring about being right, but rather to be big enough to admit that we are wrong, so we can become truly right, and then be truly happy.

2. No one who comes here but must still have hope, some lingering illusion, or some dream that there is something <u>outside</u> of himself that will bring happiness and peace to him. If everything is <u>in</u> him this

cannot be so. And therefore <u>by</u> his coming, he denies the truth about himself, and seeks for something <u>more</u> than everything, as if a part of it were separated off and found where all the <u>rest</u> of it is <u>not</u>. This is the purpose he bestows upon the body; that it seek for what he lacks, and <u>give</u> him what would make himself complete. And thus he wanders aimlessly about, in search of something that he cannot find, believing that he is what he is not.

If we came here, it is because we wanted to find something we believed we didn't have within. Why else would we come to a place of outsides, of externals? Our coming here was thus a denial that we have everything, that we *are* everything. This is why we have a body, so it can scurry around and gather all those little pieces that seem to be missing from our soul. The final line is quite poignant: "And thus he wanders aimlessly about, searching for something that he cannot find [the "more than everything" mentioned in the third sentence], believing that he is what he is not [believing he is lacking, even though he is not]."

This reminds me of a 70s movie entitled, *They Might Be Giants* (the title, incidentally, is an allusion to Don Quixote's windmills). I found this synopsis online (at www.answers.com):

> George C. Scott stars as Justin Playfair, a retired, widowed judge who labors under the delusion that he's Sherlock Holmes....[A psychiatrist, who happens to be named Dr. Watson] is drawn into Playfair's dream world, accompanying the judge [all over Manhattan] on his quest to find the elusive (and imaginary) Professor Moriarty.

I remember watching this when I was in my teens and feeling very disturbed viewing a man whose whole quest was delusional. Yet the Course is saying that this is true of all of us.

> 3. The lingering illusion will impel him to seek out a thousand idols, and to seek beyond them for a thousand more. And each will fail him, all excepting one; for he will die, and does not understand the idol that he seeks *is* but his death. Its <u>form</u> appears to be outside himself. Yet does he seek to kill God's Son within, and <u>prove</u> that he is victor over him. This is the purpose <u>every</u> idol has, for this the role that is assigned to it, and this the role that cannot <u>be</u> fulfilled.

Idols fall. That's what they do. If only we realized that they were *made* to do that! For, way deep down inside, what we are really seeking is not the idol but the emptiness after it falls. That emptiness proves that we cannot be the eternally complete Son of God. It therefore demonstrates that we have at last conquered, and killed, our true Self within.

Application: Think of an idol you are currently pursuing, something in the world that you hope to gain for yourself. Then say,

> *This idol will eventually fall.*
> *And even now, that is my plan.*
> *For I am really seeking the emptiness after it falls, because that*
>   *will prove that I am not God's Son.*
> *And thus I will at last have defeated my true Self.*
> *Yet can this goal be what I **really** want?*

4. Whenever you attempt to reach a goal in which the body's betterment is cast as major beneficiary, you try to bring about your death. For you believe that you can suffer lack, and lack *is* death. To sacrifice is to <u>give up</u>, and thus to be without and to have suffered loss. And <u>by</u> this giving up is life renounced. Seek not outside yourself. The search implies you are not whole within and fear to look upon your devastation, but prefer to seek outside yourself for what you are.

Application: Think of the latest exciting thing you are searching for, then repeat these words:

> *Is my body a major beneficiary of this?*
> *If so, then, the search for it proves to me that I am lacking.*
> *It proves that I am lacking the fullness of life.*
> *And lack of life is death.*
> *The search for this, therefore, is a search for death.*
> *Further, by searching outside, I am trying to not look within—at*
>   *the death I think is there.*
> *Yet could it be that if I really looked within, I would see only*
>   *unlimited life?*

5. Idols must fall *because* they have no life, and what is lifeless <u>is</u> a sign of death. You came to die, and what would you expect but to <u>perceive</u> the signs of death you seek? No sadness and no suffering proclaim a message <u>other</u> than an idol found that represents a parody of life which, in its lifelessness, is really death, conceived as real and given living form. Yet each must fail and crumble and decay, because a form of death cannot <u>be</u> life, and what is sacrificed cannot <u>be</u> whole.

Imagine that you came to an island and there found the man of your dreams. You seemed happy for a time, but there was also a strange emptiness. Then one day, he falls over and stops moving, and smoke starts rising from his neck. You inspect him and realize, to your horror, that he was a robot. All along, you had been relating to a lifeless mechanism. And then it all came back to you. You consciously planned this whole thing. You planned to live with a lifeless robot that would one day stop functioning. You did this because you wanted to find the total absence of life. That is why you came to this island, to escape life and find pure emptiness.

Not a happy story, but it does capture what Jesus is saying about our search for idols.

6. All idols of this world were made to keep the truth within from being known to you, and to maintain allegiance to the dream that you must find what is <u>outside</u> yourself to be complete and happy. It is vain to worship idols in the hope of peace. God dwells within, and your completion lies in Him. No idol takes His place. Look not to idols. Do not seek outside yourself.

To continue my story from the previous paragraph, you came to Idol Island because a highly respected psychic had told you that you were in fact, the next world savior, a being of incomprehensible radiance and infinite life. This was too much for you to handle, so you sought a situation that would constantly reinforce the idea that you were the opposite, that you were utterly empty inside.

Application: Repeat these words:

It is vain for me to worship idols in the hope of peace.
God dwells within me, and my completion lies in Him.

No idol takes His place.
I will not look to idols.
I will not seek outside myself.

7. Let us forget the purpose of the world the past has given it. For otherwise, the future <u>will</u> be like the past, and but a series of depressing dreams, in which all idols fail you, one by one, and you see death and disappointment everywhere.

Let us forget the purpose that brought us to this island world. The pursuit of each new idol may excite us, but after a while, we learn to guess how it will end, and then we increasingly see nothing but death and disappointment everywhere. Wouldn't we give anything for this to change?

8. To change all this, and open up a road of hope and of release in what appeared to be an endless circle of despair, you need but to decide you do not <u>know</u> the purpose of the world. You <u>give</u> it goals it does not have, and thus do <u>you</u> decide what it is for. You try to see in it a place of idols found outside yourself, with power to make complete what is within by splitting what you are <u>between</u> the two [inside and outside]. You <u>choose</u> your dreams, for they are what you wish, perceived as if it had been given you. Your idols do what you would have them do, and <u>have</u> the power you ascribe to them. And you pursue them vainly in the dream, because you want their power as your own.

Could this paragraph be right? Could it be that we assigned the world the purpose of completing us with all its (supposed) treasures? Could it be that we gave it goals it does not have? Imagine looking out at the world and seeing nothing that had power to make you complete?

According to Jesus, we set the whole thing up. *We* made up a world where there was an empty interior and a treasure-filled exterior. *We* saw in the idols the magic power to complete us. *We* wrote the story of our pursuit of them, in which we never really lay hands on them. We even affixed the expiration date for when they would fall.

9. Yet where <u>are</u> dreams but in a mind asleep? And <u>can</u> a dream succeed in making real the picture it projects outside itself? Save time, my

brother [Ur: brothers]; learn what time is <u>for</u>. And speed the end of idols in a world made sad and sick by seeing idols there. Your holy mind is altar unto God, and where He is <u>no</u> idols can abide. The fear of God is but the fear of loss of idols. It is <u>not</u> the fear of loss of your reality [see T-29.I.9:5]. But <u>you</u> have made of your reality an idol, which you must protect <u>against</u> the light of truth. And all the world becomes the means by which this idol can be saved. Salvation thus appears to <u>threaten</u> life and offer death.

If our mind is in charge of everything in this world, then this world must be a dream, and we must be asleep. How can we ever really possess the goodies of this world if they are just dream images? Okay, so they look real; they are full color and three-dimensional. But isn't this true of our dream images as well?

We set up this whole dream world to save the king of the idols—our concept of who we are, our self-image. This is why we are afraid of God, because we sense that awakening to Him means discarding this king of idols. How can we return to God when *it* is our god? This idol is what we are afraid to lose along the pathway home. Thus, when we get in touch with this fear, when we feel the fear of losing our identity by waking up to God, let us remind ourselves that we really fear shedding our *false* identity and finding our *true* Identity.

> 10. It is not so. Salvation seeks to prove there <u>is</u> no death, and <u>only</u> life exists. The sacrifice of death is <u>nothing</u> lost. An idol <u>cannot</u> take the place of God. Let Him remind you of His Love for you, and do not seek to drown His Voice in chants of deep despair to idols of yourself. Seek not outside your Father for your hope. For hope of happiness is *not* despair.

Losing the idol of our self-image seems like death itself. Yet we have got it all backwards. The *idol* is death. It is an image of our lifelessness, of our death. This is why we bemoan our self-image. This is why we sing chants of deep despair to it, for it does seem like a perennially hopeless thing, doesn't it? Our chants of despair to this god of ours (which usually have the chorus "I'm so stupid!") are, in a rather twisted fashion, meant to drown out the Voice of the real God, the God Who loves us with an everlasting Love. Yet He is where our real hope lies. The idol, as we have surmised, is indeed hopeless.

VIII. The Anti-Christ
Commentary by Robert Perry

1. What is an idol? Do you think you know? For idols are unrecognized as such, and never seen for what they really are. That is the only power that they have. Their purpose is obscure, and they are feared and worshipped, both, *because* you do not know what they are for, and why they have been made. An idol is an image of your brother that you would value more than what he is. Idols are made that he may be replaced, no matter what their form. And it is this that never is perceived and recognized. Be it a body or a thing, a place, a situation or a circumstance, an object owned or wanted, or a right demanded or achieved, it is the same.

This paragraph contains perhaps the fullest list of idols in the Course. They can be "a body [our own or someone else's] or a thing [e.g., a car], a situation [e.g., a job] or a circumstance [e.g., happening upon a great sale], an object owned or wanted, or a right demanded or achieved." The list runs the gamut from the obvious ones, like possessions, to ones you probably wouldn't think of, like rights.

Traditionally, idols are replacements for God. Here, they are replacements for the divinity of our *brothers*. That divinity could answer all our prayers, but we are praying to idols, instead. They have become our substitute for the holy radiance of our brothers' reality. Yet this fact is something that we never allow into consciousness.

2. Let not their form deceive you. Idols are but substitutes for your reality. In some way, you believe they will complete your little self, for safety [Ur: and let you walk in safety] in a world perceived as dangerous, with forces massed against your confidence and peace of mind. They have the power to supply your lacks, and add the value that you do not have. No one believes in idols who has not enslaved himself to littleness and loss. And thus must seek beyond his little self for strength to raise his head, and stand apart from all the misery the world reflects. This is the penalty for looking not within for certainty and [Ur: for] quiet calm that liberates you from the world, and lets you stand apart, in quiet and in peace [Ur: unlimited].

170

In our brother's reality we discover our own. Thus, by replacing our brother's reality, idols also replace *our* reality. They are there to augment (and thus confirm) our *false* identity, an identity that it so little and lacking that it can barely muster the confidence to raise its head in the face of all the danger in the world, or the strength to stand apart from all the misery in the world. This is truer than we realize. Imagine that you were stripped of all your props: your morning coffee, your favorite clothes, your credentials, your reputation, your station in the world, your circle of supporters, along with a hundred other props. With how much strength would you face the world then?

Yet if you really looked within and saw the immeasurable strength there, you could do then what a thousand idols cannot enable you to do now: hold your head high and stand apart from all the world's danger and misery, "in quiet and in peace unlimited" (Urtext version).

> 3. An idol is a false impression, or a false belief; some form of anti-Christ, that constitutes a gap <u>between</u> the Christ and what you see. An idol is a wish, made tangible and given form, and thus perceived as real and seen <u>outside</u> the mind. Yet it is still a thought [Ur: Yet they remain ideas], and <u>cannot</u> leave the mind that is its [Ur: their] source. Nor is its [Ur: their] form apart from the idea it [the form] represents. All forms of anti-Christ oppose the Christ. And fall before His face like a dark veil that <u>seems</u> to shut you off from Him, alone in darkness. Yet the light is there. A cloud does not put out the sun. No more a veil can banish what it seems to separate, nor darken by one whit the light itself.

Application: Imagine a large curtain in front of you. Now begin to see sewn onto this curtain, like patches on a patchwork quilt, pictures of your idols. See the possessions you value. See the situations to which you are attached. See the bodies that are important to you. See the bodies that you wished you had. See the rights that you insist on or wish for. See more and more patches go onto this curtain, until every inch is covered, and the patches are overlapping each other.

Now see the curtain slowly lifted. Behind it is the shining face of Christ, vast, lit with glory, almost blinding in its celestial radiance. This is your reality. This is what has been obscured by the heavy veil of idols.

Realize that all those patches are the anti-Christ. They all oppose

Christ. They take a tangible form, but each one is really the *wish* to not know the Christ.

Finally, realize that though they obscure the Christ from your sight, He still is there. A veil cannot "darken by one whit the light itself." Christ remains your one and only reality.

> 4. This world of idols *is* a veil across the face of Christ, <u>because</u> its purpose is to separate your brother from yourself. A dark and fearful purpose, yet a thought without the power to change one blade of grass from something living to a sign of death. Its form is nowhere, for its source abides within your mind where God abideth not. Where <u>is</u> this place where what is everywhere has been excluded and been kept apart? What hand could be held up to block God's way? Whose voice could make demand He enter not? The "more-than-everything" is <u>not</u> a thing to make you tremble and to quail in fear. Christ's enemy [anti-Christ] is nowhere. He can take <u>no</u> form in which he <u>ever</u> will be real.

In the end, that veil of idols is the entire world. The whole thing is one big veil across the face of Christ. Its purpose is to keep us from seeing the Christ in our brother, so that we don't see the Christ in ourselves. And it has done its job well.

Thus, the source of this world is a dark and fearful purpose, the purpose of anti-Christ. Yet this purpose is powerless, for it abides in a place in our mind that has shut God out, and how can God really be shut out? That would be like holding your hand to stop the tide coming in. And so the world spins out of *nothingness* into *nowhere*. If Christ is all, how could the anti-Christ ever take a form in which he would be real?

> 5. What is an idol? Nothing! It must be believed <u>before</u> it seems to come to life, and <u>given</u> power that it may be feared. Its life and power are its believer's gift, and this [life and power] is what the miracle restores to what *has* life and power worthy of the gift of Heaven and eternal peace. The miracle does not restore the truth, the light [that] the veil between has <u>not</u> put out. It merely <u>lifts</u> the veil, and <u>lets</u> the truth shine unencumbered, being what it is. It [the light] does not <u>need</u> belief to be itself, for it <u>has been</u> created; so it *is*.

An idol is like a doll. What is a doll, really? Just some cloth and plastic and stuffing. But in the child's mind the doll comes to life. Does this life reside in the doll or in the child? Likewise, does life reside in that cherished keepsake of ours or in the mind which gave it life? Krishnamurti once spoke of putting "a piece of stick you have picked up in the garden on the mantelpiece and giv[ing] it a flower every day. In a month you will be worshipping it and not to put a flower in front of it will become a sin."

We have given the life in us away to lifeless things. The miracle's job is to restore that life to *us*. How does it do that? The miracle is what lifts the veil of idols, allowing us to see the shining face of Christ, the face of our true Identity.

> 6. An idol is <u>established</u> by belief, and when it is withdrawn the idol "dies." This is the anti-Christ; the strange idea there is a power <u>past</u> omnipotence, a place <u>beyond</u> the infinite, a time transcending the eternal. Here the world of idols has been set by the idea this power and place and time are given form, and shape the world where the impossible has happened. Here the deathless come to die, the all-encompassing to suffer loss, the timeless to be made the slaves of time. Here does the changeless change; the peace of God, forever given to all living things, give way to chaos. And the Son of God, as perfect, sinless and as loving as his Father, come to hate a little while; to suffer pain and finally to die.

What is the anti-Christ? Is it that creepy kid with the 666 birthmark on his scalp? No, it is just an idea. It is the idea that animates all of our dolls, including our life-sized ones. It is the idea that animates this entire world. It is "the strange idea there is a power past omnipotence, a place beyond the infinite, a time transcending the eternal." This strange idea is, of course, the *tiny, mad* idea. And you can see the madness of it here in this paragraph. How can there be a power past omnipotence? Any omnipotence that had another power beyond it wouldn't be omnipotence. Likewise, how can there be a place beyond the infinite? How can there be a time transcending eternity, which is infinite and without limit? At the heart of all these is the notion that there can be a wish in opposition to God, a wish that is *anti-Christ*.

This crazy wish then takes form, to give itself the illusion of reality. It thus becomes the world we (seem to) live in, a "world where the impossible has happened." And because the wish that made this world is a bundle of contradictions, so the world itself is. It is a fundamentally upside-down place where "the deathless come to die." How can that really happen? It is a place where "the all-encompassing [come] to suffer loss." Again, how is that possible? And a place where "the timeless [come] to be made the slaves of time." It is a place where the changeless changes and where the peace of God is overcome and degenerates into chaos. Can we really imagine that this actually happens? Most ironic of all, it is a place where "the Son of God, as perfect, sinless and as loving as his Father, come[s] to hate a little while; to suffer pain and finally to die."

Look around you and you will see that this indeed is what happens in this world. You will see what one small, upside-down idea can do. But can it? According to Jesus, it cannot and has not done anything. There is no world.

> 7. <u>Where</u> is an idol? Nowhere! Can there be a gap in what is infinite, a place where time can <u>interrupt</u> eternity? A place of darkness set where all is light, a dismal alcove separated off from what is endless, *has* no place to be. An idol is beyond where God has set all things forever, and [where God] has left no room for anything to be <u>except</u> His Will. Nothing and nowhere <u>must</u> an idol be, while God is everything and everywhere.

Application: Look about you, letting your eyes light on anything you see, especially things you value. With each one, say,

> *This idol is nothing and nowhere, for God is everything and*
> *   everywhere.*
> *There can be no gap in what is infinite.*

Conclude by letting your eyes rove about without resting on any one thing, and saying,

> *This world is nothing and nowhere, for God is everything and*
> *   everywhere.*
> *There can be no gap in what is infinite.*

174

8. What purpose has an idol, then? What is it <u>for</u>? This is the only question that has many answers, each depending on the one of whom the question has been asked. The world <u>believes</u> in idols. No one comes unless he worshipped them, and still attempts to seek for one that yet might offer him a gift reality does <u>not</u> contain. Each worshipper of idols harbors hope his <u>special</u> deities will give him <u>more</u> than other men possess. It <u>must</u> be more. It does not really matter more of what; more beauty, more intelligence, more wealth, or even more affliction and more pain. But more of <u>something</u> is an idol for. And when one fails another takes its place, with hope of finding more of something <u>else</u>. Be not deceived by forms the "something" takes. An idol is a means for getting <u>more</u>. And it is <u>this</u> that is against God's Will.

The truth of this paragraph pierces us like an arrow through the heart. What is an idol for? To make us special. Jesus' language in this paragraph evokes images of primitive religion, where each person would have his special collection of stone figurines to which he would pray. Those special deities were there to give him better crops than other men, or a prettier wife, or a more successful son; they were there, in other words, to make him more special. Our modern-day idols are no different.

Application: Look at your body, one of your chief idols, and ask yourself, "In what way is this special deity supposed to give me more than others have?" Then make a list (such as, more youth, more attention, more health, more brainpower, more status, etc.). When you are done, read over the list and after each one, say, *"Having more than my brothers is against God's Will."*

9. God has not many sons, but only one. Who can have more, and who be given less? In Heaven would the Son of God but laugh, if idols could intrude upon his peace. It is for <u>him</u> the Holy Spirit speaks, and tells you idols <u>have</u> no purpose here. For <u>more</u> than Heaven can you never have. If Heaven is within, why would you seek for idols that would make of Heaven less, to give you <u>more</u> than God bestowed upon your brother <u>and</u> on you, as one with Him? God <u>gave</u> you all there is. And to be sure you could not lose it, did He <u>also</u> give the same to every living thing as well. And thus <u>is</u> every living thing a part of you, as of Himself. No idol can establish you as <u>more</u> than God. But <u>you</u> will never be content with being <u>less</u>.

God gave us everything, all of Heaven, all of Himself. And He gave the exact same thing to our brother. Thus, when we try to use our idols to get more than our brother, we are really seeking more than the everything that God gave us. And what happens when you say "I want more than this"? The "this" that you want more than fades from your mind, which now focuses entirely on the "more" that you want.

Thus, when we want more than our brother, the totality that God gave both him and us fades from our mind. We lose the awareness of the Heaven that is already ours. And we replace it with—what? A few pieces of junk that will break down and turn to dust in a few years? This is nuts. It is laughable. And that is what we would see if we were in Heaven.

Imagine the Son of God is in Heaven with his Father. Then some shady character with a big overcoat walks up and says, "Psst! Hey, bub, get a load of these." He then opens his coat to show us a glittering collection of cheap, knock-off watches. The Son of God says, "What will it cost me?" And the guy says, "Heaven." Can we imagine any reaction but laughter? This needs to become our reaction as well.

IX. The Forgiving Dream
Commentary by Robert Perry

1. The slave of idols is a <u>willing</u> slave. For willing he <u>must</u> be to let himself bow down in worship to what has no life, and seek for power in the powerless. What happened to the holy Son of God that this could <u>be</u> his wish; to let himself fall lower than the stones upon the ground, and look to idols that they raise him up? Hear, then, your story in the dream you made, and ask yourself if it be not the truth that you believe that it is <u>not</u> a dream.

How could we, the Son of God, have willingly enslaved ourselves to idols? How could we kneel in worship to something that is lifeless? How could we, God's Own Son, "fall lower than the stones upon the ground" and then pray to lifeless idols to raise us up? This is what we are all doing. We are so dependent on all the gadgets and paraphernalia of our lives that it seems ridiculous to believe we *are* the Son of God.

How did this happen? This section promises to provide an answer. It is an answer that we would never have come to on our own. It is a difficult answer to understand, but it is well worth the effort. For if we do understand it, we will never see our lives the same way again.

2. A dream of judgment came into the mind that God created perfect as Himself. And in that dream was Heaven changed to hell, and God made enemy unto His Son. How can God's Son <u>awaken</u> from the dream? It is a dream of judgment. So must he judge <u>not</u>, and he <u>will</u> waken. For the dream will seem to last while he is <u>part</u> of it. Judge not, for he who judges <u>will</u> have need of idols, which will hold the judgment off from resting on himself. Nor <u>can</u> he know the Self he has condemned. Judge not, because you make yourself a <u>part</u> of evil dreams, where idols are your "true" identity, and your salvation from the judgment laid in terror and in guilt upon yourself.

This paragraph contains the promised explanation for how we became the slaves of idols. We can think of this in three concentric zones, which I will present here slightly out of order:

1. The inner zone is us. We are the dreamer of the dream. As it happens, our dreams spill out of our own judgment. "It is a dream of judgment."

3. The outer zone, then, is the punishment we think we have coming to us. Because we have judged, we then turn and judge ourselves, and pronounce a sentence on ourselves. What is the sentence? It is comprised of all those horrible things that could happen to us in this world, all those things we spend our lives keeping at bay: earthquakes, cancer, injury, public humiliation, fire, etc.

2. The middle zone is our idols. In this section, idols are primarily people—our friends, family, supporters, protectors, defenders. With calamity constantly threatening on the horizon of our dream (calamity that is our own sentence on ourselves), we now desperately need friends, supporters, and protectors to make sure that that calamity never reaches us. These are our idols. They hold off the judgment (outer zone) from resting on us. They are our salvation from the judgment we laid on ourselves.

As an analogy of the three zones, imagine this. You (inner zone) feel that you have been so mercilessly judgmental and attacking that you decide you don't deserve to live. In a moment of profound guilt, you pick up the phone and hire a hit man to kill you (outer zone). You don't know when he'll do it and you don't know how. All you know is that he's out there and he's coming to get you.

Then your moment of profound guilt passes, and you decide you don't want to die. Since you can't stop the hit man (that's how it works in the movies, at least), you now hire a bunch of people to protect you (middle zone). You hire bodyguards. You hire friends to advise you and to tell you that you don't deserve this death. You hire police to patrol outside your house. And you hire therapists to help you deal with the terror you are experiencing. Even though you hired them to protect you, you now become their slave. When they say, "Go into that room and lock the door; it's for your own safety," you do it. When they say, "I need more money to better perform my job of keeping you safe," you give it to them.

This is the story of our lives. This is how we became the slave of idols.

3. All figures in the dream are idols, made to save you <u>from</u> the dream. Yet they are <u>part</u> of what they have been made to save you *from*. Thus does an idol <u>keep</u> the dream alive and terrible, for who could wish for one <u>unless</u> he were in terror and despair? And this the idol <u>represents,</u> and so its worship <u>is</u> the worship of despair and terror, and the dream from which they come. Judgment is an <u>in</u>justice to God's Son, and it *is* justice that who judges <u>him</u> will not escape the penalty he laid upon <u>himself</u> within the dream he made. God knows of justice, <u>not</u> of penalty. But in the dream of judgment you attack and <u>are</u> condemned; and <u>wish</u> to be the slave of idols, which are interposed <u>between</u> your judgment and the penalty it brings.

This world is a dream of terror and despair. Even though idols are supposed to *save* us from the dream, they are also an integral part of the dream. Thus, when we say to ourselves, "Thank God my lawyer protects me from those sharks out there," you are really saying, "I'm in danger." When you say, "Thank God my spouse defends my self-esteem when people say all those mean things about me," you are really saying, "I'm under attack." Idols, in the end, just reinforce the reality of the dream of terror and despair.

And, again, what each person is so afraid of, what he needs the idols to protect him from, is "the penalty he laid upon *himself* within the dream he made" (Urtext version). The things we are using our idols (middle zone) to keep away from us (inner zone) are the things we secretly believe we deserve (outer zone).

4. There <u>can</u> be no salvation in the dream as <u>you</u> are dreaming it. For idols <u>must</u> be part of it, to save you from what you believe you have accomplished, and have done to make you sinful and put out the light within you. Little child, the light is there. You do but dream, and idols are the toys you dream you play with. Who has need of toys but children? They pretend they rule the world, and give their toys the power to move about, and talk and think and feel and speak for them. Yet everything their toys appear to do is in the minds of those who play with them. But they are eager to forget that they made up the dream in which their toys are real, nor recognize their wishes are their own.

The people in our lives are real Sons of God with real minds of their own. However, they have agreed to appear as dream figures in our dream on condition that they play the part we have scripted for them. In a sense, then, they have become our toys. Have you ever felt as if you were someone's toy? If so, don't you think there are people who have felt that they were *your* toy?

It's as if we are a child playing at being a king, and the people in our lives are our little plastic army men. We move them around the board, wherever we want, so that they can halt the advance of the dark invading menace out there. The army men, however, are just our pawns. We think that they move about, talk, think, and speak. "Yet everything [our] toys appear to do is in the minds of those who play with them." What does this mean for the actions of *our* supporters and protectors? It means that as we watch them act, we are watching our own hand puppet.

> 5. Nightmares are childish dreams. The toys have turned against the child who thought he made them real. Yet <u>can</u> a dream attack? Or <u>can</u> a toy grow large and dangerous and fierce and wild? This does the child believe, <u>because</u> he fears his thoughts and gives them to the toys instead. And their reality becomes his own, because they seem to <u>save</u> him from his thoughts. Yet do they <u>keep</u> his thoughts alive and real, but seen <u>outside</u> himself, where they can turn against him for his treachery to them. He thinks he <u>needs</u> them that he may escape his thoughts, because he thinks the <u>thoughts</u> are real. And so he makes of <u>anything</u> a toy, to make his world remain outside himself, and play that <u>he</u> is but a part of it.

How often have we seen in fiction the toys turn against the child, or the inventions turn against the inventor? Yet, of course, we also see it in real life. Eventually, our pawns turn on us. Why? We assume it is because they get fed up with being controlled by our will and so eventually turn against our will.

Yet there is a deeper reason, only part of which is revealed in this paragraph. What Jesus says here is that our idols are not just there to protect us from all the hit men out there that we have secretly hired to kill us. They are there to protect us from our own thoughts of judgment (the thoughts which earned us the death penalty that the hit men are trying to carry out). How do they do that? They act out those thoughts for us, thus making it appear as if the thoughts are theirs, not ours. Judgment excludes, and the idols are there to *exclude* certain awful things from our lives (the outer zone). They fight our battles for us, and by being the ones that act out the aggression, they make it appear that the aggression is theirs, not ours. We thus come out looking innocent and harmless. Once you are aware of this dynamic, you will see it everywhere. Just the other night I saw a movie in which an entertainer described his agent as the person that gets to be nasty on his behalf so he can look nice.

For some reason, however, the job of acting out our thoughts of judgment entails the idols eventually turning against us. We'll see why later.

> 6. There is a time when childhood should be passed and gone forever. Seek not to retain the toys of children. Put them all away, for you have need of them no more. The dream of judgment is a children's game, in which the child becomes the father, powerful, but with the little wisdom of a child. What hurts him is destroyed; what helps him, blessed. Except he judges this as does a child, who does not <u>know</u> what hurts and what will heal. And bad things seem to happen, and he is afraid of all the chaos in a world he thinks is governed by the laws he made. Yet is the real world unaffected by the world he thinks is real. Nor have its laws been changed because he does not understand.

Here is yet another familiar theme from fiction: the little tyrant who is in way over his head. He rules with an iron fist, punishing his enemies and rewarding his friends. But he lacks the wisdom to know who is really his enemy and who is really his friend. And so he bungles it all, and everything comes crashing down on his head.

This is a picture of us. We are like the little tyrant. We order everyone about. We smile on our friends and command them to mercilessly punish our enemies. But, lacking wisdom, we don't realize that our real enemy is *judgment*, and our real friend is *everyone*. Therefore, the whole thing backfires. And when it all comes crashing down around us, we have no idea that it's because of us, that we sowed the seeds of our own destruction.

We need to step out of the role of the little god. After all, we are just children. How do we step out of this role? By ceasing to treat people like our toy army men who are there to protect us from the enemy at the gates.

> 7. The real world still is but a dream. Except the figures have been changed. They are not seen as idols which betray. It is a dream in which

no one is used to substitute for something else, nor interposed between the thoughts the mind conceives and what it sees. No one is used for something he is not, for childish things have all been put away. And what was once a dream of judgment now has changed into a dream where all is joy, because that is the <u>purpose</u> that it has. Only forgiving dreams can enter here, for time is almost over. And the forms that enter in the dream are now perceived as brothers, not in judgment, but in love.

In the current dream, we grab hold of someone and say, "I love you! Now you're my very favorite person. And one of your jobs as my new favorite is to protect me from my old favorite." It is a dream of substitution. It is also a very childish dream. We're just using people.

In forgiving dreams, we say, "I forgive you, my old favorite, for how you have betrayed me. And I forgive you, my new favorite, for how you will betray me." We withdraw all the judgment we laid on those dream figures. When we do so, we find that each one is a brother to be loved, not a toy to be used. "And what was once a dream of judgment now has changed into a dream where all is joy."

8. Forgiving dreams have little need to last. They are not made to separate the mind from what it thinks. They do not seek to prove the dream is being dreamed by someone <u>else</u>. And in these dreams a melody is heard that everyone remembers, though he has not heard it since before all time began. Forgiveness, once complete, brings timelessness so close the song of Heaven can be heard, not with the ears, but with the holiness that never left the altar that abides forever deep within the Son of God. And when he hears this song again, he knows he <u>never</u> heard it not. And where <u>is</u> time, when dreams of judgment have been put away?

In our current dreams, our thoughts seem to be outside of us. Our thoughts of judgment are out there in the idols, impelling them to attack our enemies. Our thoughts of self-condemnation are out there in the enemies, impelling them to punish us. We seem to be just a figure in the dream, tossed about by the dream. But even though we seem to be just a character on the stage, the whole thing is our own puppet show, being controlled by secret strings coming out of our own mind.

In forgiving dreams, we let all the strings go lax. And we look around the stage and find, to our surprise, that the puppets are really our brothers. Then all the characters on stage, including us, go still—and listen. We all begin to hear the faint melodies of the song of Heaven. And when we hear this song, we know that we never really *stopped* hearing it, and we know that it won't be long until it is *all* we hear, until we are off this ramshackle stage and back in our real home.

> 9. Whenever you feel fear in any form,—and you *are* fearful if you do not feel a deep content, a certainty of help, a calm assurance Heaven goes with you,—be sure you made an idol, and believe it will betray you. For beneath your hope that it will save you lie the guilt and pain of self-betrayal and uncertainty, so deep and bitter that the dream cannot conceal completely all your sense of doom. Your self-betrayal <u>must</u> result in fear, for fear *is* judgment, leading surely to the frantic search for idols and for death.

Now we are finally told why the toys turn on us. It's not because they are tired of being controlled by our will and finally revolt against it. It's because they are *carrying out* our will. We have hired them, remember, to carry out our thoughts of judgment for us. They are there to say and do all those things that would make us look terrible if *we* said and did them.

Yet the very thoughts they are carrying out for us are also a *betrayal* of us. Judgment is a betrayal of our loving nature; it is an act of self-betrayal. So when we give these thoughts to the idols to act out for us, we are really giving the idols two tasks, the same two tasks the judgments themselves perform: We are giving the idols the task of judging and attacking our enemies, and we are giving them the task of *betraying us*.

Application: Are you feeling a deep content, an unshakable certainty that you are helped, and a calm assurance that Heaven goes with you now and always? If not, then you are in a state of fear. You are in this state because you believe an idol of yours is going to betray you. Whom in your life are you anxious about? Whom do you expect will possibly not hold up his or her end of the bargain? Say to this person:

> *I hired you to be my toy, to protect me by acting out my thoughts of judgment against my enemies.*
> *But since my thoughts of judgments are a betrayal of me, I also hired you to act out that betrayal of me.*
> *I hired you to betray me.*
> *I forgive you for doing what I hired you to do.*
> *And I release you from being my toy.*

10. Forgiving dreams remind you that you live in safety and have <u>not</u> attacked yourself. So do your childish terrors melt away, and dreams become a sign that you have made a new beginning, <u>not</u> another try to worship idols and to <u>keep</u> attack. Forgiving dreams are kind to everyone who figures in the dream. And so they bring the dreamer full release from dreams of fear. He does not fear his judgment for he has judged no one, nor has sought to be released <u>through</u> judgment from what judgment <u>must</u> impose. And all the while he is remembering what he forgot, when judgment seemed to be the way to <u>save</u> him from its penalty.

In the usual dream, we are unkind to everyone. We judge, and then we lay a penalty on ourselves for judging. Then, when this penalty comes knocking (in the form of enemies and calamities), we hire "friends" to fight it and keep it bay. They act out our judgments against *it*. Thus, we use judgment to try to stave off the penalty of judgment. In the process, our enemies are attacked and our friends are used.

In forgiving dreams, we "are kind to everyone who figures in the dream." What a change! No one is chained to some role that we ordain. No one is used like a puppet to act out the thoughts that we disown. Hence, forgiving dreams bring us full release from all the terror evoked by our dream of judgment. Now perhaps this line at last makes sense: "He does not fear his judgment for he has judged no one, nor has sought to be released *through* judgment from what judgment *must* impose" (Urtext version).

Try to take some time and look around at your life, past and present. Try to see how the picture in this section might explain certain things. Whom have you hired to protect you? Protect you against *what* and against *whom*? Could the danger they were meant to protect you from be a punishment that you yourself dreamt into your life, as the self-imposed penalty for your judgments? Could your protectors be there to act out your judgments so that those judgments no longer seemed to be yours? Could your protectors' betrayal of you be simply part of their job of acting out your judgments, since your judgments betray you?

Commentaries on Chapter 30

THE NEW BEGINNING

Introduction
Commentary by Greg Mackie

1. The new beginning now becomes the focus of the curriculum. The goal is clear, but now you need specific methods for attaining it. The speed by which it can be reached depends on this one thing alone [Ur: only this]; your willingness to practice every step. Each one will help a little, every time it is attempted. And together will these steps lead you [Ur: together they will lead you both] from dreams of judgment to forgiving dreams and out of pain and fear. They are not new to you, but they are more ideas than rules of thought to you as yet. So now we need to practice them awhile, until they are the rules by which you live. We seek to make them habits now, so you will have them ready for whatever need [Ur: ready, and for *any* need].

The end of the last section spoke of the "new beginning" (T-29. IX.10:2) that comes with the acceptance of forgiving dreams. Now, Jesus gives us the means to bring about and sustain this new beginning. After 29 chapters of the Text, we know the goal is salvation, which comes from forgiving dreams. But how do we attain this goal in the rough and tumble of our daily lives?

We attain it by following specific steps, specific *rules of thought*—the rules that will be described in the following section. We need to practice those rules until they become such firmly established habits that they are the rules by which we live. We may balk at the whole idea of living by "rules," but there is simply no other way to achieve the goal of salvation. In fact, the speed by which we reach that goal depends solely on our willingness to follow the rules, our "willingness to practice every step."

I. Rules for Decision
Commentary by Greg Mackie

This is an amazing section—a kind of proto-Workbook lesson. I encourage you to really follow these rules for decision and try to experience the "happy day" they promise.

> 1. Decisions are continuous. You do not always know when you are making them. But with a little practice with the ones you recognize, a set begins to form which sees you through the rest. It is not wise to let yourself become preoccupied with every step you take. The proper set, adopted consciously each time you wake, will put you well ahead. And if you find resistance strong and dedication weak, you are not ready. *Do not fight yourself.* But think about the kind of day you want, and tell yourself there is a way in which this very day can happen just like that. Then try again to <u>have</u> the day you want.
> 2. (1) The outlook starts with this:

> *Today I will make <u>no</u> decisions by myself.*

This is the fundamental rule for decision if we want to attain the goal of salvation: Instead of making decisions by ourselves, we should place every one of them into the hands of the Holy Spirit. But how can we do this when our decisions are so rapid-fire that we're not even consciously aware of many of them? We do this by giving the decisions we *are* aware of to the Holy Spirit. This will enable us to form a "set"—a *mindset*—that will place the decisions we're not aware of into His hands as well.

We get this started by adopting that mindset consciously when we wake. There seem to be three steps to doing this:

Step 1. We establish our goal by imagining the kind of day we want. We imagine a day that reflects our goal of salvation, a day the section later calls a "happy day." What mental states would we cultivate? What kinds of things would we do? What would our encounters with others look like? How would we deal with problems that arise? The idea here is not to program specific events into our day, but to vividly imagine

188

the *kinds* of things that would occur in a truly happy day. To aid in this process, you might even want to write your "ideal day" on a card and carry it with you throughout the day.

Step 2. We tell ourselves that we can have that day—that there is a means to accomplish our goal. This is the essence of that well-known Course instruction, *"Do not fight yourself."* This doesn't mean that we should respond to our resistance to practice by giving up. Instead, it means we should remind ourselves of the day we really want, and that practicing will *give* us the day we want. This will lower our resistance so we can try again to have the day we want through our practice.

Step 3. We remind ourselves of the means to our goal: *"Today, I will make no decisions by myself. I will make all of them with the Holy Spirit."*

> This means that you are choosing <u>not</u> to be the judge of what to do. But it must <u>also</u> mean you will not judge the situations where you will be called upon to make response. For if you judge them, you <u>have</u> set the rules for how you should react to them. And then <u>another</u> answer cannot <u>but</u> produce confusion and uncertainty <u>and fear</u>.
> 3. This is your major problem now. You still make up your mind [Ur: minds], and *then* decide to ask what you should do. And what you hear may not resolve the problem <u>as you saw it first</u>. This leads to fear, because it contradicts what you perceive and so you feel attacked. <u>And therefore angry</u>. There are rules by which this will not happen. But it does occur at first, while you are learning how to hear. [Ur: But it does occur, at first, to everyone who listens well.]

Making no decisions by ourselves means both asking the Holy Spirit about what to do *and* about how to perceive the situations in which we are called to do something. The second aspect here is crucial. Without it, we will resist His guidance on what to do—even if we hear it very clearly—because it doesn't seem to solve the problem as we perceive it. The process goes something like this:

- We decide what a situation means.
- This defines what is wrong with the situation—the perceived *problem*.
- This defines what *question* should be asked to get an answer that will solve the problem.

- This defines the range of *answers* we will accept as valid solutions to the problem.

For example, let's say you're getting married. An old friend has heard about this and writes to offer congratulations. You ended your friendship with this guy years ago because your former girlfriend left you for him, and you hold him responsible. You're still angry after all these years. The situation as you see it is that this snake is trying to slither his way into your life again (maybe to steal your bride-to-be), and the problem is how to keep him out. This defines the question you might ask and the range of answers you're willing to accept: "What should I do to get rid of this jerk? Should I write back and tell him to go to hell, or should I just give him the silent treatment and hope he gets the hint?"

What will happen now if the Holy Spirit gives you this answer: "Forgive your old friend and invite him to the wedding"? You'll probably say, "You talkin' to *me*? I don't think You quite understand the situation here." You'll be angry at Him for this crazy answer and afraid to ask Him for any advice in the future. This nutty Holy Spirit just doesn't give you what you want.

> 4. (2) Throughout the day, at any time you think of it and have a quiet moment for reflection, tell yourself again the kind of day you want; the feelings you would have, the things you want to happen to you [Ur: the things you *want* to happen], and the things you <u>would</u> experience, and say:
>
> *If I make no decisions by myself, this is the day that will be <u>given</u> me.*
>
> These two procedures, practiced well, will serve to let you be directed <u>without</u> fear, for opposition will not <u>first</u> arise and <u>then</u> become a problem in itself.

After getting ourselves into the right mindset in the morning, our next step is to maintain it throughout the day. This is very much like frequent reminders in the Workbook, where we take a moment whenever we can and reflect on the theme for the day. Here, we recollect that happy day we want to have (if you wrote it on a card, you may want to look at that card again). Then, we remind ourselves (using the words we are given here) that making no decisions by ourselves is the *means* to that happy day.

This will help us to avoid that whole scenario from the last paragraph, in which we resist the Holy Spirit's answer because it doesn't seem like a valid solution to our perceived problem.

> 5. But there will still be times when you have judged <u>already</u>. Now the answer will provoke attack [your attack on the Holy Spirit], unless you quickly straighten out your mind to <u>want</u> an answer that will work. Be certain this has happened if you feel yourself unwilling to sit by and ask to have the answer <u>given</u> you. This means you <u>have</u> decided by yourself, <u>and can not see the [real] question</u>. Now you need a quick restorative <u>before</u> you ask again.

Ideally, we would use those two steps and just sail through our day making decisions with the Holy Spirit. But given our investment in the ego, we will inevitably run into situations that throw us for a loop— situations in which we've already determined for ourselves the problem, the question, and a range of acceptable answers. I find that this happens most often with difficult situations and those in which I have a lot of emotional investment. We know we've fallen into this trap when we refuse the Holy Spirit's help, either overtly defying Him or covertly "forgetting" to ask. We've now made a decision by ourselves, and we need a "quick restorative" to get our minds back on track.

> 6. (3) Remember once again the day you want, and recognize that something has occurred that is not part of it. Then realize that you have asked a question by yourself, and <u>must</u> have set an answer in your terms. Then say:
>
> *I <u>have</u> no question. I forgot what to decide.*
>
> This cancels out the terms that you have set, and lets the <u>answer</u> show you what the question <u>must</u> have really been.

Here's the "quick restorative":

1. We remember the happy day we want (if you put it on a card, this would be a great time to use that card).
2. We acknowledge that because of this situation, our day is no longer that happy day.

3. We acknowledge that the reason is that we've thrown away the means to that happy day: We've decided by ourselves what the real question is, and thus have set by ourselves a range of acceptable answers.

4. We say the words we are given here, which mean: *"I don't know what really needs solving about this situation. I forgot that I was deciding only with the Holy Spirit today."*

This gets us back to making no decisions by ourselves—once again, we are asking the Holy Spirit both how to perceive the situation and what to do. Now we can hear His answer with an open mind, and thus recognize the question *He's* answering instead of the question as *we* defined it. In the wedding example, you realize that the real question was not "What should I do to get rid of this jerk?" but rather some version of "How can I have a truly happy day?"

> 7. Try to observe this rule without delay, <u>despite</u> your opposition. For you have <u>already</u> gotten angry. And your fear of being answered in a different way from what <u>your</u> version of the question asks will gain momentum, until you believe the day you want is one in which you get *your* answer to *your* question. And you will not get it, for it would destroy the day by robbing you of what you <u>really</u> want. This can be very hard to realize, when once you have decided by yourself the rules that <u>promise</u> you a happy day. Yet this decision [Ur: these decisions] still can be undone, by simple methods that you <u>can</u> accept.

I have found that it is indeed critical to "observe this rule without delay." Once I start down the road of deciding things for myself, it's like the proverbial snowball rolling down the hill—it becomes more and more difficult to stop. I look up at the clock and realize that it's been hours since I asked the Holy Spirit anything. I've been cruising through my day on autopilot, which really means having the ego as my pilot. And I find that the happy day I wanted has gone up in smoke, as I've followed my own agenda instead of His.

The good news, though, is that the snowball *can* be stopped. That is the focus of the rest of the section. In the paragraphs that follow, it describes what can be called a "longer restorative," a way of getting ourselves back on track when the quick restorative doesn't do the trick.

In essence, this longer restorative is a process of reasoning in which we gently but firmly lead our minds back to *wanting* to make decisions with the Holy Spirit.

> 8. (4) If you are so unwilling to receive you cannot even let your <u>question</u> go, you can begin to change your mind with this:
>
> *At least I can decide I do not <u>like</u> what I feel now.*
>
> This much is obvious, and paves the way for the next easy step [Ur: which follows this].

Remember: When we evaluate a situation without the Holy Spirit's guidance, we will come up with our own version of the problem we're facing, which in turn determines the question we'll ask Him. We've decided that instead of getting the Holy Spirit's answer to the question as He perceives it, our happiness will come from getting *our* answer to *our* question.

Yet does this really make us happy? Hardly. We're afraid of asking the Holy Spirit for help. We're angry at Him for not giving us the answer we want. We're probably feeling guilty that our lofty goal of following the Holy Spirit's guidance in everything has seemingly gone down the tubes. And our perception of the situation is likely a depressing one. Think of the example I used earlier, in which an old friend you think betrayed you offers wedding congratulations. Is *any* answer to the question "What should I do to get rid of this jerk?" a truly happy one?

The first step of the longer restorative is simply getting in touch with these feelings.

> 9. (5) Having decided that you do not like the way you feel, what could be easier than to continue with:
>
> *And so I <u>hope</u> I have been wrong.*
>
> This works <u>against</u> the sense of opposition, and reminds you that help is not being thrust upon you but is something that you want and that you need, <u>because</u> you do not like the way you feel. This tiny opening will be enough to let you go ahead with just a few more steps you need to <u>let</u> yourself be helped.

10. Now you have reached the turning point, because it has occurred to you that <u>you</u> will gain if what you have decided is <u>not</u> so. Until this point is reached, you will believe your happiness <u>depends</u> on being right. But this much reason have you now attained; <u>you</u> would be better off if you were <u>wrong</u>.

"Wrong" is such a taboo word in alternative spiritual circles. Yet here, Jesus not only speaks of being wrong, but invites us to say that we *hope* we've been wrong—wrong about our interpretation of the situation, which has led us to our wrong-headed decision to jettison the Holy Spirit's guidance. Why should we hope we're wrong? Because our view of the situation has generated all those feelings we don't like: the fear, the anger, the guilt, the depression. If we're right, then we're stuck with those feelings. But if we're wrong, we still have a shot at happiness. Perhaps another view of our situation can deliver that happiness. Perhaps getting a little help with our decisions isn't such a bad idea.

11. (6) This tiny grain of wisdom will suffice to take you further. You are <u>not</u> coerced, but merely hope to get [Ur: have] a thing you <u>want</u>. And you can say in perfect honesty:

I <u>want</u> another way to look at this.

Now you have changed your mind about the day, and have <u>remembered</u> what you really want. Its <u>purpose</u> has no longer been obscured by the insane belief you want it for the goal of being <u>right</u> when you are <u>wrong</u>. Thus is the <u>readiness</u> for asking brought to your awareness, for you <u>cannot</u> be in conflict when you ask for what you want, and <u>see</u> that it is this for which you ask.

Once we realize that the way we've been looking at the situation has caused us nothing but pain, we can honestly say that we want a *another* way of seeing it. Our pig-headed insistence that we can do it ourselves has gotten us nowhere. We're now ready to give the Holy Spirit another shot at our problem situation.

12. (7) This final step is but acknowledgment of <u>lack</u> of opposition to be helped. It is a statement of an open mind, not certain yet, but willing to be shown:

I. Rules for Decision

Perhaps there <u>is</u> another way to look at this.
What can I <u>lose</u> by asking?

> Thus you now can ask [Ur: Thus are you made ready for] a question that makes sense, and so the <u>answer</u> will make sense as well. Nor will you fight <u>against</u> it, for you see that it is <u>you</u> who will be helped by it.

Finally, we affirm our new willingness to receive the Holy Spirit's help. We're not sure yet that His answer will really bring us happiness, but we *are* sure that our own answer has *not*. So, what the heck? Why not try on a new pair of glasses—what can it hurt? Perhaps the Holy Spirit really does have a better view of this situation. Since our own way has failed so miserably, what have we got to lose by asking Him for advice about this situation?

Think once again about that wedding example. You thought the question was how to get rid of this backstabbing former friend trying to worm his way back into your life. The whole idea of forgiving him and inviting him to the wedding was simply ludicrous. But now you see that your view of the situation has brought you nothing but pain. Thus you really do want a way to look at it that will relieve the pain. As you offer your now open mind to the Holy Spirit, He gently reminds you of the only thing that will really make you happy here: forgiveness, the means of salvation. Now the Holy Spirit's answer makes perfect sense. Imagine how happy you'll feel if you achieve a true reconciliation with your old friend.

Once we've reached this point, the longer restorative has done its work. We've successfully returned to our original goal of having a happy day by making no decisions by ourselves.

> 13. It <u>must</u> be clear that it is easier to have a happy day if you <u>prevent</u> unhappiness from entering at all. But this takes practice in the rules that will <u>protect</u> you from the ravages of fear. When <u>this</u> has been achieved, the sorry dream of judgment has <u>forever</u> been undone. But meanwhile, you have need for practicing the rules for its undoing. Let us, then, consider once again the very first of the decisions which are offered here.

We may resist following these rules, especially given the aversion to rules so common in alternative spirituality. We may be tempted to say, "I'll just turn everything over to the Holy Spirit; I don't need to follow restrictive *rules*. I'll just be spontaneous." But the simple fact is, our minds are not that disciplined yet. As the very first paragraph of the section said, we're making countless decisions without even knowing it. Therefore, we *need* these rules. We *need* to practice them. Only through this kind of disciplined mind training can we bring ourselves to the point where "the sorry dream of judgment has *forever* been undone."

> 14. We said you can begin a happy day with the determination <u>not</u> to make decisions by yourself. This <u>seems</u> to be a real decision [Ur: free decision] in itself. And yet, you *cannot* make decisions by yourself. The only question really is <u>with what</u> you choose to make them. That is really all. The first rule, then, is not coercion, but a simple statement of a simple fact. You <u>will</u> not make decisions by yourself whatever you decide. For they are made with idols or with God. And you ask help of anti-Christ or Christ, and which you choose <u>will</u> join with you and tell you what to do.
>
> 15. Your day is <u>not</u> at random. It is set by what you choose to live it <u>with,</u> and <u>how</u> the friend whose counsel you have sought perceives your happiness. You <u>always</u> ask advice before you can decide on <u>anything</u>. Let <u>this</u> be understood, and you can see there cannot <u>be</u> coercion here, nor grounds for opposition that you may be free. There <u>is</u> no freedom from what must occur. And if you think there is, you <u>must</u> be wrong.

Again, we may resist following these rules. We may say to Jesus, "Hey, don't fence me in. I would much rather make decisions by myself than be chained to an advisor." But now Jesus throws in a twist as he revisits the first rule: Not only *should* we make no decisions by ourselves, but it is actually *impossible* to do anything else. We always consult an advisor, be it the ego or the Holy Spirit. Every time we make a decision, we listen to either the insane rantings of our idols or the gentle counsel of the Voice for God. Therefore, we aren't being forced to follow the first rule; we're just asked to make better use of a rule we cannot help but follow anyway. Since we always consult an advisor no matter what, why not consult the One who will actually give us a happy day?

> 16. The second rule as well is but a fact. For you and your adviser must <u>agree</u> on what you want <u>before</u> it can occur. It is but this <u>agreement</u> that permits all things to happen. <u>Nothing</u> can be caused without some form

of union, be it with a dream of judgment or the Voice for God. Decisions cause results *because* they are not made in isolation. They are made by you and your adviser, for yourself <u>and for the world as well</u>. The day you want you offer to the world, for it <u>will</u> be what you have asked for, and will reinforce the rule of your adviser in [Ur: through] the world. Whose kingdom is the world for you today? What kind of day will you decide to have?

To paraphrase the second rule: If we make no decisions by ourselves, we will get the day we choose. Now we are told that precisely because we *never* make decisions by ourselves, we cannot help but get the day we choose. Why? Because agreement is what gives decisions power to actually happen, and we always make an agreement with whatever advisor we have chosen as our guide. What's more, the day we choose to have is not for ourselves alone; we offer it to the entire world, for it "will reinforce the rule of your adviser in through the world."

Application: In the morning, before you begin your day, ask yourself:

Whose kingdom is the world for me today? The ego's or the Holy Spirit's?
Will I join today with a dream of judgment or the Voice for God?
What kind of day do I want to have today?

17. It needs but two who would have happiness this day to promise it to all the world. It needs but two to understand that they cannot decide alone, to <u>guarantee</u> the joy they asked for will be wholly shared. For they have understood the basic law that <u>makes</u> decision powerful, and gives it all effects that it will <u>ever</u> have. It needs but two. These two <u>are</u> joined before there <u>can</u> be a decision. Let this be the <u>one</u> reminder that you keep in mind, and you will have the day you want, and give it to the world by having it yourself [Ur: yourselves]. Your judgment has been <u>lifted</u> from the world by your decision for a happy day. And as you have received, so <u>must</u> you give.

We've just been told that agreement is what gives decisions the power to actually happen, and that all decisions are made for the entire world. Therefore, it must be that when two people agree to have a particular kind of day, they will have that day and offer it to the world. Remember, this material was originally dictated to two people, Helen and Bill. So, as the section closes, Jesus reminds Helen and Bill—and all of us—that joining together and following these rules for decision will *guarantee* not only a happy day devoted to the goal of salvation, but that this blessed day will be shared with all the world.

I think this is an amazing section, and as I said at the beginning, I encourage you to actually give these rules for decision a try. I've been using them the past few days, and it has been a truly wonderful experience.

What strikes me most about these rules is that they illustrate an attitude that Jesus wants us to cultivate toward all of our Course practice: an attitude that he later calls "gentle firmness" (W-pI.73.10:1). The rules are firm in that they give us no wiggle room: We are to apply them in a rigorous, disciplined way, and no matter how far we get off track, we are given practices that we are expected to use to get us back *on* track. Yet they are also gentle in that they never force us to do anything: We are told again and again that the reason we should follow them is simply because they give us the happy day we really want. The longer restorative in particular is simply a process in which we gently convince ourselves that listening to the Holy Spirit is truly in our best interests.

This combination of gentleness and firmness keeps us from either 1) forcing ourselves to follow the Holy Spirit out of a sense of "sacrifice" or 2) giving up at the first sign of resistance. Either of these options will result in us not listening to the Holy Spirit, either because we're tired of the constant sacrifice or because we just don't put in the necessary effort. But these rules for decision enable us to gently but firmly place ourselves in His hands, so we can find the happiness we seek.

II. Freedom of Will
Commentary by Greg Mackie

1. Do you not understand that to oppose the Holy Spirit *is* to fight *yourself?* [Ur: *is* to fight yourself?] He tells you but <u>your</u> will; He speaks for <u>you</u>. In <u>His</u> Divinity is but your own. And all He knows is but <u>your</u> knowledge, saved for <u>you</u> that you may do <u>your</u> will through Him. God *asks* you do your will. He joins with *you*. He did not set His Kingdom up alone. And Heaven itself but represents your will, where everything created is for you. No spark of life but was created with your glad consent, as you would have it be. And not one Thought that God has ever had but waited for your blessing to be born. God is no enemy to you. He asks no more than that He hear you call Him "Friend."

The previous section instructed us not to fight ourselves (T-30.I.1:7), and emphasized that making decisions with the Holy Spirit is something we really want. Now Jesus brings these two ideas together in a striking way: To fight the Holy Spirit *is* to fight ourselves because He speaks for our true will, what we really want.

The power and extent of our will are truly amazing. Remember when we were told that our own creation happened only with our own consent (T-28.VI.6)? Now we are told that *everything* God created was with our consent; every Thought God ever had came into being with our blessing. Therefore, making decisions with the Holy Spirit is not turning our lives over to some alien will that is enemy to our wants and needs. It is joyously joining with the Friend Whose Will is our own.

2. How wonderful it is to do your will! For that *is* freedom. There is nothing else that ever should be called by freedom's name. <u>Unless</u> you do your will you are <u>not</u> free. And would God leave His Son <u>without</u> what he has chosen for himself? God but ensured that you would never <u>lose</u> your will when He gave you His perfect Answer. Hear It now, that you may be reminded of His Love and learn <u>your</u> will. God would not have His Son made prisoner to what he does not want. He <u>joins</u> with you in willing you be free. And to <u>oppose</u> Him is to make a choice against <u>yourself</u>, and choose that <u>you</u> be bound.

199

A generic definition of "freedom" is the ability to do your will without anything getting in the way. Everyone would probably agree with this definition. Yet in this world, we don't understand what true freedom really is. We think freedom is the freedom of our *body* to do the will of our *ego* without anything getting in the way. Yet in the Course's view, this is really imprisonment, for the ego is not our true will; it is an alien will. It's as if we were a victim of identity theft, and we then decided that freedom meant doing the will of the guy who stole our credit cards and is now going by our name.

Real freedom is the freedom of the *mind* to do our *true* will, the will we share with God. "There is nothing else that ever should be called by freedom's name." God created the Holy Spirit to remind us of this, to speak for our true will in a world where we have foolishly chained ourselves to an identity thief. That is why we should make all of our decisions with Him: "that you may be reminded of His Love and learn *your* will."

> 3. Look once again upon your enemy, the one you chose to hate instead of love. For thus was hatred born into the world, and thus the rule of fear established there [Ur: here]. Now hear God speak to you, through Him Who is His Voice and <u>yours</u> as well, reminding you that it is <u>not</u> your will to hate and be a prisoner to fear, a slave to death, a <u>little</u> creature with a <u>little</u> life. Your will is boundless; it is <u>not</u> your will that it be bound. What lies in you has joined with God Himself in all creation's birth. Remember Him Who has created you, and through <u>your</u> will created everything. Not one created thing but gives you thanks, for it is by your will that it was born. No light of Heaven shines except for you, for it was set in Heaven by your will.

Our imprisonment to an alien will began when we chose to hate instead of love—a decision that was completely alien to the loving will we share with God. This decision established the entire world we see, in which we seem to be tiny, terrified creatures trapped in the prison of a body, at the mercy of countless attackers and doomed to die. But it is not truly our will to hate and to suffer at the hands of the world our hate has spawned. Our true will is still to love as God loves. And we remember this each time we listen to the Holy Spirit guiding us to love our brother with the Love of God.

Application: Bring to mind someone whom you dislike or hold some sort of grievance against; a person you regard as an "enemy." Realize that your decision to hate this person is imprisoning you in this cruel world. Your hatred is the cause of all the suffering you experience. Now, hear God speak to you through the Holy Spirit:

> It is **not** your will to hate and be a prisoner to fear,
> a slave to death,
> a **little** creature with a **little** life.
> Your will is boundless;
> it is **not** your will that it be bound.
> Your will, joined with Mine, created everything in love.
> Therefore, your will is only to love this brother
> with the boundless love you share with Me.

Let this love extend from you to this person. See this person beam with gratitude, both for the healing love you have just given, and for the fact that by your will was he born.

4. What cause have you for anger in a world that merely waits your blessing to be free? If you be prisoner, then God Himself could not be free. For what is done to him whom God so loves is done to God Himself. Think not He wills to bind you, Who has made you co-creator of the universe along with Him. He would but keep your will forever and forever limitless. This [Ur: The] world awaits the freedom you will give when you have recognized that you are free. But you will not forgive the world until you have forgiven Him Who gave your will to you. For it is by your will the world is given freedom. Nor can you be free apart from Him Whose holy Will you share.

Deep down (sometimes not so deep down), we're angry at the world for imprisoning us. We're also angry at God for apparently putting us into this hellhole, and for giving us guidance that seems to make us sacrifice what we really want. But God doesn't imprison us; in fact, we *can't* be imprisoned. We are so beloved of our Father, so indissolubly joined with Him, that imprisoning us would be imprisoning Him. Is it really possible to imprison *God*? (The second sentence here reminds me of Workbook Lesson 278, "If I am bound, my Father is not free.") Only our own decision to hate *seems* to imprison us, but if it is *our* decision we can't truly be imprisoned by it.

In response to our apparent imprisonment, God has given everyone a "get out of jail free" card. How do we redeem it? We forgive God for all the things He didn't do to us. This reveals our true will to us, the will we share with Him, which sets us free. This then enables us to set the entire world free.

> 5. God turns to <u>you</u> to ask the world be saved, for by your <u>own</u> salvation is it healed. And no one walks upon the earth but must depend on <u>your</u> decision, that he learn death <u>has</u> no power over him, because he shares <u>your</u> freedom as he shares your will. It *is* your will to heal him, and because you have decided <u>with</u> him, he is healed. And now is God forgiven, for you chose to look upon your brother as a friend.

This final paragraph continues the discussion of the "get out of jail free" process, adding an element that seems confusing. The previous paragraph said that forgiving God leads to setting the world free. But this paragraph seems to suggest that setting the world free leads to forgiving God. Which is it?

I'm not sure of the answer. Perhaps it is a cycle, in which you start with forgiving God, which then leads to you freeing the world through forgiving it, which then leads to you forgiving God more deeply, etc. But I'm also wondering if the step of choosing "to look upon your brother as a friend" might be distinct from the step of freeing the entire world. Paragraph 3 asked us to start the process it described with a version of looking upon your brother as a friend. Perhaps, then, the order is something like this:

1. We set an individual brother free by loving instead of hating him, by seeing him as a friend, by forgiving him.
2. This enables us to forgive God.
3. This reveals our true will to us, the will we share with God, which sets us free.
4. This enables us to set the entire world free.

However it works, the bottom line is that we are free, and have the power to set everyone free by showing them that the entire Sonship shares the infinitely free will of God. God turns to us and asks us if we would claim our freedom and save the world from the bitter illusion of imprisonment. What is our answer?

III. Beyond All Idols
Commentary by Greg Mackie

1. Idols are quite specific. But your will is universal, being limitless. And so it has <u>no</u> form, nor is content for its expression in the terms of form. Idols are <u>limits</u>. They are the belief that there are <u>forms</u> that will bring happiness, and that, <u>by</u> limiting, is all attained. It is as if you said, "I have no need of everything. This <u>little</u> thing I want, and it will <u>be</u> as everything to me." And this <u>must</u> fail to satisfy, because it <u>is</u> your will that everything be yours. Decide for idols and you ask for <u>loss</u>. Decide for truth and everything <u>is</u> yours.

Our true will is universal, limitless, formless, and cannot be content with anything less than the eternal inheritance given to us by God, which is *everything*. But we have thrown all of this away for our false gods, our idols. We now believe that "there are *forms* that will bring happiness."

I'll bet a few forms you like have probably popped into your mind already. We've become an extra-twisted version of Steve Martin in *The Jerk*, saying, "I don't need everything. All I need is this ashtray…and this paddle game…and this remote control…and these matches…" Our idols are not limited to physical things, of course. Our self-image is an idol. So are all those things from that list we saw in T-29.VIII: "a body or a thing, a place, a situation or a circumstance, an object owned or wanted, or a right demanded or achieved" (T-29.VIII.1:9). But whatever form we seek, it is by definition less than the everything that is really ours. To seek for idols is therefore to seek for loss.

2. <u>It is not form you seek</u>. What form can be a substitute for God the Father's Love? What form can take the place of all the love in the Divinity of God the Son? What idol can make two of what <u>is</u> one? And <u>can</u> the limitless be limited? You do not <u>want</u> an idol. It is <u>not</u> your will to have one. It will <u>not</u> bestow on you the gift you seek. When you decide upon the <u>form</u> of what you want, you <u>lose</u> the understanding of its purpose. So you see <u>your</u> will within the idol, thus reducing it to a <u>specific</u> form. Yet this could never <u>be</u> your will, because what shares in all creation <u>cannot</u> be content with <u>small</u> ideas and <u>little</u> things.

204

III. Beyond All Idols

When we seek idols—which we do any time we think some particular form will make us happy—it's as if we're taking our limitless will and cramming it into a thimble. It's like some strange fetish, where instead of loving a whole person, we become infatuated with her big toe. But as much as we seek idols, deep down we don't really want them, because no form could actually satisfy us. Again, we can be satisfied with nothing less than our limitless inheritance as divine Sons of our loving Father.

> 3. Behind the search for <u>every</u> idol lies the yearning for completion. Wholeness has no form <u>because</u> it is unlimited. To seek a special person or a thing to <u>add</u> to you to make yourself complete, can <u>only</u> mean that you believe some <u>form</u> is missing. And by finding <u>this</u>, you will achieve completion in a <u>form</u> you like. This is the purpose of an idol; that you will not look <u>beyond</u> it, to the source of the belief that you <u>are</u> incomplete. <u>Only</u> if you had sinned could this be so. For sin is the <u>idea</u> you are alone and separated <u>off</u> from what is whole. And thus it <u>would</u> be necessary for the search for wholeness to be made beyond the boundaries of limits on yourself.

What we really want is not idols, but what we think they will bring: *completion*. We think that we are incomplete and lacking, so we need to acquire something outside ourselves to fill all the holes we see in us. Think about it: Isn't every form you seek in the world intended to fill some sort of emptiness in you? We acquire food to fill our empty bellies, special people to fill the gaping hole of loneliness, special things to bolster our deflated self-esteem, etc. We think if we can just acquire the right forms, we'll achieve completion.

But we're not truly incomplete. The only reason we think we are is our hidden belief that we are *sinners*, thrown out of the limitless paradise we once shared with God and now forced to scrape by on our own in this bitter, painfully limited world "east of Eden." The purpose of idols, we are told here, is to keep this belief hidden. If we saw that our sense of incompletion stems from our belief that we are sinners, we might wise up and change our minds. But as long as we're chasing idols, we'll continue to believe that lack is just part of our nature, and completion can come only from acquiring the right collection of forms.

> 4. It <u>never</u> is the idol that you want. But what you think it <u>offers</u> you [completion], you want indeed and have the <u>right</u> to ask for. Nor could

it be <u>possible</u> it be denied. Your will to be complete <u>is</u> but God's Will, and this is given you <u>by</u> being His. God knows not form. He <u>cannot</u> answer you in terms that have no meaning. And <u>your</u> will could not <u>be</u> satisfied with empty forms, made but to fill a gap that is not there. It is not this you <u>want</u>. Creation gives no <u>separate</u> person and no <u>separate</u> thing the power to complete the Son of God. What idol <u>can</u> be called upon to give the Son of God what he already <u>has</u>?

We think we want idols because we think they will bring us completion. As we've just seen, the real reason we want idols is to mask our underlying belief that we are sinners who don't *deserve* to ask for completion. But underneath this is the changeless truth that we are not sinners, and therefore have every right to ask God for completion.

This request cannot be denied because we and God share the will to be complete, and therefore, we are already complete. There is no need, then, to seek desperately for completion in forms that could never satisfy us. All we need do is ask God for the completion that is ours already.

Application: Bring to mind some form that you think will bring you happiness. Now, say the following:

> *I do not really want this idol.*
> *I want the completion I think it offers me, and I have the right to ask God for completion.*

> *God, I ask for my completion now.*
> *I know this request cannot be denied, for my completion is Your will and mine, and therefore I am already complete.*

5. Completion is the *function* of God's Son. He has no need to <u>seek</u> for it at all. Beyond <u>all</u> idols stands his holy will to be but what he <u>is</u>. For <u>more</u> than whole is meaningless. If there were change in him, if he could be reduced to <u>any</u> form and limited to what is <u>not</u> in him, he would not <u>be</u> as God created him. What idol <u>can</u> he need to be himself? For can he give a part of him away? What is not whole [idols] cannot <u>make</u> whole. But what is <u>really</u> asked for [wholeness, completion] <u>cannot</u> be denied. Your will *is* granted. <u>Not</u> in any form that would content you not, but in the whole completely lovely Thought God holds of you.

III. Beyond All Idols

Our function is to complete God, and we do this simply by being what we are as God created us. Beyond our foolish quest for completion through securing the right forms is the eternal completion that is our birthright as God's Sons. The quest for idols is rooted in the belief that we have somehow changed ourselves from limitless creations beloved of God to tiny lumps of flesh with gaping holes that need to be filled up from outside. But we cannot change ourselves; we remain as God created us.

We can choose to stop seeking idols and instead ask for the completion that is already ours. At one point, the Workbook asks us: "Would you refuse to take the function of completing God, when all He wills is that you be complete?" (W-pII.7.5:4). If we *don't* refuse—if we ask for our true completion, for our true will—our request will answered not with yet another unsatisfying form, but with "the whole completely lovely Thought God holds of you.

> 6. Nothing that God knows not exists. And what He knows exists forever, changelessly. For thoughts endure as long as does the mind that thought of them. And in the Mind of God there is no ending, nor a time in which His Thoughts were absent or could suffer change. Thoughts are not born and cannot die. They share the attributes of their creator, nor have they a separate life apart from his. The thoughts you think are in your mind, as you are in the Mind Which thought of you. And so there are no separate parts in what exists within God's Mind. It is forever one, eternally united and at peace.

The rest of this section speaks of the true source of our completion: "the whole completely lovely Thought God holds of you." We begin with a few basic principles about thoughts: 1) they endure as long as the mind that thought of them, 2) they share the attributes of the mind that thought of them, and 3) they are not separate from the mind that thought of them. These principles are true both of the thoughts in our own minds and the Thoughts in the Mind of God.

Since we are Thoughts in the Mind of God, this must mean that, whatever we think we have become, the truth is that 1) we are eternal, since the Mind that thought of us is eternal, 2) we share all of God's attributes, and 3) we have no separate life apart from God.

> 7. Thoughts <u>seem</u> to come and go. Yet all this means is that you are sometimes <u>aware</u> of them, and sometimes not. An unremembered thought is born again to <u>you</u> when it returns to your awareness. Yet it did not die when you forgot it. It was <u>always</u> there, but <u>you</u> were unaware of it. The Thought God holds of you is perfectly unchanged by your forgetting. It will <u>always</u> be exactly as it was before the time when you forgot, and will be just the same when you remember. And it is the same <u>within</u> the interval when you forgot.

We've forgotten the Thought God holds of us so completely that it's as if it never existed. But we've all had the experience of remembering something that was long forgotten. When this happens, we realize that what we had forgotten didn't just pop into existence when we remembered it; it must have been there, buried in our minds, all along. So it is with the Thought God holds of us. When we forgot it and accepted the ridiculous notion that we had somehow turned ourselves into needy sinners, the Thought of God in which our completion lies remained in our minds, as it remained in God's Mind. It can be remembered right now, and when we remember it, we will realize that it has always been there.

> 8. The Thoughts of God are <u>far</u> beyond all change, and shine forever. They await not birth. They wait for welcome and remembering. The Thought God holds of you is like a star, unchangeable in an eternal sky. So high in Heaven is it set that those outside of Heaven know not it is there. Yet still and white and lovely will it shine through all eternity. There was no time it was not there; no instant when its light grew dimmer or less perfect ever was.

Now Jesus begins an extended metaphor to describe the Thought God holds of us: the metaphor of a star. This metaphor draws its power from the fact that from time immemorial, human beings have regarded stars as symbols of the eternal, changeless, and heavenly. For this metaphor to have its full impact, we have to realize that the Thought of God is who we really are. This metaphor describes *us*.

What we are like, Jesus says, is an eternal star in an eternal sky. This star is so far away from earth that it can't even be seen from earth. Yet it is still there. It has always been there, and "no instant when its light grew dimmer or less perfect ever was." This sheer, unchanging, radiant perfection is our reality *right now*, even though we can't see it, even as we lament our many lacks and imperfections, even as we muddle through this world in which it seems that we will never be complete.

> 9. Who knows the Father knows this light, for He is the eternal sky that holds it safe, forever lifted up and anchored sure. Its perfect purity does not depend on whether it is seen on earth or not. The sky embraces it and softly holds it in its perfect place, which is as far from earth as earth from Heaven. It is not the distance nor the time that keeps this star invisible to earth. But those who seek for idols <u>cannot</u> know the [Ur: this] star is there.

The eternal sky in this metaphor is God Himself. Think of that! We are perfect, radiant stars shining in the sky of God's everlasting Love. Again, this is true even though we can't see it. Far beyond this crazy world that seems to be our reality, our true reality continues to shine in changeless, timeless, perfect peace. Yet now Jesus gives us a twist: It is not actually distance or time that keeps us from seeing our radiant reality. Instead, it is our futile search for idols. We're so busy scavenging on the ground for scraps to get us through another day that we never bother to look up and see the light that would satisfy every need forever.

> 10. Beyond all idols is the Thought God holds of you. Completely unaffected by the turmoil and the terror of the world, the dreams of birth and death that here are dreamed, the myriad of forms that fear can take; quite undisturbed, the Thought God holds of you remains <u>exactly</u> as it always was. Surrounded by a stillness so complete no sound of battle comes remotely near, it rests in certainty and perfect peace. Here is your <u>one</u> reality kept safe, completely unaware of all the world that worships idols, and that knows not God. In perfect sureness of its changelessness and of its rest in its eternal home, the Thought God holds of you has never left the Mind of its Creator, Whom it knows as its Creator knows that it is there.

Think of the vast sweep of human history: all the people who have come and gone, all the empires rising and falling, the wars, the turmoil, the terror. Through it all, the stars have shined upon the earth like silent sentinels, the fixed firmament circling through the days, weeks, months, years, centuries, and millennia, unaffected by all the drama unfolding below.

Like the stars, the Thought God holds of us stands forever beyond the battleground, unaffected by the drama of life on earth. As we frantically search for idols to keep us going in this crazy world, our reality shines on in the vast expanse of the eternal sky of God, resting in perfect peace, secure in the everlasting certainty of our eternal home.

> 11. Where could the Thought God holds of you <u>exist</u> but where you are? Is your reality a thing <u>apart</u> from you, and in a world which your reality knows <u>nothing</u> of? Outside you there <u>is</u> no eternal sky, no changeless star and <u>no</u> reality. The mind of Heaven's Son in Heaven is, for there the Mind of Father and of Son joined in creation which can <u>have</u> no end. You have not two realities, but one. Nor can you be <u>aware</u> of more than one. An idol *or* the Thought God holds of you is your reality. Forget not, then, that idols <u>must</u> keep hidden what you are, <u>not</u> from the Mind of God, but from your own. The star shines still; the sky has never changed. But you, the holy Son of God Himself, are unaware of your reality.

As we're reading this beautiful description of our reality, we may be tempted to think: "Well, that's all well and good, but it's pretty remote from where I'm living right now." We may even think that we have two realities: a lower self that lives life on earth, and a higher Self that stands above it all. This, however, is not the case. This exalted description is describing our *only* reality: "You have not two realities, but one." All that we really are is that eternal star shining in the eternal sky of God, *right now*.

As long as we keep up our idol collecting, we will remain unaware of the star we are. But when we decide to identify with the Thought of God that is our true Identity, we will recognize the glorious truth that "the star shines still; the sky has never changed." We will remember the Heaven we never left.

Application: The description of "the Thought God holds of you" in these closing paragraphs is so beautiful that we should really take it to heart. Below, I've laid out some lines from these paragraphs in iambic pentameter and put them in first person (with a few minor modifications). Read them slowly and let them sink in. These lines are describing *you*. This is who *you* really are.

III. Beyond All Idols

The Thought God holds of me is like a star, unchangeable in an eternal sky.
So high in Heaven is it set that those outside of Heaven know not it is there.
Yet still and white and lovely will it shine through all eternity.
There was no time it was not there; no instant when its light grew dimmer or less perfect ever was.

Who knows the Father knows this light, for He is the eternal sky that holds it safe, forever lifted up and anchored sure.
Its perfect purity does not depend on whether it is seen on earth or not.
The sky embraces it and softly holds it in its perfect place, which is as far from earth as earth is far from Heaven's gate.

Beyond all idols is the Thought God holds of me.
Completely unaffected by the turmoil and the terror of the world, the dreams of birth and death that here are dreamed, the myriad of forms that fear can take; quite undisturbed, the Thought God holds of me remains exactly as it always was.
Surrounded by a stillness so complete no sound of battle comes remotely near, it rests in certainty and perfect peace.
Here is my one reality kept safe, completely unaware of all the world that worships idols, and that knows not God.
In perfect sureness of its changelessness and of its rest in its eternal home, the Thought God holds of me has never left the Mind of its Creator, Whom it knows as its Creator knows that it is there.

My search for idols has not dimmed my light.
The star shines still; the sky has never changed.
For I am still as God created me.

IV. The Truth behind Illusions
Commentary by Greg Mackie

1. You <u>will</u> attack what does not satisfy, and thus you will not see you made it up. You <u>always</u> fight illusions. For the truth behind them is so lovely and so still in loving gentleness, were you <u>aware</u> of it you would forget defensiveness entirely, and rush to its embrace. The truth could never <u>be</u> attacked. And this you knew when you made idols. They were made that this might be forgotten. You attack but <u>false</u> ideas, and <u>never</u> truthful ones. All idols <u>are</u> the false ideas you made to fill the gap you think arose between yourself and what is true. And you attack them for the things you think they <u>represent</u>. What lies <u>beyond</u> them cannot <u>be</u> attacked.

The last section told us that idols are inherently unsatisfying, because they are limits; the only thing that could possibly satisfy us is the truth of who we really are, which gives us everything. Now we are told that "this you knew when you made idols." We knew that truth is so completely satisfying that we would "rush to its embrace" if we saw it as it is. We knew that truth can't even *be* attacked. But we also wanted to attack the truth and stay separate.

To solve this dilemma, we made unsatisfying idols and placed them in the gap between us and the truth. Now these unsatisfying idols seem to *be* the truth, which both gives us a good reason to attack "truth" and— precisely *because* we attack—keeps us from seeing that we made these idols up, which reinforces their "truth" even more. Real truth is now nowhere to be found, which is exactly the point.

2. The wearying, dissatisfying gods you made are blown-up children's toys. A child <u>is</u> frightened when a wooden head springs up as a closed box is opened suddenly, or when a soft and silent woolly bear begins to squeak as he takes hold of it. The rules he made for boxes and for bears have failed him, and have broken his "control" of what surrounds him. And he is afraid, because he thought the rules <u>protected</u> him. Now must he learn the boxes and the bears did <u>not</u> deceive him, broke no rules, nor mean his world is made chaotic and unsafe. <u>He was mistaken</u>. He misunderstood what <u>made</u> him safe, and thought that it had <u>left</u>.

212

Recall the earlier discussion of toys in T-29.IX. In that discussion, the toys—our idols—seem to protect us, but always end up betraying us. It is the same here. The child has made "rules" for her toys that seem to enable her to control them and thus keep herself safe. She is safe (she thinks) because the rules tell her how her toys work. This enables her to anticipate what they will do, and thus stay in control.

When they do unexpected things, though—like a Jack-in-the-Box popping out or a woolly bear squeaking—her whole illusion of control is shattered, and she is afraid. She now realizes that her rules were mistaken; she doesn't really know how her toys work. But her very fear is based on two other mistakes: She is mistaken in believing that harmless toys can hurt her, and mistaken about the true source of her safety. To ease her fear, she needs to realize that these toys *can't* hurt her, precisely because the real sources of her safety—her loving parents—have made sure that nothing harmful is placed within her reach.

This metaphor, of course, is meant to describe *us*. Our idols—all those people, places, things, situations, and circumstances that we think will make us happy and safe, but always seem to be fouling up—are nothing more than "blown-up children's toys," just inflated versions of the toys that seem to betray the child.

> 3. The gap that is not there is filled with toys in countless forms. And each one seems to break the rules you set for it. It never <u>was</u> the thing you thought. It <u>must</u> appear to break your rules for safety, since the <u>rules</u> were wrong. But *you* are not endangered. You can laugh at popping heads and squeaking toys, as does the child who learns they are no threat to him. Yet [Ur: But] while he likes to play with them, he still perceives them as obeying rules he made for his enjoyment. So there still are rules that they can seem to break and frighten him. Yet *is* he at the mercy of his toys? And *can* they represent a threat to him?

Like the child who develops rules for her toys, we spend our lives learning the "rules" for how everything works. If we can just learn the traffic rules, the rules of etiquette, the rules for romantic relationships, the rules for keeping the body healthy, etc., we will be in control and thus be able to avoid harm. But what actually happens? Everyone and everything around us is constantly breaking the rules, so we live in constant terror of what horrible thing is going to pop up when we least expect it. Yet remember, this is exactly what we *want* to happen. Our idols are designed to be unsatisfying. So, they *must* break our rules, because this gives us the dissatisfaction that justifies our attacks on them.

We need to learn exactly what the child needs to learn. We need to learn that our rules are wrong—our idols behaving the way they're supposed to won't make us safe. We need to learn that our real safety comes from the simple fact that our idols are *harmless toys*, so it doesn't matter how they behave. If we can learn this, then we can laugh at our toys just as the child learns to laugh at hers—not because we still enjoy playing with them, but simply because we realize that we aren't at the mercy of them.

Application: Think of things in your life that would frighten you if they didn't go the way you want. Now, apply the following sentences to them:

> *My idols will inevitably break my rules for them.*
> *But since my rules are not the source of my safety, I am not endangered.*
> *Therefore, I can laugh at [the thing that is frightening me now].*

4. Reality observes the laws of God, and <u>not</u> the rules you set. It is His laws that <u>guarantee</u> your safety. All illusions that you believe about yourself obey <u>no</u> laws. They seem to dance a little while, according to the rules you set for them. But then they fall and cannot rise again. They are but toys, my child, so do not grieve for them. Their dancing never brought you joy. But neither were they things to frighten you, nor make you safe if they obeyed your rules. They must be neither cherished <u>nor</u> attacked, but merely looked upon as children's toys without a <u>single</u> meaning of their own. See <u>one</u> in them and you will see them all. See <u>none</u> in them and they will touch you not.

Just as the real source of the child's safety is her parents, so the real source of *our* safety is our Divine Parent. Our reality is forever safe in His embrace, kept inviolate by the changeless laws of Heaven. Our idols are nothing but lawless illusions that are absolutely meaningless. Therefore, we need to take Paul's advice and "put away childish things" (1 Corinthians 13:11). We need to look at all the idols in our lives that have danced for a while only to fall, and hear Jesus say to us: "They are but toys, my child, so do not grieve for them. Their dancing never brought you joy"—nor did they bring us safety or danger. When we recognize this, we will be free of them.

> 5. Appearances [idols] deceive *because* they are appearances and not reality. Dwell not on them in <u>any</u> form. They but <u>obscure</u> reality, and they bring fear *because* they hide the truth. Do not attack what you have made to <u>let</u> you be deceived, for thus you prove that you <u>have been</u> deceived. Attack <u>has</u> power to make illusions real. Yet what it makes is nothing. Who could be made fearful by a power that can have no <u>real</u> effects at all? What could it <u>be</u> but an illusion, making things appear like to itself? Look calmly at its toys, and understand that they are idols which but dance to vain desires. Give them not your worship, for they are not there. Yet [Ur: But] this is <u>equally</u> forgotten in attack. God's Son needs <u>no</u> defense against his dreams. His idols do not threaten him at all. His <u>one</u> mistake is that he thinks them real. What can the power of illusions <u>do</u>?

This paragraph really ties us back to the first paragraph, which said that through attacking our idols, we won't see that we made them up—we will see them as real, and thus hide true reality from our sight. Here, we are told much the same thing. When we attack our idols for not satisfying us, we have fallen for our own ruse. We have made our idols real, which is frightening precisely because it hides true reality, which is love.

Fortunately, our attack on our idols cannot truly make them real. We will learn this as we look calmly at the idols made "real" by attack and realize they are truly nothing. They need be neither worshipped for the joy we hope they'll bring nor attacked for the disappointment they inevitably *do* bring. They are mere toys, no more enjoyable or frightening than the popping head or the squeaking woolly bear.

> 6. Appearances can but deceive the mind that <u>wants</u> to be deceived. And you can make a simple choice that will forever place you far <u>beyond</u> deception. You need not concern yourself with <u>how</u> this will be done, for this you <u>cannot</u> understand. But you <u>will</u> understand that mighty changes have been quickly brought about, when you decide one very simple thing; you do not <u>want</u> whatever you believe an idol gives. For thus the Son of God declares that he is free of idols. And thus *is* he free.

What do we believe an idol gives? Think of what this section has told us. We think that idols will bring us safety and happiness. But actually, we designed them to be unsatisfying, so we could attack them, make them real, and thus push truth away. Deep down, this obliteration of truth is what we believe an idol gives. If we decide we don't want to play this crazy game anymore, the entire game is up, and we will be free of idols and see "mighty changes" in our lives.

Application: With all this in mind, bring to mind various idols in your life—the people, things, and situations that seem to bring you joy when they do what you want, and justification to attack when they don't. Say to each one in turn:

> *I do not **want** whatever I believe this idol gives.*
> *I do not want to push truth away.*

7. Salvation is a paradox indeed! What could it be <u>except</u> a happy dream? It asks you but that you forgive all things that no one ever did; to overlook what is not there, and not to look upon the unreal as reality. You are but asked to let your will be done, and seek no longer for the things you do not want. And you are asked to let yourself be free of all the dreams of what you never were, and seek no more to substitute the strength of idle wishes for the Will of God.

Throughout this section, we've seen an emphasis on the fact that everything that seems to both attract and frighten us, everything that we worship and attack, is really *nothing*. Seeing this is the essence of salvation, and it truly is paradoxical: All we're asked to do is give up things that never existed, that we never really had, and that we never even wanted in the first place. We're simply asked to forgive things that didn't happen, stop seeing things that aren't there, give up what was never real, ask only for what we really want, stop imagining that we're something we're not, and replace our painful fantasies with the loving Will of God. In short, salvation is a happy dream: a *dream* because we're releasing things that never really existed, and *happy* because we're releasing things we never really wanted.

8. Here does the dream of separation start to fade and disappear. For here the gap that is not there begins to be perceived without the toys

of terror that you made. No more than this is asked. Be glad indeed salvation asks so little, <u>not</u> so much. It asks for <u>nothing</u> in reality. And even in illusions it but asks forgiveness be the substitute for fear. Such is the <u>only</u> rule for happy dreams. The gap is emptied of the toys of fear, and then its unreality is plain. Dreams are for nothing. And the Son of God <u>can</u> have no need of them. They offer him no single thing that he could ever want. He is <u>delivered</u> from illusions by his will, and but restored to what he <u>is</u>. What could God's plan for his salvation <u>be</u>, except a means to give him to Himself?

If we realized that all salvation asks of us is that we release things that never really existed and that we never really wanted, what could we be but *glad*? This release is accomplished by forgiveness, "the *only* rule for happy dreams." (This recalls both the "rules" we set for our toys, and the rules for decision in T-30.I, which are the rules for a happy day.) How do we live this rule in daily life? When an idol inevitably doesn't satisfy us and we're tempted to attack it, we forgive it instead. We forgive our spouse for not taking out the garbage. We forgive the car for breaking down. We forgive the weather for raining on our picnic. We forgive the computer for losing our e-mail. We forgive the human resources manager for not giving us the job we wanted. We forgive Osama bin Laden for 9/11.

If we do this, the gap we have filled with our idols, our "blown-up children's toys," will be seen as empty, and therefore unreal. We will have no need of idols any more. We will recognize what we really want, and thus be restored to what we really are: God's Son, happy and safe forever in the Arms of our Beloved.

V. The Only Purpose
Commentary by Greg Mackie

1. The real world is the state of mind in which the <u>only</u> purpose of the world is seen to be forgiveness. Fear is <u>not</u> its goal, for [Ur: and] the <u>escape</u> from guilt becomes its aim. The <u>value</u> of forgiveness is perceived and <u>takes the place</u> of idols, which are sought no longer, for their "gifts" are not held dear. No rules are idly set, and no demands are made of anyone or anything to twist and fit into the dream of fear. Instead, there is a wish to understand all things created as they really <u>are</u>. And it is recognized that all things must be <u>first</u> forgiven, and *then* understood.

The insane world we see is devoted to the purpose of pursuing guilt and the fear that stems from guilt. Guilt is what our idols really bring us, both because they affirm we are abject sinners full of limitation and lack (T-30.III.3) and because, as the last section said, we attack them for not obeying our "rules" for satisfaction, an attack which reinforces our guilt.

The real world, on the other hand, is "the state of mind in which the *only* purpose of the world is seen to be forgiveness." There, our goal is *escape* from guilt and fear. Because of this new goal, we now value the means of escape—forgiveness—instead of the idols that reinforce guilt and fear. We no longer make demands on people or things to satisfy us by following our rules. Our goal now becomes not to twist things to suit our wishes but to understand them as they really are, an understanding that comes only through forgiveness.

2. <u>Here</u> [in this world], it is thought that understanding is <u>acquired</u> by attack. <u>There</u> [in the real world], it is clear that <u>by</u> attack is understanding <u>lost</u>. The folly of pursuing guilt as <u>goal</u> is fully recognized. And idols are not wanted there, for guilt is understood as the sole cause of pain in <u>any</u> form. No one is tempted by its vain appeal, for suffering and death have been perceived as things <u>not</u> wanted and not striven <u>for</u>. The possibility of freedom has been grasped and welcomed, and the means by which it can be gained can now be understood. The world becomes a place of hope, because its only purpose is to <u>be</u> a place where hope

218

of happiness can be fulfilled. And no one stands outside this hope, because the world has been united in belief the purpose of the world is one which all must <u>share</u>, if hope be more than just a dream.

Again, the previous section talked about how we attack our idols for not satisfying us. It is often at this point of dissatisfaction and disillusionment that we think we finally understand the truth about something: "I used to trust my husband, but now that he has run off with his secretary I see him for the snake he really is." But in the real world, we see that understanding *cannot* come through attack. Moreover, we see that the only reason we pursued idols and attacked them when they failed us was to accumulate guilt and thus bring ourselves pain and death. Who really wants *that*? When we choose the real world, all of this insanity will be replaced by a world "where hope of happiness can be fulfilled," a hope everyone shares because everyone recognizes it *must* be shared to be fulfilled.

Application: The fourth sentence here is a doozy. Think of something that is giving you pain right now, and consider the perceived "causes" of this pain. Now, repeat these words:

> *Guilt is the sole cause of this pain, and of all pain I have ever experienced.*
>
> *I have pursued the guilt that causes this pain, but this pursuit is folly.*
>
> *Let me no longer be tempted by idols which bring me guilt, pain, and death.*
>
> *The real world found through forgiveness is all I really want.*

3. Not yet is Heaven quite remembered, for the purpose of forgiveness still remains. Yet everyone is certain he will go <u>beyond</u> forgiveness, and he but remains until it is made perfect in himself. He has no wish for anything but this. And fear has dropped away, because he is united in his purpose with <u>himself</u>. There is a hope of happiness in him so sure and constant he can barely stay and wait a little longer, with his feet still touching earth. Yet is he glad to wait till every hand is joined, and every heart made ready to arise and go with him. For thus is <u>he</u> made ready for the step in which is all forgiveness left behind.

What a beautiful picture of a time when everyone is in the real world. Each person is devoted solely to the purpose of forgiveness. Each person is certain that when this forgiveness is perfectly attained, the infinite happiness of remembering Heaven will be hers. She is so eager to reach this goal that she can hardly bear to wait any longer for it. Yet she is happy to wait for all of her fellow travelers to be made ready for Heaven, for she realizes that their readiness will help *her* be ready for God's final step.

> 4. The final step is God's, because it is but God Who could create a perfect Son and share His Fatherhood with him. No one outside of Heaven knows how this can be, for understanding this is Heaven itself. Even the real world has a purpose still beneath creation and eternity. But fear is gone because its purpose is forgiveness, <u>not</u> idolatry. And so is Heaven's Son prepared to be himself, and to remember that the Son of God knows everything his Father understands, and understands it perfectly with Him.

We can make ourselves ready for Heaven through forgiveness, but the final step *to* Heaven is God's. Why? Because only God could create a perfect Son who is himself a creator, and there is no way we could understand this in our current state. There is a suggestion here that God's final step is tied somehow to God's original creation of us, a suggestion which is echoed elsewhere in the Course: "Yet the last step must be taken by God, because the last step in your redemption, which seems to be in the future, was accomplished by God in your creation" (T-13.VIII.3:2). And it makes sense that the last step to Heaven can only be accomplished by Someone Who is fully aware of Heaven. How could we reach Heaven ourselves when we have no idea what Heaven is like?

Rather than trying to understand Heaven and lift ourselves up by our own bootstraps, then, we should simply devote ourselves to the task of forgiveness. As the first paragraph told us, "all things must be *first* forgiven, and *then* understood." The real world with the purpose of forgiveness prepares us for Heaven by removing everything that stands in the way of our awareness of Heaven. Then God takes His final step, and we gain the understanding that only being fully aware of Heaven can give us.

5. The real world still falls short of this, for this [having a Son who perfectly shares His knowledge] is God's Own purpose; <u>only</u> His, and yet completely shared and perfectly fulfilled. The real world is a state in which the mind has learned how easily do idols go when they are still perceived but wanted not. How willingly the mind can let them go when it has understood that idols are nothing and nowhere, <u>and are purposeless</u> [see T-29.VIII]. For only then can guilt and sin be seen <u>without</u> a purpose, and as meaningless.

The real world is not Heaven, but again, it removes everything that stands in the way of our awareness of Heaven—including our idols. In the world we see, letting go of idols is difficult, because we believe in them and have a strong investment in them. But in the real world, letting go of them is easy, because although they can still be perceived, they are seen as *nothing, nowhere, purposeless,* and *unwanted.* When we see this, we will also see that the sin and guilt our idols serve are equally nothing, nowhere, purposeless, and unwanted.

6. Thus is the real world's purpose [forgiveness] gently brought into awareness, to <u>replace</u> the goal of sin and guilt. And all that stood <u>between</u> your image of yourself and what you <u>are</u>, forgiveness washes joyfully away. Yet God need not create His Son <u>again</u>, that what is his be given <u>back</u> to him. The gap between your brother and yourself was never there. And what the Son of God knew in creation he <u>must</u> know again.

As we let go of our idols, our goal of sin and guilt is replaced with the goal of forgiveness. When this happens, all the sin and guilt we see in the gap between our illusion of ourselves and our glorious reality as Sons of God is scrubbed clean.

We might think that once this happens, God will have to start all over, as He did in the Genesis story of the flood that washed all the sin from the earth. Yet He doesn't have to start over, because our sin is totally illusory. He doesn't have to create us again; the washing away of our "sins" through forgiveness simply reveals the radiant Son of God who was always there underneath that illusory tarnish. When this cleansing has been accomplished, we will remember what was always ours: our holy brothers and everything we knew when we were first created.

7. When brothers join in purpose in the world of fear, they stand <u>already</u> at the edge of the real world. Perhaps they still look back, and think they see an idol that they want. Yet has their path been surely set <u>away</u> from idols toward reality. For when they joined their hands it was Christ's hand they took, and they <u>will</u> look on Him Whose hand they hold. The face of Christ is looked upon <u>before</u> the Father is remembered. For He <u>must</u> be unremembered till His Son has reached <u>beyond</u> forgiveness to the Love of God. Yet is the Love of Christ accepted first. And <u>then</u> will come the knowledge They are one.

The section has been speaking of the purpose of forgiveness. Now, it speaks of two brothers *joined* in the purpose of forgiveness, two holy relationship partners journeying to God together. This simple act of joining in a common purpose—think of Helen and Bill's joining in the search for a better way—has turned them away from the vain search for idols and brought them to the border of the real world.

They aren't out of the woods yet—they will still be tempted, like Lot's wife, to look back at what they're leaving behind. Some of those idols still look awfully good. But once they took each other's hands they took Christ's hand, and their destiny was set: As we were told in the "Obstacles to Peace" section, they will look upon the face of Christ together and then disappear into God.

Application: Think of a person you feel you've truly joined with, but whom you still sometimes see as an idol meant to satisfy your personal needs. Say these words silently to this person:

> *I may still be tempted to see you as an idol, but when we joined, our path was set away from idols toward reality.*
> *When we joined, it was Christ's hand each of us took, and we **will** look on Him whose hand we hold.*
> *We **will** look on the face of Christ together, and then remember God our Father.*

8. How light and easy is the step across the narrow boundaries of the world of fear when you have <u>recognized</u> Whose hand you hold! Within your hand is everything you need to walk with perfect confidence away from fear forever, and to go straight on, and quickly reach the gate of

Heaven itself. For He Whose hand you hold was waiting but for you to join Him. Now that you have come, would <u>He</u> delay in showing you the way that He must walk with <u>you</u>? His blessing lies on you as surely as His Father's Love rests upon Him. His gratitude to you is past your understanding, for you have enabled Him to rise from chains and go with you, <u>together</u>, to His Father's house.

Jesus never seems to tire of extolling the benefits of joining with another person. Before we join, we seem trapped in this terrifying world of pain and suffering with no exit to be found except death. But once we join with another person in a common goal and realize that this joining is with Christ, *everything* changes. Christ has been waiting long for us to make this choice. It has released him from prison and now, with gratitude that "is past [our] understanding," he journeys with us to God. He gives the journey His blessing and shows us the way to Heaven's gate. He gives us everything we need to reach our goal. Once we see that Christ's hand is leading us, we no longer feel trapped in this world. Stepping out of terror into the joy of the real world becomes "light and easy." We now have perfect confidence that we will leave the nightmare behind forever and make our way quickly to our Father's house.

All of this comes simply from taking our *brother's* hand. Will we take it?

> 9. An ancient hate is passing from the world. And with it goes <u>all</u> hatred and <u>all</u> fear. Look back no longer [at your idols], for what lies ahead is all you <u>ever</u> wanted in your heart [Ur: hearts]. Give up the world! But <u>not</u> to sacrifice. You never <u>wanted</u> it. What happiness have you sought here that did not bring you pain? What moment of content has not been bought at fearful price in coins of suffering? Joy <u>has</u> no cost. It is your sacred right, and what you pay for is <u>not</u> happiness. Be speeded on your way by honesty, and let not your experiences here deceive in retrospect. They were <u>not</u> free from bitter cost and joyless consequence.

Again, even after we have joined each other on the journey to God, we will still be tempted to look back at our precious idols. That certainly happened with Helen and Bill. In the face of this temptation, we are being asked to "Give up the world!" This sounds like a radical and nearly impossible thing to do.

What can we do to make this easier? First, we can remind ourselves that what we're journeying toward "is all you *ever* wanted in your hearts." Second, we can get rigorously honest with ourselves and realize that all the happiness we *thought* we got from our idols came at a horrific price. We have a tendency to minimize the cost of our "happiness" in hindsight—"Hey, that relationship was pretty good. Sure we fought a lot, but the sex was great"—but we must avoid this tendency now. We must reflect on our lives and see just how much we paid for our scraps of "joy." Would we not rather have real joy, which comes at *no* cost? That is what leaving the "ancient hate" of the world behind and journeying to God will bring us.

> 10. Do not look back except in honesty. And when an idol tempts you, think of this:
>
> > *There never was a time an idol brought you <u>anything</u> except the "gift" of guilt. Not one was bought <u>except</u> at cost of pain, nor was it ever paid by you alone.*
>
> Be merciful unto your brother, then. And do not choose an idol thoughtlessly, remembering that he will pay the cost as well as you. For <u>he</u> will be delayed when you look back, and <u>you</u> will not perceive Whose loving hand you hold. Look forward, then; in confidence walk with a happy heart that beats in hope and does not pound in fear [Ur: happy hearts that beat in hope and do not pound in fear].

We've been told not to look back, but now we are given a qualifier: "except in honesty." The last paragraph was all about looking with that honesty. And if in that looking back we are tempted to think that a particular idol still looks appealing, Jesus gives us a practice here to get us back to honesty. The practice line we are given tells us three things about idols. First, what we actually get when we purchase them is *guilt*. Second, the currency with which we pay for them is *pain*. Third, the price of pain is not paid by us alone, but also by our *brother*.

This last part is particularly important. When we joined with each other, we each became our brother's keeper. We now have a responsibility to each other. If I choose an idol, you will suffer. Both of us will be delayed on our journey. I will forget that I hold Christ's hand, which scuttles our journey to the real world. Is this what I want? No. I want happiness, so I must be merciful to you. I must look at that tempting idol with unflinching honesty, turn away from it, and resume the happy journey to God with you.

Application: The practice here is a great one to use whenever you are tempted by an idol. Think of some idols that are currently attracting you and apply the italicized practice lines to them right now.

> 11. The Will of God forever lies in those whose hands are joined. <u>Until</u> they joined, they thought He was their enemy. But when they joined and <u>shared</u> a purpose, they were free to learn their will is one. And thus the Will of God <u>must</u> reach to their awareness. Nor can they forget for long that it is but their own.

The section concludes with a brief description of what happens when we join in a shared purpose. Before we join, we think God is our enemy (this reminds me of T-30.II, where we think God is an enemy, and forgiving our brother is linked with forgiving Him). But when two of us join in a common purpose, we discover that our wills are one. This then enables the Will of God to reach our awareness, which leads to the discovery that our joined wills and *God's* Will are one. Thus, as we take our brother's hand and realize he is our friend, we realize that God is our Friend as well. Once we see this, can returning to our Heavenly home with Him be far behind.

VI. The Justification for Forgiveness
Commentary by Robert Perry

1. Anger is *never* justified. Attack has *no* foundation. It is here escape from fear begins, and will be made complete. Here is the real world given in exchange for dreams of terror. For it is on this forgiveness rests, <u>and is but natural</u>. You are <u>not</u> asked to offer pardon where attack is due, and <u>would</u> be justified. For that would mean that you forgive a sin by overlooking what is <u>really</u> there. <u>This is not pardon</u>. For it would assume that, by responding in a way which is <u>not</u> justified, your <u>pardon</u> will become the answer to attack that <u>has</u> been made. And thus is pardon inappropriate, by being granted where it is <u>not</u> due.

This paragraph (and indeed this section) is a crucial explanation of Course-based forgiveness. For its latter sentences describe exactly how forgiveness is normally seen, but then tell us that that isn't it. Normally, of course, when we believe we have been attacked, our anger and retaliation appear to be fully justified. Forgiveness (as usually understood) doesn't challenge this perception at all. It simply says that even though we have a *right* to be angry and to retaliate, we will forego anger and retaliation for the sake of being good. In this view, forgiveness overlooks the sin that, in its view, is really there.

Yet responses are supposed to fit the action they are responding to. Responding to a sinful attack with forgiveness is like giving the sprinter who just earned his gold medal a lump of coal instead. Where's the connection? No, Jesus says, forgiveness has to fit the act. Forgiveness only makes sense if the attack on us doesn't really *deserve* a response of anger or retaliation.

2. Pardon is *always* justified. It has a sure foundation. You do <u>not</u> forgive the unforgivable, nor overlook a <u>real</u> attack that calls for punishment. Salvation does not lie in being asked to make unnatural responses which are inappropriate to what is real. Instead, it merely asks that you respond appropriately to what is <u>not</u> real by not perceiving what has not occurred. If pardon <u>were</u> unjustified, you <u>would</u> be asked to sacrifice your rights when you return forgiveness for attack. But you are merely

asked to see forgiveness as the <u>natural</u> reaction to distress that rests on error, and thus calls for help. Forgiveness is the <u>only</u> sane response. It *keeps* your rights from being sacrificed.

Notice the contrast between the first two sentences in this paragraph and in the first.

Anger is *never* justified (1st para.).	Pardon is *always* justified (2nd para.).
Attack has *no* foundation (1st para.).	[Pardon] has a sure foundation (2nd para.).

It seems that anger and attack are the appropriate response to being attacked. They seem to fit the act. And that is why forgiveness is so hard; it seems to be a response that does not fit the act. Yet Jesus says here that that's not how salvation works. "Salvation does not lie in being asked to make unnatural responses which are inappropriate to what is real." Thank God! The reason that anger and attack are inappropriate is that they are a response to *sin*, and attack is not sin. It's as if we believed that harmless Mr. Smith is really the devil in disguise, and we thought the only way to keep him from enslaving the world in an everlasting reign of evil was to kill him, no matter how much he claims to not know what we are talking about. At that point, the truly appropriate response to him would be to not perceive the devil that is not there.

Application: This paragraph contains two of my favorite lines for practicing forgiveness. Let's use them now. Think of someone you are itching to attack (or see someone else attack), and say:

> *Forgiving [name] is the natural reaction to distress that rests on error, and thus calls for help.*
> *Forgiving [name] **keeps** my rights from being sacrificed.*

3. This understanding is the <u>only</u> change that lets the real world rise to take the place of dreams of terror. Fear cannot <u>arise</u> unless attack is justified, and if it <u>had</u> a real foundation pardon would have none. The

real world is achieved when you perceive the basis of <u>forgiveness</u> is quite real and fully justified. While you regard it as a gift unwarranted, it <u>must</u> uphold the guilt you would "forgive." Unjustified forgiveness <u>is</u> attack. And this is all the world can <u>ever</u> give. It pardons "sinners" sometimes, but remains <u>aware</u> that they have sinned. And so they do not <u>merit</u> the forgiveness that it gives.

Imagine saying to someone, "I'll forgive you, but you don't deserve it. The fact is that you sinned, you're guilty, and you deserve my wrath. But I give you the gift of my forgiveness anyway, even though it is totally unmerited." How forgiven do you think that person would feel? Yet this *is* conventional forgiveness. This is its thought system exactly. The conclusion is inescapable: Conventional forgiveness cannot really forgive. It does not deserve the name.

Conventional forgiveness not only cannot release the attacker from his guilt but also cannot truly release the forgiver. It cannot reveal to him the real world. The real world will not arise before our sight until we realize that forgiveness is the *natural, appropriate, justified* response.

4. This is the false forgiveness which the world employs to <u>keep</u> the sense of sin alive. And recognizing God is just, it seems impossible His pardon <u>could</u> be real. Thus is the fear of God the sure result of seeing pardon as unmerited. No one who sees himself as guilty <u>can</u> avoid the fear of God. But he is <u>saved</u> from this dilemma if <u>he</u> can forgive. The mind <u>must</u> think of its Creator as it looks upon itself. If you can see your brother <u>merits</u> pardon, you have learned forgiveness is <u>your</u> right as much as his. Nor will you think that God intends for you a fearful judgment that your brother does not merit. For it is the truth that you <u>can</u> merit neither more nor less than he.

Deep in our minds, we assume that whatever our brother fundamentally is—evil or good—*we* must be as well. We also assume that God can't be too different from us. If we are judgmental, God must be, too. Therefore, by judging our brother as evil, we accomplish two things. We think we must be like our brother—we must be evil. And we think that God must be like us—He must be judgmental. Put those two together and you get: God must judge us as evil. Therefore, conventional forgiveness, which is inherently judgmental, leads directly to the belief that we are evil and should live in fear of God's judgment.

Think, for instance, about someone you consider to be evil, or as close to it as one can get. After identifying someone, try to get in touch with a belief, perhaps lodged in the back of your mind, that God engages in judgment that is not so different from yours. The inevitable result of these two beliefs (this person is evil; God is judgmental) is that somewhere in your mind is the feeling of God frowning upon this person. Try to locate your belief that God will not protect this person from the dangers that inevitably come his way, but instead will make sure that bad things happen to him.

Now ask yourself, "How different from this person can I really be?" Realize that all the traits you despise in this person have their (apparently) milder counterparts in you. Then ask yourself, "Given this, what does that say about how God must look on me?"

> 5. Forgiveness <u>recognized</u> as merited will heal. It gives the miracle its strength to <u>overlook</u> illusions. This is how you learn that you must be forgiven too. There <u>can</u> be no appearance that can <u>not</u> be overlooked. For if there were, it would be necessary <u>first</u> there be some sin that stands <u>beyond</u> forgiveness. There would be an error that is <u>more</u> than a mistake; a special <u>form</u> of error that remains unchangeable, eternal, and beyond correction or escape. There would be one mistake that had the power to <u>undo</u> creation, and to make a world that could <u>replace</u> it and <u>destroy</u> the Will of God. Only if this were possible could there be <u>some</u> appearances that could withstand the miracle, and <u>not</u> be healed by it.

Forgiveness seen as unmerited sends a subtle message of condemnation. In contrast, "Forgiveness recognized as merited will heal." Such forgiveness can overlook any attack, however real and destructive it appears to be. But how can it be that *every* attack can be overlooked? Jesus turns that question around: How can it not be? For if there were a single mistake that couldn't be forgiven, that would mean that mistake was so real that it couldn't be undone—ever. It would therefore be eternal. Being eternal, it would be like an evil foot in the door of Heaven. It would have the power to ultimately undo God's creation (the Sonship), and replace it with a world that was creation's opposite, a world that would destroy God's Will of perfect Love.

Are you willing to believe that this is possible? Are you willing to grant your brother's mistake, so tiny in the grand scheme of things, the power to destroy the Will of God?

> 6. There is no surer proof idolatry is what you wish than a belief there are some forms of sickness and of joylessness forgiveness <u>cannot</u> heal. This means that you prefer to keep <u>some</u> idols, and are not prepared, as yet, to let <u>all</u> idols go. And thus you think that <u>some</u> appearances are real and not appearances at all. Be not deceived about the <u>meaning</u> of a fixed belief that <u>some</u> appearances are harder to look past than others are. It <u>always</u> means you think forgiveness must be limited. And you have set a goal of partial pardon and a limited escape from guilt <u>for you</u>. What can this be except a false forgiveness of <u>yourself</u>, and everyone who seems <u>apart</u> from you?

Jesus now brings the discussion back to idolatry. If we think we cannot forgive a certain attack, it's not because that attack is actually unforgivable. It's because *we* are attached to it. We clutch it tight because we secretly want it to bring down God (as the last paragraph explained). We cling to it as His replacement. We have, in other words, made it an idol. Our worship of this idol is really the worship of *limited* forgiveness. What this means, though, is that "you have set a goal of partial pardon and a limited escape from guilt *for you*" (Urtext version).

> 7. It <u>must</u> be true the miracle can heal <u>all</u> forms of sickness, or it <u>cannot heal</u>. Its purpose cannot be to judge which <u>forms</u> are real, and which <u>appearances</u> are true. If one appearance must remain <u>apart</u> from healing, one illusion must be part of truth. And you could <u>not</u> escape all guilt, but only <u>some</u> of it. You must forgive God's Son <u>entirely</u>. Or you will keep an image of yourself that is not whole, and will remain afraid to look within and find escape from <u>every</u> idol there. Salvation rests on faith there <u>cannot</u> be some forms of guilt that you can<u>not</u> forgive. And so there cannot be appearances that have replaced the truth about God's Son.

The very foundation of salvation is the idea that all forms of guilt can be forgiven, all mistakes can be corrected, all forms of sickness can be healed. This allness is what gives the miracle its power to heal. Without this allness, the miracle is a wimp that cannot overcome big problems and has only partial power over the small ones. And when it finally stands before the biggest problem of all—your guilt—it will be like a little man with a pickaxe standing in front of a mountain. Is that what you want? Wouldn't you rather see the miracle facing your guilt as the *sun* shining upon *mists*? To claim this second picture there is only one thing you need do: "You must forgive God's Son *entirely*" (Urtext version).

> 8. Look on your brother with the willingness to see him as he is. And do not keep a part of him outside your willingness that he be healed. To heal is to make whole. And what is whole can have no missing parts that have been kept outside. Forgiveness rests on recognizing this, and being <u>glad</u> there cannot be some forms of sickness which the miracle must <u>lack</u> the power to heal.

If you are really willing for your brother to be healed, then you can't set to one side some part of him and say, "But not this. This thing is unforgivable and can't be healed." For to be healed is to be whole, and in this picture he is obviously not whole. The choice, therefore, is either "Do I want him healed entirely?" or "Do I want him in pieces?"

> 9. God's Son is perfect, or he cannot be God's Son. Nor will you <u>know</u> him, if you think he does not merit the escape from guilt in all its consequences and its forms [Ur: in *all* its forms and *all* its consequence]. There <u>is</u> no way to think of him but this, if you would know the truth about yourself.

> *I thank You, Father, for Your perfect Son, and in his glory will I see my own.*

> Here is the joyful statement that there are <u>no</u> forms of evil that can overcome the Will of God; the glad acknowledgment that guilt has <u>not</u> succeeded by your wish to make illusions real. And what is this except a simple statement of the truth?

This is one of the most powerful practices in the Course, in my view. It is the entire section boiled down into one sentence. This section, therefore, functions very much like a Workbook lesson, which begins with abstract teaching and ends with a practice that condenses that teaching into a sharp point and aims it at specifics in our lives.

The whole section has expressed the idea that, when a brother attacks, that attack is an entirely correctable mistake that has no power to undo my brother's perfect nature as God's creation. It has also said that how I see my brother will determine how I see myself. This practice combines both of those ideas. But rather than spending its time negating wrong perceptions of my brother's mistakes, it leaves those mistakes behind and lifts off into celebrating and thanking God for his untainted perfection. In my experience, it is this note of joyous thanksgiving, which simply ignores the apparent sin in front of me, that makes the practice so powerful.

Application: Use this practice with anyone at any time. As a start, you might want use it with several people right now, especially people you have been consciously resenting. Call the person to mind and then say to God with as much sincerity as you can muster,

> *I think you, Father, for Your perfect Son, and in his glory will I see my own.*

Try to treat both parts of the statement with equal sincerity. Try to genuinely be thankful for this person who is in reality God's perfect Son. And try to really acknowledge that only by seeing his glory—the aura of his holiness—will you come to believe that you shine with the same glory.

10. Look on your brother with this hope in you, and you will understand he <u>could</u> not make an error that could change the truth in him. It is <u>not</u> difficult to overlook mistakes that have been given no effects. But what you see as having power to make an idol of the Son of God you will <u>not</u> pardon. For he has become to you a graven image and a sign of death. Is <u>this</u> your savior? Is his Father <u>wrong</u> about His Son? Or have <u>you</u> been deceived in him who has been given you to heal, for <u>your</u> salvation and deliverance?

We have two choices of how we see our brother. We can see him as God's Own Son, whose errors have never changed the glorious perfection that God placed in him. Or we can see him as a false god who carries within himself the energy of anti-God, an energy so dark and evil that it can actually overthrow God.

Though the second option is very popular, it has some real problems with it. First, this brother is supposed to be our savior, but how can someone like this actually save us? Only if he is holy can he save us. Second, God is sure that this brother is His Own Son. Can God really be wrong about him, while we are right instead? Third, this person was sent for us to heal, yet this view of him guarantees that we will never heal him. And since healing him is what brings about our own salvation, that's not going to happen either. Given these three things, isn't it safer to assume that we have been wrong about him?

VII. The New Interpretation
Commentary by Robert Perry

1. Would God have left the meaning of the world to <u>your</u> interpretation? If He had, it *has* no meaning. For it cannot be that meaning changes constantly, and yet is true. The Holy Spirit looks upon the world as with <u>one</u> purpose, changelessly established. And <u>no</u> situation can affect its aim, but <u>must</u> be in accord with it. For <u>only</u> if its aim could change with every situation could each one be <u>open</u> to interpretation which is different every time you think of it. You <u>add</u> an element into the script you write for every minute in the day, and all that happens now means something else. You <u>take away</u> another element, and every meaning shifts accordingly.

Imagine if God had said to us, "Okay, whatever you think the world means, that's what it means." If He had, Jesus says, then the world would have no meaning whatsoever. Because the meaning that we give things (which comes from the *purpose* that we assign them) is constantly in flux. And a world whose meaning is forever changing is a world that *has* no meaning.

The last three sentences are a penetrating account of how we assign meaning and purpose. It says that we have a script for how the day should go: "At breakfast, my eggs should be cooked just right. On my drive to work, at least ninety percent of the lights I hit should be green. At work, I should breeze through my responsibilities without any curve balls to upset my schedule." This script, of course, has thousands of details. With each situation, I assign an implicit purpose that it's supposed to fulfill, and that purpose determines what it means.

Yet here's the problem: Every time I think of a situation, I assign a slightly different meaning and purpose to it. With each passing minute, I think about some situation, and thereby shift the meaning I see in it. And as I do, that new element casts a different light on *everything* in the script. If you have ever written fiction, you know that if you change one element in the story, everything in the story looks slightly different, often requiring you to tamper with other events to bring them into accord

234

with the new element. Thus, the fact that we constantly change particular elements means that literally *everything* in our script for the day is always in flux. This really should come as no surprise.

(Please take note that this "script" is not the familiar one that Course students talk about. That script is the script my ego writes which actually *determines* the happenings of my life. As a result, the events of my life are *always* in accord with that script. The script in this section, however, is one that is frequently frustrated and contradicted by the day's events. Chances are, for instance, that ninety percent of the traffic lights I hit *won't* be green. Strangely, you will not find any references to "script" in the Course that refer to that other, more metaphysical script.)

All of this stands in sharp contrast to how the Holy Spirit sees the world. In His perception, everything has one purpose, which never changes from time to time or situation to situation.

> 2. What do your scripts reflect except your plans for what the day *should* be? And thus [according to these plans] you judge disaster and success, advance, retreat, and gain and loss. These judgments all are made according to the roles the script assigns [see T-29.IV, "Dream Roles"]. The fact they have no meaning in themselves is <u>demonstrated</u> by the ease with which these labels change with other judgments, made on different aspects of experience [of the script]. And then, in looking back, you think you see <u>another</u> meaning in what went before. What have you really done, except to show there <u>was</u> no meaning there? But <u>you</u> assigned a meaning in the light of goals that change, with <u>every</u> meaning shifting as they change.

Our script is essentially our plans for what the day should be in order to fulfill the goals we have for it. This script, then, becomes our standard for evaluating the day. If, for example, I did hit ninety percent green lights, I would think that that part of the day was a success.

That all makes a certain amount of sense. What doesn't make sense, however, is how my script for one situation is altered when I change the script for *another* situation. Let's say, for instance, that before I head off to work, I consider it imperative that my wife agree to go out to dinner and a movie with me tonight. I have a whole list of reasons of why it is important that we do so. When I arrive at work, however, I find that I have been given a hefty raise. Even though the two situations are for all intents and purposes unrelated, I find that my need to go out tonight suddenly evaporates. None of my original reasons for going out had anything to do with how much I'm earning at my job. In fact, I'm now more able to afford a night out. Nevertheless, my raise does away with my insistent urge to go out this evening.

Or let's turn this around a bit. Let's say that, in the morning, my wife tells me that she just doesn't feel like going out tonight, and besides, she needs the time to get pressing things done. I am very disappointed. Then I go to work and get my big raise. Now I look back on her decision, and it doesn't seem so bad. I'm totally fine about it.

(I just got a call from an old friend I grew up with. He said, "My business is going to hell and I have this sudden urge to go golfing." I mentioned that I had never played golf, to which he replied, "That makes three of us!")

The point is that, if I were really in touch with the actual meaning of going out to dinner and a movie, that meaning would not alter, especially not in response to an *unrelated* situation. Yet let's face it, this is the norm with us. This demonstrates that we are not in touch with actual meaning. Rather, all we are doing is juggling an assortment of totally subjective, fanciful, self-made "meanings." How does it feel to really consider that?

> 3. Only a <u>constant</u> purpose can endow events with stable meaning. But it must <u>accord</u> *one* <u>meaning to them all</u>. If they are given <u>different</u> meanings, it <u>must</u> be that they reflect but different purposes. And this is <u>all</u> the meaning that they have. Can this <u>be</u> meaning? Can confusion <u>be</u> what meaning means? Perception <u>cannot</u> be in constant flux, and make allowance for stability of meaning <u>anywhere</u>. Fear is a judgment <u>never</u> justified. Its presence has no meaning but to show you wrote a fearful script, and are afraid accordingly. But <u>not</u> because the thing you fear has fearful meaning in itself.

To be in touch with real meaning, I need to see the same unvarying meaning in a situation over time. It can't change. But that's not all. I need to see the same unvarying meaning in *every* situation. Why? Remember, meaning is determined by purpose. Consequently, if I see a different meaning in each situation, that means that I see each one as fulfilling a different *purpose*.

The implication is that I am managing a collection of dueling purposes, each one vying for its place in the sun, each one shining a different meaning on the situation with which it is associated. But then *should* it be associated with that situation? Maybe that situation should really be fulfilling another one of my purposes. I think, for instance, that my work should fulfill my purpose of making money, but maybe it should fulfill my drive to serve a higher cause (or in my own case, vice versa). I just don't know. It makes me very confused just to think about it.

Again, this shows that I am simply not in touch with real meaning. Further, all this instability makes me quite anxious and genuinely afraid. Yet maybe all the fearful meaning I see in things is not really in them. Maybe it's just a product of my own capricious process of assigning meaning.

> 4. A common purpose is the <u>only</u> means whereby perception can be stabilized, and <u>one</u> interpretation given to the world and all experiences here. In this shared purpose is one judgment [Ur: meaning] shared by everyone and everything you see. You do not have to judge, for you have learned one meaning has been <u>given</u> everything, and you are <u>glad</u> to see it everywhere. It cannot change *because* you would [want to] perceive it everywhere, unchanged by circumstance. And so you <u>offer</u> it to all events, and <u>let</u> them offer you stability.

Aren't we sick and tired of all this instability of meaning? It's as if everything in our lives is not resting on the ground but rather hanging from a string, and the string is constantly going up and then down. We think we are used to everything ceaselessly bobbing up and down like this. We think we have adjusted. But we haven't.

Wouldn't it be great if, instead, we never had to judge what something means or what it is for? Wouldn't it be great if we settled that whole question once and for all by deciding that everyone and everything has *one* meaning, *one* purpose, which never changes? What a relief that would be!

> 5. Escape from judgment simply lies in this; all things have but one purpose, which you share with all the world. And nothing <u>in</u> the world can <u>be</u> opposed to it, for it belongs <u>to</u> everything, as it belongs to you. In <u>single</u> purpose is the end of all ideas of sacrifice, which <u>must</u> assume a <u>different</u> purpose for the one who gains and him who loses. There

could be no thought of sacrifice apart from this idea. And it is this idea of different goals that makes perception shift and meaning change. In one united goal does this become impossible, for your agreement makes interpretation stabilize and last.

Now the notion of one purpose expands. It is not just a situation having a purpose that is stable over time. It is not just all the situations in my life having the same unvarying purpose. Now, that one purpose goes beyond my situations to encompass the situations of others. Now it is a purpose that I share with others. And since we have the same purpose, I can't gain at your expense. We gain together. This one purpose, in other words, does not just save me from instability, confusion, and judgment, it also saves me from *conflict* and *separateness*.

6. How can communication really be established while the symbols that are used mean different things? The Holy Spirit's goal gives one interpretation, meaningful to you and to your brother. Thus can you communicate with him, and he with you. In symbols that you both can understand the sacrifice of meaning is undone. All sacrifice [of meaning?] entails the loss of your ability to see relationships among events. And looked at separately [in separation from your brother] they have no meaning. For there is no light by which they can be seen and understood. They have no purpose. And what they are for cannot be seen. In any thought of loss there is no meaning. No one has agreed with you on what it means. It is a part of a distorted script, which cannot be interpreted with meaning. It must be forever unintelligible. This is not communication. Your dark dreams are but the senseless, isolated scripts you write in sleep. Look not to separate dreams for meaning. Only dreams of pardon can be shared. They mean the same to both of you.

Jesus now continues the theme of a single purpose that unites ourselves and others. Without this, he says, we can't really communicate. To understand what he means, imagine that when I say the word "dog," you think it refers to a toaster. Thus, the sentence "I had to spank my dog" will mean very different things to you and me.

Actually, Jesus says, this is the condition we live in. Because my goals are separate from yours, the meaning I give things is different from the meaning you give them. For instance, if I hand you money, do you think we see the same meaning in that money? For me, it is "money that is not mine anymore." For you, it is "money that is now mine." Those are two very different pieces of money! This is the ultimate source of our communication breakdowns.

Only when we agree on a common purpose can we see the see the same meaning in things. And only when we all see the same meaning can *each* of us see a meaning that blankets everything. For while we live in our own world of meaning, we are painfully aware that others are living in their very different worlds of meaning. Thus we see a landscape chopped into countless segments, countless islands of meaning, separated by invisible international boundaries. Isn't this why the world seems like such a meaningless place?

That fractured landscape means that we have lost touch with meaning. We will only escape this anxiety-producing sacrifice of meaning when we stop writing our own isolated scripts in which everyone else is just a bit player in *our* story. The only way to find a stable, all-encompassing meaning is to see the story as being about *us*, all of us. It must be a story about forgiveness, a need that we all share.

> 7. Do not interpret out of solitude, for what you see means nothing. It will shift in what it stands for, and you will believe the world is an uncertain place, in which you walk in danger and uncertainty. It is but your <u>interpretations</u> which are lacking in stability, for they are <u>not</u> in line with what you really are. This is a state so seemingly unsafe that fear <u>must</u> rise. Do not continue thus, my brother. We have <u>one</u> Interpreter. And through His use of symbols are we joined, so that they mean the same to <u>all</u> of us. Our common language lets us speak to all our brothers, and to understand with them forgiveness has been given to us all, and thus we <u>can</u> communicate again.

Jesus now takes the teaching from the first six paragraphs and turns it into injunctions. "Do not interpret out of solitude," he says. This means solitude in the sense of separateness from each other *and* separateness from the Holy Spirit. This solitude means that we write our private script, in which we are the hero. If we do, the meanings that we see will constantly change. We will live on an ice floe, with moving and fragmenting blocks of ice under our feet at all times. We will live a life of fear.

But if we let the Holy Spirit be our Interpreter, He will assign one purpose and therefore one meaning to everything and everyone. And we will see a meaning that is the same for us and for our brothers. Then we can communicate with them. Then we can all live within the same story, a story of forgiveness.

Application: Let's apply this teaching now. Say:

> *Holy Spirit, be my Interpreter.*
> *I want a stable, unvarying purpose for this current situation.*
> *I want the same purpose for all my situations.*
> *And I want the same purpose for me and for my brothers, a*
> *   purpose that unites us.*
> *What is this purpose?*

Then listen within. And when you get a sense of what that purpose is, try to embrace it as yours. And try to keep it with you as you go through your day, applying it to everything.

VIII. Changeless Reality
Commentary by Robert Perry

1. Appearances deceive [see IV.5:1], <u>but can be changed</u>. Reality is changeless. It does not deceive at all, and if you fail to see <u>beyond</u> appearances you *are* deceived. For everything you see will change, and yet you thought it real before, and now you think it real again. Reality is thus reduced to form, and <u>capable</u> of change. Reality is changeless. It is this that <u>makes</u> it real, and <u>keeps</u> it separate from all appearances. It <u>must</u> transcend all form to be itself. It <u>cannot</u> change.

It is an axiom that appearances can be deceiving. We have all learned to not trust a book's cover, a body's clothing, or *any* form of advertising, for that matter. Jesus, however, takes it one step farther. It's not just that appearances *can* deceive; they *do* deceive. They are deceptive by nature. For they *change*. Think of a person's body. Within a short space of time, it can announce to you a series of messages: "This person is happy." "This person is beautiful." "This person is angry." "This person is selfish." "This person is sick." "This person is dead."

Can the truth about that person really change like that? No. Hence, appearances, which are continually changing, must be deceiving you. For "reality is changeless." This is its defining characteristic. It must therefore be beyond appearance (form) and beyond all change.

2. The miracle is means to demonstrate that <u>all</u> appearances can change <u>because</u> they <u>are</u> appearances, and <u>cannot</u> have the changelessness reality entails. The miracle attests salvation <u>from</u> appearances by <u>showing</u> they can change. Your brother has a changelessness in him beyond appearance and deception, both. It is obscured by changing views of him that you <u>perceive</u> as his reality. The happy dream about him takes the form of the appearance of his perfect health, his perfect freedom from all forms of lack, and safety from disaster of all kinds. The miracle is proof he is not bound by loss or suffering in any form, <u>because it can so easily be changed</u>. This demonstrates that it was never real, and <u>could</u> not stem from his reality. For that is changeless, and has no effects that anything in Heaven or on earth could ever alter. But appearances are shown to be unreal *because* they change.

Though appearances change, there are certain appearances that seem beyond our power to change. We all know what these are. They are the grim appearances that seem to hold us in their grip, no matter how hard we try to break that grip. Given their unyielding persistence, those appearances seem genuinely real. They seem to have the power to define who we are.

The miracle's job is to show that none of this is true. Its job is to come in and change the appearance of sickness, lack, and disaster as easily as one would change one's shirt. It thereby proves that those things could not have been real, for see how easily they can be changed?

Think about Jesus' miracles. A man lying on his pallet next to a pool for thirty-eight years. A woman with a vaginal hemorrhage for twelve years. In their eyes, this had become their reality. By changing that condition so instantly and easily, Jesus did more than show that it was no longer their reality. He showed that it couldn't have been their reality in the first place. For see how flimsy an appearance it ended up being?

In this paragraph, Jesus also decisively answers those who say that the miracle would not heal form because form is not real. He says that the miracle does heal form, in order to *prove* that it's not real.

> 3. What is temptation but a wish to make illusions real? It does not <u>seem</u> to be the wish that <u>no</u> reality be so. Yet it <u>is</u> an assertion that some <u>forms</u> of idols have a powerful appeal that makes them <u>harder</u> to resist than those you would not <u>want</u> to have reality. Temptation, then, is nothing more than this; a prayer the miracle touch not some dreams, but <u>keep</u> their unreality obscure and <u>give</u> to them reality instead. And Heaven gives no answer to the prayer, nor <u>can</u> a miracle be given you to heal appearances you do not like. <u>You have established limits</u>. What you ask *is* given you, but not of God Who knows no limits. <u>You</u> have limited <u>yourself</u>.

This paragraph begins a theme that carries through to the end of the Text, the theme of temptation. In fact, the phrase here—"What is temptation but a wish [or 'the wish']"—occurs three times.

The temptation here is the temptation to value something of the world, to value an idol. It says, "I may not want these unpleasant appearances over here to be real, but *this* appearance (fill in your favorite one) has a powerful appeal. This I want to be real." Actually, Jesus says that this is a prayer: "Holy Spirit, I pray that you not send me a miracle to heal this appearance. Please don't change it and thereby prove it to be unreal. I want it to be real, and real means permanent."

What we don't realize is that making one appearance real implies that they all are real. And being real, they cannot be changed, not even by a miracle. Now a miracle cannot be given us to heal even the appearances that we *don't* like. Now we wonder why the Holy Spirit won't answer our prayer and heal those painful appearances. We don't realize that He *did* answer our prayer—our prayer that He back off.

> 4. Reality is changeless. Miracles but show what you have interposed <u>between</u> reality and your awareness is unreal, and does not interfere at all. The cost of the belief there must be some appearances <u>beyond</u> the hope of change is that the miracle cannot come forth from you consistently. For you have <u>asked</u> it be withheld from power to heal all dreams. There is no miracle you cannot have when you <u>desire</u> healing. But there is no miracle that <u>can</u> be given you <u>unless</u> you want it. <u>Choose</u> what you would heal, and He Who gives all miracles has not been given freedom to bestow His gifts upon God's Son. When he is tempted [to value certain appearances], he <u>denies</u> reality. And he becomes the willing slave [see T-29.IX.1:1] of what he chose instead.

In commenting on the previous paragraph, I implied that valuing a pleasant appearance amounts to saying no to all miracles. This paragraph softens the picture. When I say, "I want this appearance to be permanent but this one to be healed," I am really saying to the Holy Spirit, "I want inconsistent miracles." And that's what I get: "The miracle cannot come forth from you consistently." Inconsistency seems to be the very nature of miracles, which leads us to assume that that's how God is. He works in mysterious ways, which, translated, means He can't be trusted. Could it be that He is consistent, but that we have said to Him, "I want Your consistency to shine through only every now and then"?

> 5. *Because* reality is changeless is a miracle already there to heal all things that change, and offer them to you to see in happy form, devoid of fear. It <u>will</u> be given you to look upon your brother thus. But <u>not</u> while you would have it otherwise in some respects. For this but means you would not have him healed and whole. The Christ in him is perfect. Is it this that you would look upon? Then let there be no dreams about

him that you would <u>prefer</u> to seeing this. And you <u>will</u> see the Christ in him because you <u>let</u> Him come to you. And when He has appeared to you, you will be certain you are like Him, for He is the changeless in your brother <u>and</u> in you.

Now it gets more specific. Why can't we offer a miracle to our brother consistently? Because we value some changing appearance of him more than we value the changeless reality in him. Maybe we want to feast our eyes on his attractive body. Maybe we want to gloat over his misfortune. Either way, now the miracle cannot come forth from us consistently.

Yet if instead, we value the changeless Christ in him, the miracle will come forth from us to heal our brother's painful appearances "and offer them to you to see in happy form, devoid of fear." And we will receive an even greater gift. We will see the Christ in him. "And when He has appeared to you, you will be certain you are like Him" (possibly a reference to 1 John 3:2).

> 6. This will you look upon when you decide there is not one appearance you would hold in place of what your brother really <u>is</u>. Let no temptation to prefer a dream allow uncertainty to enter here. Be not made guilty and afraid when you are tempted by a dream of what he is. But do not give it power to <u>replace</u> the changeless in him in your sight of him. There is no false appearance but will fade, if you request a miracle instead. There is no pain from which he is not free, if you would have him be but what he is. Why should you fear to see the Christ in him? You but behold yourself in what you see. As he is healed are <u>you</u> made free of guilt, for his appearance <u>is</u> your own to you.

Application: Think of someone you know and love, and then think of some outward appearance or circumstance of this person that you are attached to because you find that it pleases you, or entertains you, or comforts you. Now repeat:

> *I am being tempted to value a dream of what [name] is.*
> *I will not let this make me feel afraid or guilty.*
> *But I will not give it power to replace the changeless in my sight*
> *   of [name].*

VIII. Changeless Reality

I behold the changeless Christ in [name].
I value this sight over any appearance.
For this gives me power to free [name] from all painful appearances.
*And it lets me behold the Christ in **me**.*

Commentaries on Chapter 31

THE FINAL VISION

I. The Simplicity of Salvation
Commentary by Robert Perry

1. How simple is salvation! All it says is what was never true is not true now, and never will be. The impossible has <u>not</u> occurred, and <u>can</u> have no effects. And that is all. Can this <u>be</u> hard to learn by anyone who <u>wants</u> it to be true? <u>Only</u> unwillingness to learn it could make such an easy lesson difficult. How hard is it to see that what is false can not be true, and what is true can not be false? You can no longer say that you perceive no differences in false and true. You have been told <u>exactly</u> how to tell one from the other, and just what to do if you become confused. Why, then, do you persist in learning <u>not</u> such simple things?

Jesus likes to say that the Course is simple. And by simple, he doesn't mean "simple but not easy." He explicitly says, "This course is easy" (T-23.III.4:1). Yet he is also fully aware that we *experience* it as extremely difficult, especially the longer we're with it and the more serious we get about it. You have probably wondered yourself why the Course seems so hard. This paragraph begins a penetrating discussion of why.

All salvation says is that the false is not true and the impossible has not happened. In principle, this is extremely easy to learn, especially since the Course has taught us how to tell the difference between the false and true. Yet, as we have no doubt observed in life, if someone doesn't want to learn something, it doesn't matter how simple you make it.

2. There <u>is</u> a reason. But confuse it not with difficulty in the simple things salvation asks you learn. It teaches but the very obvious. It merely goes from one apparent [clear, easily understood] lesson to the next, in easy steps that lead you gently from one to another, with no strain at all. This <u>cannot</u> be confusing, yet you <u>are</u> confused. For somehow you believe that what is <u>totally</u> confused is easier to learn and understand. What you have taught yourself is such a giant learning feat it is indeed incredible. But you accomplished it because you wanted to, and did not pause in diligence to judge it hard to learn or too complex to grasp.

Let's not kid ourselves that salvation is objectively difficult. It teaches the simple and obvious. It goes from one clear lesson to the next, in small, gentle steps. This is especially evident in the Workbook. Why on earth does such a gentle process seem hard to us? Because we have accomplished the "giant learning feat" of teaching ourselves a totally confused thought system, that of the ego. Sure, it was hard to learn, but that didn't stop us. We forged ahead and learned it anyway. Because of it, the clear and simple thought system presented in the Course seems virtually impenetrable.

Notice how Jesus has turned the tables on us. We say to him, "The thought system you are trying to teach me is so complex and convoluted!" He replies, "The complex, convoluted thought system is what you believe *now*. Compared to it, the Course is the essence of simplicity." We complain, "But the Course takes so much effort to learn." He replies, "Learning your current thought system is what took the gargantuan effort, and in *that* case you didn't moan about it. You just made up your mind and did it." You can almost hear him thinking, "We could do with a little of that attitude now."

> 3. No one who understands what you have learned, how carefully you learned it, and the pains to which you went to practice and repeat the lessons endlessly, in every form you could conceive of them, could <u>ever</u> doubt the power of your learning skill. There is no greater power in the world. The world was <u>made</u> by it, and even now depends on nothing else. The lessons you have taught yourself have been so overlearned and fixed they rise like heavy curtains to obscure the simple and the obvious. Say not you cannot learn them. For your power to learn is strong enough to teach you that your will is <u>not</u> your own, your thoughts do <u>not</u> belong to you, and even <u>you</u> are someone else.

We simply have no idea just how powerful our learning skill is. We can learn anything if we want to. Look around you. The furniture, the trees, the bodies—all are nothing more than crystallizations of lessons you taught yourself. That's how powerful your learning skill is. You repeated these lessons to yourself endlessly—using the very same process the Course teaches in the Workbook. You even went on to *overlearn* the lessons that made this world—you continued to study and practice even after attaining efficiency (which is the meaning of "overlearn").

These lessons took so much practice because they were crazy. You taught yourself that your will (of love) is not your real will at all, that your thoughts are really residing not in you but in the people you projected them on, and that you, the Son of God, are somebody else entirely (a human being). Who but a master learner could successfully teach himself such mind-bogglingly nutty ideas as these?

The problem is that these crazy, contradictory lessons are interfering with the simple and obvious lessons the Course wants to teach you. Jesus mentioned this idea to Helen privately:

> I told you the next part of the course will place increasing emphasis on Atonement, and I defined this as "undoing." You know very well that changing learning patterns requires undoing the old ones. The real meaning of retroactive inhibition is simply that when two kinds of learning coexist, they interfere with each other.
>
> You were wise in setting up William Rockford to allow measuring both the old and new learnings, thus permitting *ratio measurement.* Actually, I helped you with this one [Helen interrupts here: "I am mad about this"] because most studies just measure learning decrement [loss] caused by new learning with the old. But the emphasis *should* be on how to minimize the effect of the old on the new. This is a much more helpful area to work in. (*Absence from Felicity*, p. 237-238)

Normally, "retroactive inhibition" refers to new learning inhibiting the retention of old learning. Jesus, however, says that the emphasis should be on how the *old* learning inhibits the learning of the *new*. That's what he is talking about in this section.

> 4. Who could maintain that lessons such as these are easy? Yet you have learned more than this. You have continued, taking every step, however difficult, without complaint, until a world was built that suited you. And every lesson that makes up the world arises from the first accomplishment of learning; an enormity so great the Holy Spirit's Voice seems small and still before its magnitude. The world began with one strange lesson, powerful enough to render God forgotten, and His Son an alien to himself, in exile from the home where God Himself established him. You who have taught yourself the Son of God is guilty, say not that you cannot learn the simple things salvation teaches you!

It all began with "one strange lesson": the idea that God's Own Son could actually be guilty. Think about that idea for a moment. Do you see the insanity of it? Imagine being in Heaven, surrounded and permeated by endless fields of pure holiness, and slowly convincing yourself through continual repetition and sheer force of will that God's Own Son is actually a sinner. What a massive learning feat! All the other crazy lessons we taught ourselves were based on this one. And we continued, "without complaint" (another subtle swipe at our complaints about learning the Course), until a whole world was built, a world that was just a vast intermeshing web of these lessons.

If we did all that, surely we can learn *A Course in Miracles*!

> 5. Learning is an ability you made and gave yourself. It was <u>not</u> made to do the Will of God, but to uphold a wish that it <u>could</u> be opposed, and that a will <u>apart</u> from it was yet more real than it. And this has learning sought to demonstrate, and you <u>have</u> learned what it was made to teach. Now does your ancient overlearning stand implacable before the Voice of truth, and teach you that Its lessons are not true; too hard to learn, too difficult to see, and too opposed to what is <u>really</u> true. Yet you <u>will</u> learn them, for their learning is the <u>only</u> purpose for your learning skill the Holy Spirit sees in all the world. His simple lessons in forgiveness have a power mightier than yours, because they call from God and from your Self to you.

We invented learning in order to teach ourselves that God's Will could be opposed and then forgotten, replaced by a new will (the ego's) that was more powerful than it. And it worked—we learned that. Now the Holy Spirit comes and softly knocks on a door we thought we had closed forever. He shows up in the form of this blue book and says, "God's Will is still the only real will." Our natural response is, "I beg your pardon?"

What this book says can seem so pie in the sky, like such a leap of faith. Yet despite our skepticism, something stirs in us, some inexplicable attraction, which grows into an irrevocable determination. For the fact remains that the only true use of our learning skill is to learn the lessons presented in this course. And the fact remains that the Will these lessons represent is still far stronger than the will with which we identify. Therefore, no matter how much we dilly-dally and stall, we *will* learn these lessons.

> 6. Is this a <u>little</u> Voice, so small and still It cannot rise above the senseless noise of sounds that have no meaning? God willed not His

Son forget Him. And the power of His Will is in the Voice That speaks for Him. Which lesson will you learn? What outcome is inevitable, sure as God, and far beyond all doubt and question? <u>Can</u> it be your little learning, strange in outcome and incredible in difficulty will withstand the simple lessons being taught to you in every moment of each day, since time began and learning had been made?

The Holy Spirit, of course, is not just speaking to us through this blue book. He has been whispering in our ear every second since time began. He has been sending us lessons in every situation, potential holy encounters in every interaction. And despite conventional images of Him, He is no "small voice." He is the Voice for God Himself, Who wills that His Son not forget Him.

So the mighty Voice of God Himself is speaking to us every minute, teaching us an incredibly simple lesson. Can our tiny, senseless, incredibly difficult learning withstand all of this? Whom do we think we're kidding?

> 7. The lessons to be learned are only two. Each has its outcome in a different world. And each world follows surely from its source. The certain outcome of the lesson that God's Son is guilty is the world you see. It <u>is</u> a world of terror and despair. Nor <u>is</u> there hope of happiness in it. There <u>is</u> no plan for safety you can make that ever will succeed. There <u>is</u> no joy that you can seek for here and hope to find. Yet this is <u>not</u> the only outcome which your learning can produce. However much you may have overlearned your chosen task, the lesson that reflects the Love of God is stronger still. And you <u>will</u> learn God's Son is innocent, and see <u>another</u> world.

There are only two lessons to learn: God's Son is *guilty* or God's Son is *guiltless*. Each lesson is the foundation for an entire world. You can guess which lesson our current world is founded on. Do you find these lines to be an accurate description of this world?

It *is* a world of terror and despair.
Nor *is* there hope of happiness in it.
There *is* no plan for safety you can make that ever will succeed.
There *is* no joy that you can seek for here and hope to find.
(Urtext version)

253

Why is a world like this the only outcome of the lesson "God's Son is guilty"? The answer is simple: *This is the only world the guilty deserve.*

Yet even though we have overlearned this miserable world, the lesson that God's Son is guiltless is actually stronger. In the end, we will learn it, for it reflects our real will. It's what we really want.

> 8. The outcome of the lesson that God's Son is guiltless is a world in which there is no fear, and everything is lit with hope and sparkles with a gentle friendliness. Nothing but calls to you in soft appeal to be your friend, and let it join with you. And never does a call remain unheard, misunderstood, nor left unanswered in the selfsame tongue in which the call was made. And you will understand it was <u>this</u> call that everyone and everything within the world has <u>always</u> made, but <u>you</u> had not perceived it as it was. And now you see <u>you</u> were mistaken. You had been deceived by forms the call was hidden in. And so you did not hear it, and had lost a friend who <u>always</u> wanted to be part of you. The soft eternal calling of each part of God's creation to the whole is heard throughout the world [that] this second lesson ["God's Son is guiltless"] brings.

Application: This is such a poignant paragraph. Let's try to make it real to ourselves.

Imagine a world in which there is no fear, a world in which everything is lit with hope, in which everything and everyone sparkles with a gentle friendliness.

In this world, everyone calls to you in soft appeal to be your friend, and to let him or her join with you.

And you hear every call, and understand it, and answer it in the same language in which the call was made.

Now you understand it was this call that everyone and everything has always made, but you had not perceived it as it was.

You had been deceived by the harsh and inconsiderate forms the call was hidden in, and so you did not hear it, and had lost a friend who always wanted to be part of you.

(Does someone come to mind?)

But now the soft, eternal calling of each part of God's creation to the whole is heard by you at last.

Indeed, it is heard throughout the world that the second lesson brings, the lesson that God's Son is guiltless.

9. There is no living thing that does not share the universal Will that it be whole, and that you do not leave its call unheard. Without your answer is it left to die, as it is saved from death when you have heard its calling as the ancient call to life, and understood that it is but your own. The Christ in you remembers God with all the certainty with which He knows His Love. But <u>only</u> if His Son is innocent can He <u>be</u> Love. For God were fear indeed if he whom He created innocent could be a slave to guilt. God's perfect Son remembers his creation. But in guilt he has forgotten what he really is.

10. The fear of God results as surely from the lesson that His Son is guilty as God's Love must be remembered when he learns his innocence. For hate must father fear, and look upon its father as itself.

Application: Think of someone whom you have been holding at arm's length, perhaps because this person has, in your eyes, mistreated you. Then say,

You are calling to me in soft appeal to be my friend.
Your calling is the ancient call to life.
How can I leave your call unanswered when my answer saves you from death?
How can I leave it unanswered when I understand that your call is but my own?

The paragraph ends by making the point that only if God's Son is guiltless can God be Love. Why? Because if God would let His Own Son be a slave to guilt, how much can we really trust Him? Actually, paragraph 10 contains a more developed answer (which I think I understand accurately): We think we are guilty because we hate. Our hate then fathers fear (of punishment). Then we then project both hate and fear onto God; we see a hateful God Who is the source of our fear.

How wrong are you who fail to hear the call that echoes past each seeming call to death, that sings behind each murderous attack and pleads that love restore the dying world. You do not understand Who calls to you beyond each form of hate; each call to war. Yet you will recognize Him as you give Him answer in the language that He calls. He will appear [see 30.VIII.5:9] when you have answered Him, and you will know in Him that God is Love.

We look out and see a world of murderous attacks, a world in which people are just asking for it—for different kinds of punishment, different forms of death. How wrong are we to see this! How wrong are we when we fail to hear the lovely call that constantly sings beneath those superficial calls to war. It is the call to be our friend. It is the call "that love restore the dying world." This call is ceaselessly singing from every living creature all over the world. The world is dying because this call is going unanswered. Little do we realize that the One really calling to us is Christ, the guiltless Son of God Himself. But when we at last hear a brother's true call and answer it, then Christ will appear to us in all His guiltlessness. And we will know in Him that God is Love.

11. What is temptation but a wish [the same phrase we saw in 30.VIII.3:1] to make the wrong decision on what you would learn, and have an outcome that you do not want? It is the <u>recognition</u> that it [the outcome you have learned] is a state of mind <u>unwanted</u> that becomes the means whereby the choice is reassessed; another outcome seen to be preferred. You are deceived if you believe you want disaster and disunity and pain. Hear not the call for this within yourself. But listen, rather, to the deeper call beyond it that appeals for peace and joy. And all the world will <u>give</u> you joy and peace. For as you hear, you answer. And behold! Your answer is the proof of what you learned. Its outcome is the world you look upon.

Now the theme of temptation gets woven into the discussion. The temptation to value certain illusions is really just a wish to learn the wrong lesson, the one we don't want (God's Son is guilty). However, once we obtain the outcome of this lesson—a world of "disaster and disunity and pain," we can look at that and say, "I *must* have learned the wrong lesson."

Therefore, let us not follow the call of our false will, the will that pulls us in the direction of learning the wrong lesson. Let us instead hearken to the call of our true will, our will for peace and joy. For the call we listen to within ourselves will determine the call we hear in our brother. If we listen to our own call for peace and joy, that is the call we will hear in him. And when we hear it in everyone, then we will be living in the second world, the real world.

> 12. Let us be still an instant, and forget all things we ever learned, all thoughts we had, and every preconception that we hold of what things mean and what their purpose is. Let us remember not our own ideas of what the world is for. We do not know. Let every image held of everyone be loosened from our minds and swept away.
> 13. Be innocent of judgment, unaware of any thoughts of evil or of good that ever crossed your mind of anyone. Now do you know him not. But you <u>are</u> free to learn of him, and learn of him anew. Now is he born again to you, and you are born again to him, <u>without</u> the past that sentenced him to die, and you with him. Now is he free to live as you are free, because an ancient learning passed away, and left a place for truth to be reborn.

These are such beautiful paragraphs. I think they are some of the first sentences I heard from *A Course in Miracles*. To really appreciate them, however, we need to see them in the context of the whole section. Since before time began, we have been teaching ourselves an ancient lesson, the lesson that God's Son is guilty. That lesson has been the dark lens, the distorted filter, through which we experience everything. Our brother says, "Can we be friends?" but through the filter of this lesson we hear him say, "I declare war on you!" We look at our holy brother, but through our warped lens we see the devil formerly known as God's Son. What we see of him and what we hear of him leave room for only one conclusion: He deserves to die. We then act accordingly, and so goes the world.

Little do we realize that we are not seeing the world as it is. We are merely looking at that ancient lesson we taught ourselves in the mirror. It is high time that we unlearn that lesson. It is time to learn a new lesson. Therefore, "Let us be still an instant, and forget all things we ever learned…"

II. Walking with Christ
Commentary by Greg Mackie

1. An ancient lesson ["God's Son is guilty"—see T-31.I.7:4 and T-31.I.4:6] is not overcome by the <u>opposing</u> of the new and old. It is not <u>vanquished</u> that the truth be known, nor fought against to <u>lose</u> to truth's appeal. There is no battle that must be prepared; no time to be expended, and no plans that need be laid for bringing in the new. There *is* an ancient battle being waged <u>against</u> the truth, but truth does not respond. Who <u>could</u> be hurt in such a war, unless he hurts himself? He <u>has</u> no enemy in truth. And <u>can</u> he be assailed by dreams?

The last two paragraphs of the previous section said that the way to let go of our "ancient learning" (T-31.I.13:5) is to be still an instant and let go of all the thoughts that make up that ancient learning. That is what we must do instead of fighting against it. Truth does not fight against illusions at all; it doesn't even respond to the furious battle illusions are waging against *it*. As long as we fight on the side of illusions, we will hurt ourselves as our weapons aimed against truth backfire on us. But if we will simply rise above the battleground, we will recognize that neither side of this war can hurt us. Illusions *can't* hurt us because they are not real, and truth *won't* hurt us because it is not our enemy.

2. Let us review again what seems to stand <u>between</u> you and the truth of what you are. For there are steps in its relinquishment. The first is a decision that <u>you</u> make. But afterward, the truth is <u>given</u> you. You would <u>establish</u> truth. And by your wish you set two choices to be made, each time you think you must decide on anything. <u>Neither</u> is true. Nor <u>are</u> they different. Yet must we see them both, before you can look <u>past</u> them to the <u>one</u> alternative that *is* a different choice. But not in dreams you made, that this might be <u>obscured</u> to you.

The previous section spoke of what stands between us and the truth: the ancient lesson that God's Son is guilty. To let go of that ancient lesson, there are two steps: 1) we decide to let it go, and then 2) truth is given us. Before we can make the decision in step 1, though, we must look honestly at what we've done to establish and maintain that ancient lesson. First, we decided that we wanted to establish truth for ourselves. This led us to establish two illusory alternatives for each decision we make. We established them to obscure the *real* alternative, the choice that will enable us to fulfill step 1 and let go of our ancient lesson. We will begin looking at these illusory alternatives in the next paragraph.

> 3. What you would choose between is not a choice and gives but the illusion it is free, for it will have one outcome either way. Thus is it really not a choice at all. The leader and the follower emerge as separate roles, each seeming to possess advantages you would not want to lose. So in their fusion there appears to be the hope of satisfaction and of peace. You see yourself divided into both these roles, forever split between the two. And every friend or enemy becomes a means to help you save yourself from this.

Now we are given the two illusory alternatives, which are not truly alternatives because they both produce the same result. The illusory alternatives, which I suspect no one would have guessed, are *leader* and *follower*. Each of these roles seems to have its benefits, so we want to hold on to both of them. This makes us feel split between them, a split that we use other people to "resolve" (as the next paragraph will explain).

Think about your own life: Are there not some times and situations where you desire the role of leader, and others where you prefer the role of follower? Each does seem to have its advantages. As leader, we get to be in control. We get the credit when things go well. We get admiration, prestige, and respect. As follower, we are relieved of the pressure and responsibility of being in control. We don't get the blame when things go poorly—in fact, *we* can blame the leader when they do. We get to be guided and taken care of by the leader, and can relax in the comfortable anonymity of just being a hired hand.

Note: This section is not saying that there is anything inherently wrong with the roles of leader and follower. In fact, elsewhere the Course smiles on these roles. For instance:

> *My brothers all can follow in the way I lead them. Yet I merely follow in the way to You, as You direct me and would have me go.* (W-pII.324.1:6-7)

> Let us together follow in the way that truth points out to us. And let us be the leaders of our many brothers who are seeking for the way, but find it not. (W.Fl.In.2:5-6)

In these cases, the roles of leader and follower are chosen by the Holy Spirit for His purpose. The leader is meant to follow Him, the roles of leader and follower are temporary, and the inherent equality of leader and follower is assumed. The present section is speaking of *our* version of leading and following, in which we choose the roles ourselves for the ego's purpose. This inevitably promotes inequality and separateness.

> 4. Perhaps you call it love. Perhaps you think that it is murder justified at last. You hate the one you gave the leader's role when <u>you</u> would have it, and you hate as well his <u>not</u> assuming it at times you want to let the follower in you arise, and give away the role of leadership. And this is what you made your brother <u>for</u>, and learned to think that this his purpose <u>is</u>. Unless he serves it, he has not fulfilled the function that was given him by you. And thus he merits death, because he has no purpose and no usefulness to you.

Here's how we use others to "resolve" our split between the roles of leader and follower: We give them the purpose of taking the role we don't currently want. When another person fulfills this purpose, we "love" her for it. But this role-playing game inevitably turns into "murder justified at last," for two reasons. First, the person may not decide to take the role we want her to take. Second, even if she does take it, she's bound to not fulfill that role to our satisfaction. Either way, she's not fulfilling the function we assigned her, so we (apparently) have reason to hate her. She's guilty, and thus she merits death.

> 5. And what of him? What does he want of <u>you</u>? What <u>could</u> he want, but what you want of him? Herein is life as easily as death, for what you choose you choose as well for him. Two calls you make to him, as he to you. Between these two *is* choice, because from them there <u>is</u> a different outcome. If he be the leader or the follower to you it matters not, for you have chosen death. But if he calls for death or calls for life, for hate or for forgiveness and for help, is <u>not</u> the same in outcome. Hear the one, and you are separate from him and are lost. But hear the other, and you join with him and in your answer is salvation found. The

voice you hear in him is but your own. What does he ask you for? And listen well! For he is asking what will come to you, because you see an image of yourself and hear your voice requesting what you want.

The other person is playing the same role-playing game we are, trying to assign us the role of leader or follower and hating us when we don't do what she wants. Both of us are thus reinforcing the lesson that God's Son is guilty and calling for death. But each of us is also making a deeper call. This is the call for the real alternative to the death that inevitably results from the game of "follow the leader or lead the follower": the call for *life*—the call for forgiveness and help instead of hatred and death. Which call will we choose to hear in the other person? Which alternative do we ourselves call for? These two questions are the same. And when we choose to hear the call for life in the other, our loving answer to that call joins us together and brings salvation to both of us.

6. Before you answer, pause to think of this:

> *The answer that I give my brother is what I am asking for. And what I learn of him is what I learn about myself.*

Then let us wait an instant and be still, forgetting everything we thought we heard; remembering how much we do not know. This brother neither leads nor follows us, but walks beside us on the selfsame road. He is like us, as near or far away from what we want as we will let him be. We make no gains he does not make with us, and we fall back if he does not advance. Take not his hand in anger but in love, for in his progress do you count your own. And we go separately along the way unless you keep him safely by your side.

The real alternative to the musical-chairs game of leading and following is the recognition that our brother walks neither ahead or behind "but walks beside us on the selfsame road." In truth, there *is* no leader and follower. The assumption behind the leader-follower game is that we do not have common interests: Each of us thinks that we gain at the other's expense when we cajole the other into fulfilling the role we assign. But hearing the call for life enables us to see that we have common interests, so we gain or lose together.

Application: Think of someone in your life that you've assigned the role of leader or follower—in particular, someone with whom you are angry for either not taking the role you wanted him to take, or for not fulfilling the role you gave him to your satisfaction.

Realize that your anger at him means that you are hearing his call for death, but that you could just as easily hear his call for life. What does he ask you for? Does he ask for death or for life? Before you answer, repeat these lines and really let them sink in:

> *The answer that I give [name] is what I am asking for. And what I learn of [name] is what I learn about myself.*

Now, wait an instant and be still, forgetting everything you thought you heard before, remembering how much you do not know. In stillness, let the answer be given you.

> 7. <u>Because</u> he is your equal in God's Love, <u>you</u> will be saved from all appearances and answer to the Christ Who calls to you. Be still and listen. Think not ancient thoughts. Forget the dismal lessons that you learned about this Son of God who calls to you. Christ calls to all with <u>equal</u> tenderness, seeing no leaders and no followers, and hearing but <u>one</u> answer to them all. Because He hears one Voice, He cannot hear a <u>different</u> answer from the one He gave when God appointed Him His only Son.

The previous section told us that it is Christ who calls for life through our brother (see T-31.I.10:4). As we listen to our brother's call, we are to set aside "ancient thoughts": the ancient lesson that God's Son is guilty, our brother's call for death. Instead, we are to hear in him Christ's call for life, and answer that call with the same answer Christ gave God when He (Christ) was created.

What is this answer? Recall what God said when He created Christ: "You are beloved of Me and I of you forever. Be you perfect as Myself, for you can never be apart from Me" (T-28.VI.6:4-5). Christ's answer to this was "I will," and in this answer was He born (T-28.VI.6:6). Our answer to the Christ in our brother is an acknowledgment of his perfection and God's eternal Love for him. And because we are equally beloved of God, our answer to Christ's call in our brother saves us as well.

8. Be very still an instant. Come without all thought of what you ever learned before, and put aside all images you made. The old will fall away before the new without your opposition or intent. There will be no attack upon the things you thought were precious and in need of care. There will be no assault upon your wish to hear a call that never has been made. Nothing will hurt you in this holy place, to which you come to listen silently and learn the truth of what you really want. No more than this will you be asked to learn. But as you hear it, you will understand you need but come away <u>without</u> the thoughts you did not want, and that were <u>never</u> true.

"Be very still an instant." This is the third time in recent paragraphs that we've been given this injunction (the others are T-31.I.12:1 and the sixth paragraph of this section). This paragraph loops back to the first two paragraphs. The second paragraph invited us to let go of our ancient lesson (that God's Son is guilty), so truth could be given us. The first paragraph emphasized that this ancient lesson is not overcome through a battle between the old and the new, between illusions and the truth. There will be no attack on our desire to hear an illusory call for death, or on anything we hold dear. Rather, we listen silently to the Christ in our brother and let the truth of what we really want—the call for life and everything that comes with it—be given us.

9. Forgive your brother <u>all</u> appearances, that are but ancient lessons you have taught yourself about the sinfulness in you. Hear but his call for mercy and release from all the fearful images he holds of what <u>he</u> is and of what <u>you</u> must be. He is afraid to walk with you, and thinks perhaps a bit behind, a bit ahead would be a safer place for him to be. Can <u>you</u> make progress if you think the same, advancing only when he would step back, and falling back when he would go ahead? For so do you forget the journey's goal, which is but to decide to walk <u>with</u> him, so neither leads nor follows. Thus it is a way you go together, <u>not</u> alone. And in <u>this</u> choice is learning's outcome changed, for Christ has been reborn to <u>both</u> of you.

As long as we're both playing the game of leading and following, there's really no hope. As long as each of us advances when the other steps back and steps back when the other advances, we're engaged in a silly dance and not moving forward at all. Each of us will see the other as a sinner whose many sins reflect our own sinfulness—the ancient lesson that God's Son is guilty. But when we forgive our brother *all* appearances—not just the "sins" we see in him, but the very idea that he is a body with particular character traits—the dance will be over as we realize that the journey's goal is to walk *together*. Once we decide to walk together, Christ is reborn to both of us.

Application: As you did in the last application, think of someone in your life that you've assigned the role of leader or follower, someone whom you're angry with for not fulfilling the role you've assigned her. Say these words to this person:

> *[Name], I forgive you **all** appearances I see in you, for they are but ancient lessons of guilt that I have taught myself about the sinfulness in **me**.*
> *I hear your call for mercy and release from all the fearful images you hold of what you are and what I must be.*
> *Let us no longer trade the roles of leader and follower.*
> *Let us instead walk together, so neither leads nor follows.*
> *In this choice all ancient lessons of guilt will pass away, for in this choice is Christ reborn to **both** of us.*

10. An instant spent without your old ideas of who your great companion is and what he should be asking for, will be enough to let this happen. And you will perceive his purpose is the same as yours. He asks for what you want, and needs the same as you. It takes, perhaps, a different form in him, but it is not the form you answer to. He asks and you receive, for you have come with but one purpose; that you [Ur: both may] learn you love your brother [Ur: each other] with a brother's love. And as a brother, must his Father be the same as yours, as he is like yourself in truth.

What a beautiful paragraph! Normally we think our brother should be asking whether he is to be the leader or the follower (and of course, we already have an answer in mind for him). We thus see him as someone with a different purpose and different needs, someone fundamentally separate from us whose job is to fulfill the role we want him to fulfill. We play the leader-follower game with him, and since this game is what teaches us the ancient lesson of guilt, all we're hearing in our brother is his call for death.

But if we set aside that ancient lesson for just an instant, *everything* changes. We now see our "great companion" in a whole new way. We see that the two of us actually have the same purpose and the same needs. Whatever form our brother's asking takes—even if he's asking *us* to be the leader or the follower—underneath that call for death is the call for life, the purpose both of us truly came for. What a beautiful purpose it is: "that you both may learn you love each other with a brother's love" (Urtext version). We have come to learn simply that we are both part of the loving family of God.

> 11. Together is your joint inheritance remembered and accepted by you both. Alone it is denied to both of you. Is it not clear that while you still insist on leading or on following, you think you walk alone, with no one by your side? This is the road to nowhere, for the light cannot be given while you walk alone, and so you cannot <u>see</u> which way you go. And thus [Ur: so] there <u>is</u> confusion, and a sense of endless doubting as you stagger back and forward in the darkness and alone. Yet these are but appearances of what the journey is, and how it must be made. For next to you is One Who holds the light before you, so that every step is made in certainty and sureness of the road. A blindfold can indeed obscure your sight, but cannot make the way itself grow dark. And He Who travels with you *has* the light.

As long as we insist on leading or following, we will seem to be walking alone. This is obvious if you simply bring to mind a mental image of leading and following—the two people are not next to each other. The way of leading or following, we are told, is also a way of darkness. If we follow it, we will go groping along a dark path, full of doubt and confusion, switching leader and follower roles as we stagger around getting nowhere. Isn't this what life so often feels like: lurching about in confusion and doubt and seemingly making little progress?

Yet this is only what the journey *seems* to be. In truth, our brother stands beside us, and in him is the Christ, who lights the path before us and makes it clear. This is true *right now*; the only reason we don't see it now is that we've put on the blindfold of that ancient lesson of guilt. If we will simply be still an instant and take that blindfold off, we will see Who travels with us and journey together confidently on the brightly lit path to God.

III. The Self-Accused
Commentary by Robert Perry

> 1. Only the self-accused condemn. As you prepare to make a choice that will result in <u>different</u> outcomes, there is first one thing that must be overlearned. It must become a habit of response so typical of everything you do that it becomes your <u>first</u> response to all temptation, and to every situation that occurs. Learn this, and learn it well, for it is here delay of happiness is shortened by a span of time you cannot realize. You <u>never</u> hate your brother for <u>his</u> sins, but <u>only</u> for your own. Whatever form his sins appear to take, it but obscures the fact that you believe them to be yours, and <u>therefore</u> meriting a "just" attack.

This is a remarkable paragraph. As we prepare to make, not one of the ego's pseudo-choices (like the choice between leader or follower; see Section II), but a real choice, one that will result in different outcomes, there is one thing we need to learn. Actually, we need to *overlearn* it (just as we have overlearned the ego's thought system; see Section I). This means that we need to continue to study and practice it even after we have attained proficiency. We need to overlearn it to the point where it becomes an unconscious habit, a knee-jerk response to every upset and indeed to every situation that occurs. If we can just overlearn this *one* thing, we will bring closer our attainment of bliss by a span of time that we cannot even comprehend.

By this point, we are on the edge of our seat, wondering what this "one thing" is. Finally, Jesus tells us: "You *never* hate your brother for *his* sins, but *only* for your own" (Urtext version). In other words, our condemnation of another is really just self-accusation dressed up as something elseAre we prepared to believe this? To learn it? To *overlearn* it? And what would be the outcome if we did? Wouldn't the outcome be that we never condemned another living person again?

Application: Think of a number of different people, and with each one get in touch with the sinfulness you see in that person, and then say,

I never hate [name] for his [or her] sins, but only for my own.

Try to make a silent vow to carry this thought with you until you have made applying it to everything an automatic reflex.

> 2. Why should his sins <u>be</u> sins, if you did not believe they could not be forgiven in you? Why are they real in him, if you did not believe that they are <u>your</u> reality? And why do you attack them everywhere except you hate yourself? Are *you* a sin? You answer "yes" <u>whenever</u> you attack, for <u>by</u> attack do you assert that you are guilty, and must give [attack] as you deserve [attack]. And what <u>can</u> you deserve but what you are? If you did not believe that you <u>deserved</u> attack, it never would occur to you to <u>give</u> attack to anyone at all. Why should you? What would be the gain to you? What could the outcome be that you would <u>want</u>? And how <u>could</u> murder bring you benefit?

The first three sentences (all questions) are crucial, for they provide the logic behind the idea that the sins we condemn in our brother are really our own. Here is my attempt to unpack them.

- I see my brother's reality through the lens of how I see my own reality.
- I see my reality as sinful.
- Therefore, I see my brother's reality as sinful.

In other words, it is only my perception of myself as sinful that makes me see him as sinful. Put differently, it is only my sins that make his sins appear to *be* sins. Thus, the sinfulness in his sins is really my own sinfulness (or more accurately, my own *perceived* sinfulness). As an analogy, imagine that you are wearing red-tinted glasses. Through them, you look at another and say, "What a terrible sunburn he has." Are you seeing his sunburn, or are you seeing your own red lenses? The same with the sin we see in our brother. Are we seeing his sinfulness, or are we seeing the lens of our own sins?

There is a second line of reasoning in the paragraph. Here is my understanding of it. Just as you *see* another according to how you see yourself, so you *give* to another according to how you see yourself—how you see what you are and what you deserve. Thus, just as you only see another as *sinful* when you think you are sinful, so you only give *attack*

267

to him when you think you deserve attack (because of your attacking nature). In other words, just as you see your brother as if he is yourself, so you actually *treat* him as if he is yourself. On some unconscious level, then, as you look at him, you are looking at yourself. As you attack him, you are attacking yourself.

The reason for this, hinted at by later paragraphs, is that we want to see a world that will *confirm our self-perception*. A world full of innocent people wouldn't confirm our perception of ourselves as a sinner. Only a world full of sinners would confirm that self-perception.

> 3. Sins are in bodies. They are not perceived in minds. They are not seen as purposes, but <u>actions</u>. Bodies act, and minds do not. And therefore must the body be at fault for what it does. It is not seen to be a passive thing, obeying your commands, and doing nothing of itself at all. If you are sin you *are* a body, for the mind acts not. And purpose must be in the body, <u>not</u> the mind. The body must act on its own, and motivate itself. If you are sin you lock the mind <u>within</u> the body, and you give its purpose to its prison house, which acts <u>instead</u> of it. A jailer does not follow orders, but <u>enforces</u> orders on the prisoner.

In the end, a sin, to be a sin, must be carried out. It must be acted out in the world. For something can only be a sin if it does real damage. And in our eyes, the only way to do real damage is to act something out bodily. So the body is what carries out sin. But we also see it as what *motivates* sin. The body's needs, urges, and instincts appear to be the driving force behind its destructive behaviors. Jesus then uses this idea to add one more link onto his chain of logic. Here is the whole chain:

- If you see and attack sin in your brother, then you believe that you *are* sin.
- The body is what does sin; it is what motivates and carries out sin. The body is the author of sin.
- If you are sin, the body must be the author of *you*.

Your mind, then, must be a powerless prisoner, cooped up inside your sinning body. Your mind must be simply along for the ride as the body rampages through the countryside, destroying everything in its path. The body does the deed, while you stand helplessly by, accumulating the guilt.

4. Yet is the *body* prisoner, and <u>not</u> the mind. The body thinks no thoughts. It has no power to learn, to pardon, nor enslave. It gives no orders that the mind need serve, nor sets conditions that it must obey. It holds in prison but the willing mind that would abide in it. It sickens at the bidding of the mind that would become its prisoner. And it grows old and dies, because that mind is sick within <u>itself</u>. Learning is all that causes change. And so the body, where no learning <u>can</u> occur, could never change unless the mind <u>preferred</u> the body change in its appearances, to suit the purpose given by the mind. For mind <u>can</u> learn, and there is <u>all</u> change made.

The body is just a puppet of the mind. It has no power to imprison the mind; it is the *mind's* prisoner. It acts out exactly what the mind tells it to, for it has no will of its own. It gets sick and grows old and dies because the mind lays its own sickness onto the body. How could the body change at all on its own? For only learning brings change and the body can't learn.

Application: Say to yourself,

I am not a prisoner of my body.
My body is my puppet.
It does only what I tell it to.
It changes only because I order it to.
It is merely a figure in the dream of my mind.

5. The mind that thinks it is a sin has but <u>one</u> purpose; that the body be the source of sin, to <u>keep</u> it [the mind] in the prison house [the body] it [the mind] chose and guards and holds [uses to hold] itself [the mind] at bay, a sleeping prisoner to the snarling dogs of hate and evil, sickness and attack; of pain and age, of grief and suffering [which are all found in the body]. Here [in this prison] are the thoughts of sacrifice preserved, for here guilt rules, and orders that the world be like itself; a place where nothing can find mercy, nor survive the ravages of fear except in murder and in death. For here [in this prison] are you made sin, and sin cannot abide the joyous and the free, for they are enemies which sin must kill. In death is sin preserved, and those who think that they are sin <u>must</u> die for what they think they are.

We who believe that we are sin want only one thing: "that the body be the source of sin." You probably assume that this is because we want to displace the sin onto the body, so that our mind feels more innocent. But that's not the explanation Jesus gives here. The reason we want the body to be the source of sin is that then we are a *prisoner* of sin. There's nothing we can do about it. We are powerless to stop it. This reminds me of an awful 80s movie, *The Hand*, where Michael Caine plays a cartoonist who loses his hand in an auto accident. The hand is never found but turns up later, acting on its own, killing all the people that Caine is angry at, and making *Caine* appear to be the murderer. Have you ever felt that way about your body?

In our tiny prison of meat, "guilt rules," and orders that the world be every bit as miserable as we are, for its freedom would undermine our imprisonment. Here is the rationale for the ideas in paragraph 2. This says that we see the world through the lens of our own self-perception because we want the world we see to *reinforce* our self-perception.

> 6. Let us be glad that you <u>will</u> see what you believe, and that it <u>has</u> been given you to <u>change</u> what you believe. The body will but follow. It can <u>never</u> lead you where you would not be. <u>It</u> does not guard your sleep, nor interfere with your awakening. Release your body from imprisonment, and you will see no one as prisoner to what you have escaped. You will not <u>want</u> to hold in guilt your chosen enemies, nor keep in chains, to the illusion of a changing love, the ones you think are friends.
> 7. The innocent release in gratitude for <u>their</u> release. And what they see upholds their freedom <u>from</u> imprisonment and death. Open your mind to change, and there will be no ancient penalty exacted from your brother or yourself. For God has said there *is* no sacrifice that can be asked; there *is* no sacrifice that can be made.

It may seem like a real downer that once we believe in our own sinfulness, we will see the world through its lens. But instead, let us be glad! For by seeing our sinfulness in the world, we can realize we believe in it, and then we can change our belief in it. At this point, a little voice in our head will say, "But you aren't free to change your belief in your sinfulness. The *body* is the source of sin. It will keep on sinning no matter what you believe." We must refuse to listen to this voice. The fact is that the body will go wherever we tell it to go. If we want to go to God, the body will say, "Fine, when do we start?"

And when we finally release the body from its assignment of playing the role of our jail, we will see everyone as free of that jail. Remember, as we see our own reality, so will we see theirs. If we are free, we will see everyone as free. Thus we will stop chaining our enemies to guilt and our friends to our fantasies of love. We will be so grateful to be liberated that we will liberate everyone. We will then look out on a world that confirms that we are *free*, rather than confirming that we are prisoner.

IV. The Real Alternative
Commentary by Robert Perry

1. There is a tendency to think the world can offer consolation and escape from problems that its <u>purpose</u> is to keep. Why should this be? Because it is a place where choice among illusions seems to be the <u>only</u> choice. And <u>you</u> are [you seem to be] in control of outcomes of your choosing. Thus you think, within the narrow band from birth to death, a little time is given you to use for you alone; a time when everyone conflicts with you, but you can choose which road will lead you out of conflict, and <u>away</u> from difficulties that concern you not. Yet they *are* your concern. How, then, can you escape from them by leaving them behind? What <u>must</u> go with you, you will take with you whatever road you choose to walk along.

This paragraph accurately describes our lives. We are beset with problems, difficulties, and conflict, but we have a choice (or so we think). If we are clever, gutsy, and a bit lucky, we can choose a road which will lead us away from all this. People will still have their problems. The people with whom we competed will still be trying to grab their slice of the pie. But it won't be our concern anymore. We will be sipping our wine and enjoying the view.

Sounds about right, doesn't it? Yet, as we might expect, Jesus explodes this conventional perspective on life. First, he says, the world was actually made to keep these problems that we are trying to escape. Second, we are only choosing between different illusions (this will be expanded on later). Third, the difficulties we are trying to escape are really rooted inside of us, and thus we will take them with us wherever we go. These three add up to a single idea: No matter what we choose, no matter where we go, the problems will be there.

2. Real choice is no illusion. But the world has none to offer. <u>All</u> its roads but lead to disappointment, nothingness and death. There <u>is</u> no choice in its alternatives. Seek not <u>escape</u> from problems here. The world was made that problems could not *be* escaped. Be not deceived by all the different names its roads are given. They have but one end.

And each is but the means to <u>gain</u> that end, for it is here that all its roads will lead, however differently they seem to start; however differently they seem to go. Their end is certain, for there is no choice among them. All of them will lead to death. On some you travel gaily for a while, before the bleakness enters. And on some the thorns are felt at once. The choice is not <u>what</u> will the ending be, but <u>when</u> it comes.

The image of a road is central to this section, so it might help to clarify that Jesus is using it as a metaphor for a *direction to take in life*. We often use it in the same way. We speak of having "been down that road before."

The picture Jesus paints here is exceedingly bleak. Imagine that you stand at a crossroads, with ten roads radiating out from it. One of those signposts is there that has a sign for each road, pointing in that road's direction. You look down each one of the roads. The first one you look down looks dark, twisted, rocky, and thorny. Forget that, you think. You keep looking down the various roads, until you find one that looks perfect. It is smooth and gently winding. It passes through a beautiful landscape with trees, birds, and flowers. You even like the name of it: "Happy Trails." So you choose that one. You set off down it, whistling a happy tune. Unfortunately, however, you failed to notice something crucial on the signpost. In small letters underneath the name of Happy Trails, it said, "Death: 41 miles." Indeed, if you had looked closer at the signs, you would have seen a similar number under the name of every single road. The only thing that differed was the distance until death was reached.

This is Jesus' image for life in this world, and for what we call the power of choice.

3. There <u>is</u> no choice where every end is sure. Perhaps you would prefer to try them all, before you <u>really</u> learn they are but one. The roads this world can offer seem to be quite large in number, but the time must come when everyone begins to see how like they are to one another. Men have died [at their own hand] on seeing this, because they saw no way <u>except</u> the pathways offered by the world. And learning <u>they</u> led nowhere, lost their hope. And yet this was the time they <u>could</u> have learned their greatest lesson. All must reach this point, and go <u>beyond</u> it. It is true indeed there is no choice at all within the world. But this is <u>not</u> the lesson [the "greatest lesson" just referred to] in itself. The lesson has a <u>purpose</u>, and in <u>this</u> you come to understand what it is <u>for</u>.

We start out in life thinking we have all these exciting choices. We can go down this road or that one or that one. It's like standing in front of four hundred flavors of ice cream. But then we start trying the different roads, and each one ends unexpectedly in pain and heartache—in some form of death. The eternal optimists among us think, "Ah, but there are *more* to try." In this case, however, the optimists are in abject denial. Others figure the game out more quickly. They think, "If all these roads lead to death, why not just cut to the chase and end it all?" That is the meaning of Jesus' poignant line, "Men have died on seeing this."

It is a glimpse into the soul of the Course that Jesus actually has praise for these proponents of ultimate despair. He bemoans their suicide, but he also says, "And yet this was the time they *could* have learned their greatest lesson" (Urtext version). In fact, he says that we *all* need to reach the point they reached! But we also need to go beyond it, just as they could have. For learning that all roads in this world lead to death is just the first part of that "greatest lesson" he referred to earlier.

Recently, I read something in *What Is Enlightenment?* magazine ("Ripples on the Surface of Being," September – December 2006) that was eerily reminiscent of Jesus' rather startling claim here. Author Carter Phipps was researching the question "What does it mean to be in the world but not of it?" while also reading Eckhart Tolle's *The Power of Now*. He said,

> I was particularly struck by the opening account of his [Tolle's] awakening. Not only was it an authentic description of a powerful enlightenment, but it occurred in a very unusual psychological context. "Until my thirtieth year," Tolle writes, "I lived in a state of almost continuous anxiety interspersed by periods of suicidal depression." Now that hardly sounds like the opening line of a spiritual fairy tale, but strangely enough, it was Tolle's depression and his decision one fateful night that he simply could no longer "live with himself" that was the crucial catalyst for his subsequent enlightenment. Unafraid of dying, close to suicide, Tolle was ready to cash in his chips and walk away from this world altogether, but somehow he managed instead to walk right into the arms of a profound spiritual realization.
>
> What did it mean, I wondered, for a spiritual breakthrough to be predicated on a suicidal state of mind? How would it affect one's subsequent conclusions about how one should relate to the world?

Moreover, Tolle wasn't the only one with such a biography. His story parallels that of Byron Katie, the housewife turned popular spiritual teacher who was also speaking at the conference in La Jolla. Katie, whose accolades have also grown over the years and who was listed in the year 2000 as one of *Time* magazine's one hundred spiritual luminaries, had her own awakening while she was living in a halfway house, caught up in depression and thoughts of suicide. Both Tolle's and Katie's enlightenment experiences were deep, profound, and life-transforming. And both had come to teach a spiritual path in which transcendence was heavily emphasized and the purpose of life in the world was ultimately to liberate oneself from suffering.

4. Why would you seek to try another road, another person or another place, when you <u>have</u> learned the way the lesson starts, but do not yet perceive what it is for? Its purpose is the <u>answer</u> to the search that all must undertake who still believe there is another answer to be found. Learn now, <u>without</u> despair, there is no hope of answer [Ur: answers] in the world. But do not judge the lesson that is but <u>begun</u> with this. Seek not another signpost in the world that seems to point to still another road. No longer look for hope where there is none. Make fast your learning <u>now</u>, and understand you but waste time unless you go <u>beyond</u> what you have learned to what is yet to learn. For from this lowest point will learning lead to heights of happiness, in which you see the <u>purpose</u> of the lesson shining clear, and perfectly within your learning grasp.

Notice that he says, "You *have* learned the way the lesson starts" (Urtext version). We *have* learned how similar to each other are the roads of the world. We *have* learned that choice between them is only pseudo-choice. But we don't like the lesson. It's too depressing. So we look the other way, and keep on trying out different roads.

We are just wasting time. We are like the drug addict who has learned that his addiction brings only misery, but looks the other way, and keeps on using. What we need to do, Jesus says, is first face what we have learned without despair. Then we need to realize this is just the beginning of the lesson, and that from this low point the lesson will "lead to heights of happiness."

Application: Ask yourself honestly:

Have I learned that all the roads in the world are really the same?

If the answer is yes, then ask the Holy Spirit:

Holy Spirit, having learned this, what should I do?

Then wait for an answer. If nothing comes at first, ask again, perhaps in different words, and then listen again.

> 5. Who would be willing to be turned <u>away</u> from all the roadways of the world, <u>unless</u> he understood their real futility? Is it not needful that he should <u>begin</u> with this, to seek another way instead? For while he sees a choice where there is none, what power of decision can he use? The great <u>release</u> of power must begin with learning where it really <u>has</u> a use. And what decision has power if it be applied in situations without choice?

Now we get a hint of where the lesson is really taking us: "to seek another way instead," to choose an option that lies outside the world's options. We are not going to do this unless we first understand the real futility of the roads offered by the world. Until we get that, why on earth *would* we seek elsewhere? And as long as we don't seek elsewhere, all our energy is being poured into spinning our wheels. This is why we don't understand how much power lies in our faculty of choice—whatever we do with it leads to more or less the same results. We are like rats in an experiment that get shocked no matter what they do. Eventually, they just give up.

> 6. The learning that the world can offer but <u>one</u> choice, no matter what its form may be, is the beginning of acceptance that there is a <u>real</u> alternative instead. To fight <u>against</u> this step is to defeat your purpose here. You did not come to learn to find a road the world does not contain. The search for <u>different</u> pathways in the world is but the search for different <u>forms</u> of truth. And this would *keep* the truth from being reached.

Now we are told more about the lesson: "that there is a *real* alternative instead" (Urtext version). We first accept how the lesson begins: that all the roads within the world are the same road with different shrubbery.

Then, once we accept that, we can move on to more of the lesson: accepting that there is a real alternative instead.

Try to think about both parts. To what degree can you accept that all the roads in the world are really the same road, the road to death? If you accepted that, what changes would that mean in your life? What roads would you stop walking down? And can you accept that there really is a qualitatively different way of walking through life, a way that is not on the world's list of options?

> 7. Think not that happiness is <u>ever</u> found by following a road <u>away</u> from it. This makes <u>no</u> sense, and <u>cannot</u> be the way. To you who seem to find this course to be too difficult to learn, let me repeat that to achieve a goal you must proceed in its direction, not <u>away</u> from it. And <u>every</u> road that leads the other way will <u>not</u> advance the purpose to be found. If <u>this</u> be difficult to understand, then <u>is</u> this course impossible to learn. But only then. For otherwise, it is a simple teaching in the obvious.

While the world's roads lead to death, the Holy Spirit's road leads the other way. It leads to happiness. And you can't get somewhere by following a road that leads in the opposite direction. This is the most basic law of travel. Now Jesus says that only if this basic law is hard to understand is the Course hard to learn. Are we willing to raise our hand and say yes, the basic law of travel is actually hard to understand? If not, then Jesus says we have to admit that the Course isn't hard, either. We have to admit that it's nothing more than "a simple teaching in the obvious."

> 8. There *is* a choice that you have power to make when you have seen the real alternatives. <u>Until</u> that point is reached you <u>have</u> no choice, and you can but decide how you would choose the better to deceive yourself again. This course attempts to teach no more than that the power of decision cannot lie in choosing different forms of what is still the <u>same</u> illusion and the <u>same</u> mistake. All choices in the world depend on this;[:] you choose <u>between</u> your brother and yourself, and you will gain as much as he will lose, and what you lose is what is given him. How utterly <u>opposed</u> to truth is this, when all the lesson's purpose is to teach that what your brother loses *you* have lost, and what he gains is what is given *you*.

277

Until we recognize what the real alternatives are, we think we have a thousand alternatives in front of us, when in fact we only have one. As long as we think that, we really have no choice. Our only choice is how we will fool ourselves into thinking that this new option is genuinely different from the ones we've already tried.

In the latter part of the paragraph, Jesus finally tells us the actual content of the lesson. This is the lesson that began with learning that all the world's roads lead to the same place, and that continued with learning that there *is* an alternative to those roads. Now we learn the essence of that alternative: "that what your brother loses *you* have lost, and what he gains is what is given *you*." *This* is the lesson. This is the essence of the Holy Spirit's road. And this is what distinguishes it from the world's roads, which all share one core theme: that my gain is extracted from you, and your gain is extracted from me. Let's be honest: Isn't that the essence of the options offered by the world? And isn't this why the Holy Spirit's road is a *real* alternative?

> 9. He has not left His Thoughts! But you forgot His Presence and remembered not His Love. No pathway in the world can lead to Him, nor any worldly goal be one with His. What road in all the world will lead within, when <u>every</u> road was made to separate the journey from the purpose it must have unless it be but futile wandering? All roads that lead <u>away</u> from what you are will lead you to confusion and despair. Yet has He never left His Thoughts to die, without their Source forever in themselves.
>
> 10. He has not left His Thoughts! He could no more depart from them than they could keep Him out. In unity with Him do they abide, and in their oneness <u>Both</u> are kept complete. There <u>is</u> no road that leads away from Him. A journey <u>from</u> yourself does not exist. How foolish and insane it is to think that there <u>could</u> be a road with such an aim! Where could it go? And how could you be made to travel on it, walking there without your own reality at one with you?

The world's roads were all built to lead away from God, away from what we are, away from our home within. Yet can we actually reach that destination? How can we leave God when He refuses to leave us? We are a Thought of His. How exactly can a thinker leave his thoughts? Thus, perhaps the roadways of the world do not actually lead us away from home. "How foolish and insane it is to think that there could be a road with such an aim!" Perhaps the world's roads just lead to the progressive obscuring of the fact that we never left home.

> 11. Forgive yourself your madness, and forget all senseless journeys and all goal-less aims. They have no meaning. You can <u>not</u> escape from what you are. For God <u>is</u> merciful, and did not let His Son abandon Him. For what He is be thankful, for in that is <u>your</u> escape from madness and from death. Nowhere but where He is can <u>you</u> be found. There *is* no path that does not lead to Him.

Imagine that you travel to another planet, and on this planet you see everyone scurrying about in various directions at great speeds. You stop different ones of them to ask where they are going and they all give the same answer: "I am leaving space." You quite understandably answer, "But everywhere you are going is *within* space. You can't leave space." To which they all reply, "That's why I am traveling so fast."

That, of course, is a great symbol for this planet. Only here the inhabitants, if they were truly honest, would say, "I am leaving God," not realizing that you can't leave God, and especially not realizing that *if* you can't leave God, then the pathways that take you there do not even exist.

We have been down many such roads, haven't we? The first step is to admit that these roads all lead to the same destination: the complete absence of God. The second step is to realize that such a destination is impossible, and hence the roads that lead there cannot actually be real. The third step is to forgive ourselves for the madness of chasing a destination that does not exist on a road that was never real. And then we can head the other way.

V. Self-Concept versus Self
Commentary by Robert Perry

This is a long section. I think it is safe to say that if you understand this section, you will never look at your self-concept the same way again.

> 1. The learning of the world is built upon a concept of the self adjusted to the world's reality. It fits it well. For this an image is that suits a world of shadows and illusions. Here it walks at home, where what it sees is one with it. The building of a concept of the self is what the learning of the world is <u>for</u>. This is its purpose; that you come <u>without</u> a self, and <u>make</u> one as you go along. And by the time you reach "maturity" you have perfected it, to meet the world on equal terms, at one with its demands.

What an interesting picture of the building of our self-concept! This says that we enter the world with no self-concept. We seem to barely have any identity at all. Then, as we grow up, we slowly craft our identity, our self-concept. The guiding principle behind this crafting is that our self-concept needs to fit the world so that it can successfully interface with it. And so we constantly fine-tune it to improve this fit. We adjust our self-concept to the world, so that by the time we are grown up, we are "well adjusted." Now that our self-concept is fully in tune with the world, we can "meet the world on equal terms, at one with its demands." Can you look back over your own growing up years and see this process?

> 2. A concept of the self is made by <u>you</u>. It bears <u>no</u> likeness to yourself at all. It is an idol, made to take the place of your reality as Son of God. The concept of the self the world would teach is not the thing that it appears to be. For it is made to serve two purposes, but one of which the mind can recognize.

Imagine that you are a portrait painter. An angelic being has just arrived on earth, a being of such beauty and celestial radiance that no one here has seen anything like her. You have been given the honor of capturing her unique likeness on canvas. However, you are unsettled by her otherworldly beauty, and so, while you paint her portrait, you can't bring yourself to look at her. To keep your familiar world intact, you constantly look around at familiar faces. As a result, when you are done with her portrait, it looks just like the other people you were looking at, but nothing at all like her!

That's what you have done in painting your own self-concept. It looks nothing like you, but it does look exactly like everything else in this "world of shadows and illusions."

Now we are told that we actually have a dual self-concept, with a surface face that we can recognize and a deeper aspect that we can't see. We'll explore first the one and then the other.

> The first presents the face of innocence, the aspect acted <u>on</u>. It is this face that smiles and charms and even seems to love. It searches for companions and it looks, at times with pity, on the suffering, and sometimes offers solace. It believes that it is good within an evil world. 3. This aspect can grow angry, for the world is wicked and unable to provide the love and shelter innocence deserves. And so this face is often wet with tears at the injustices the world accords to those who would be generous and good. This aspect [in its eyes] <u>never</u> makes the first attack. But every day a hundred little things make small assaults upon its innocence, provoking it to irritation, and at last to open insult and abuse.
> 4. The face of innocence the concept of the self so proudly wears can tolerate attack [on its part] in self-defense, for is it not a well-known fact the world deals harshly with defenseless innocence?

The first aspect of our self-concept is the aspect that sits on the surface: the face of innocence. Its essence is, "I am good, I care, and I'm trying my best, but the world is terribly unfair, and so sometimes I get very sad or quite angry. I'm not the kind to attack first, but I need to defend myself, or I would get squashed." Look at that description, and the description in the above paragraphs. This does capture how we see ourselves, does it not? Did you ever think that after all your years of crafting a self-concept, you would come up with one that looked the same as everyone else's?

Our self-esteem depends on every line of this description. Look again at the above paragraphs and pick one of the sentences at random. Notice how your sense of self-worth in part rests on that sentence; how, if you gave it up, you would have to give up a chunk of your self-esteem.

Notice also that this is not real innocence. It is a *face* of innocence. Read again the above paragraphs and note that they are saturated with a sense of irony and insincerity. Can you see that? This innocence, then, is a façade. It is a face that we paint on. It is an act. We try to hide this fact from others and even from ourselves, but deep down, we know.

> No one who makes a picture of himself omits this face, for he has need of it. The other side he does not want to see. Yet it is here [on the other side] the learning of the world has set its sights, for it is here the world's "reality" is set, to see to it the idol lasts.

Now we see the real motives behind this innocent face. We are like the guy who wears the Mickey Mouse suit at Disneyland. The face we wear beams the message, "I'm just naturally sweet and innocent," but underneath the mask we are really thinking, "Look, I need to wear this because it gets me what I want." And what does it do for us? It hides the second side of our self-concept. We need to keep this side hidden, because it is the whole foundation of the world, and that's one applecart we wouldn't want to upset.

> 5. Beneath the face of innocence there is a lesson that the concept of the self was made to teach. It is a lesson in a terrible displacement, and a fear so devastating that the face that smiles above it must forever look away, lest it perceive the treachery it hides. The lesson teaches this: "I am the thing you made of me, and as you look on me, you stand condemned because of what I am." On this conception of the self the world smiles with approval, for it guarantees the pathways of the world are safely kept, and those who walk on them will not escape.

Notice that the lower level of the self-concept is what actually contains the payload, the "lesson that the concept of the self was made to teach." The top level (the face of innocence) is really just a cover. Its only purpose is to hide the lower level so that it remains unquestioned, so that we never "perceive the treachery it hides." This lesson is simply an intensified version of the darker elements of the face of innocence, the elements which claim that we are at the mercy of an evil world. That is why I call this level "the enraged victim."

Application: Imagine actually saying this to someone:

I am the thing you made of me, and as you look on me, you stand condemned because of what I am.

Imagine yourself saying it again, and as you do, search your mind for someone you would like to say this to, or someone you *have* said this to (in so many words), or someone you *are* saying this to now. How does it feel when you imagine yourself actually saying these words to that person?

Notice that this statement is indeed a self-concept. It even opens with the words "I am." Now consider that your chipper, sincere face of innocence is really there just to cover and protect *this*, your actual self-concept. Consider that, somewhere inside, this is the underlying message you are giving to the world all the time. How does that feel?

6. Here is the central lesson that ensures your brother is condemned eternally. For what <u>you</u> are has now become his sin. For this is no forgiveness possible. No longer does it matter what he does, for your accusing finger points to him, unwavering and deadly in its aim. It points to you as well, but this is kept still deeper in the mists below the face of innocence. And in these shrouded vaults are all his sins and yours preserved and kept in darkness, where they cannot be perceived as errors, which the light would surely show. You can be neither <u>blamed</u> for what you are, nor can you <u>change</u> the things it makes you do. Your brother then is symbol of your sins to you who are but silently, and yet with ceaseless urgency, condemning still your brother for the hated thing you are.

Notice that we have three levels here:

1. **The face of innocence**. This face says, "Yeah, Joan is a terrific lady. Sure she has her issues, but she is a very nice person."
2. **The enraged victim**. This level says, "What am I? I am the hated, mangled *thing* that Joan made of me. I can never go back and undo what she did. I just have to live with the grotesque, misshapen thing I became when she was done with me. Forgive

her? I live every day in silent condemnation of her. No matter what she does, no matter where she goes, my accusing finger points at her, unwavering and deadly in its aim."

3. **The pit of guilt**. This level says, "Let's face it: my victim stance is just a cowardly displacement. The truth is that I am the thing *I* made of me, and as I look on me *I* stand condemned because of what I am. Don't believe that finger that points at Joan. The real finger points at *me*."

The key here is that the lower two levels are locked inside vaults, and the vaults are shrouded in mist. Do you get the picture? We have made it exceedingly difficult to access those lower levels, for if we did, we might actually change our mind about their content. We might see that our brother's sin (victim level) was really just a harmless mistake, with no effect on us. And we might see that our own sin (level three) was also just a mistake. This means that as long as we don't open those shrouded vaults, our seemingly innocent state of goodwill toward our brothers is really just cloaked unforgiveness.

> 7. Concepts are learned. They are not natural. Apart from learning they do not exist. They are not given, so they must be made. Not one of them is true, and many come from feverish imaginations, hot with hatred and distortions born of fear. What is a concept but a thought to which its maker gives a meaning of his own? Concepts maintain the world. But they can **not** be used to demonstrate the world is real. For all of them are made **within** the world, born in its shadow, growing in its ways and finally "maturing" in its thought. They are ideas of idols, painted with the brushes of the world, which cannot make a single picture representing truth.

We take our self-concept to be gospel. We walk through our day without questioning that it accurately depicts us. This paragraph is calling on us to question it. After all, it is just a highly subjective concept, and a *concept* is something of which we have *conceived*. It is an idea that we made up. Further, we made it under the influence of this world. Our self-concept was born under the shadow of the world, grew up in the ways of the world, and finally "matured" in the thought of the world. And from birth to maturity, every brushstroke of it was painted with the brushes of the world. Given all this, of course it pictures us as a *creature* of the world.

Yet what if we are not creatures of the world? What if we have fashioned an image of ourselves that doesn't resemble us in the slightest? What if we *have* no image to be perceived?

> 8. A concept of the self is meaningless, for no one here can see what it is for, and therefore cannot picture what it <u>is</u>. Yet is all learning that the world directs begun and ended with the single aim of teaching you this concept of yourself, [so] that you will choose to follow this world's laws, and never seek to go <u>beyond</u> its roads nor realize the way you see yourself. Now must the Holy Spirit find a way to help you see this concept of the self must be undone, if <u>any</u> peace of mind is to be given you. Nor can it be unlearned except by lessons aimed to teach that you are something else. For otherwise, you would be asked to make exchange of what you now believe for total loss of self, and greater terror would arise in you.

Everything we learn in this world is designed to subtly reinforce our self-concept, the concept that says, "I am the thing you made of me." This self-concept is basically the same as "I am a slave." And if you have that self-concept, then you also think "I rise when the master says. I do what the master tells me. And I never stray beyond the master's boundaries." That's what we say every day. *Our* master is the world. Believing that we are the world's slave, we follow the world's laws and choose from the world's roads (as we discussed in the previous section).

Like any slave, we must first free our *mind*. We have to undo our oppressive self-concept. This is the Holy Spirit's aim. To accomplish this, though, He has to be gentle. He can't just say, "You are not that." He can't ask us to leap from the familiar into the void. He must give us an alternative to which we can transfer our belief. He has to say, "You aren't that; here's what you *are*."

We will see how He gently reasons us out of our current self-concept in the remaining half of the section.

Commentary by Greg Mackie

9. Thus are the Holy Spirit's lesson plans arranged in easy steps, that though there be some lack of ease at times and some distress, there is no shattering of what was learned, but just a re-translation of what seems to be the evidence on its behalf. Let us consider, then, what proof there is that you are what your brother made of you. For even though you do not yet perceive that this is what you think, you surely learned by now that you <u>behave</u> as if it were. Does he <u>react</u> for you? And does [Ur: did] he know exactly what would happen? Can [Ur: Could] he see your future and ordain, before it comes [Ur: came], what you should do in <u>every</u> circumstance? He must have made the world as well as [making] you to have such prescience in the things to come.

The previous paragraph said that the Holy Spirit must be gentle in His undoing of what we think we are. As part of this gentle process, Jesus will now reassess the apparent evidence for our self-concept.

Here, Jesus takes aim at the enraged victim level, the idea that we are what our brother made of us. We may find that idea hard to believe when it is stated so bluntly, but if you think about it, how often do we say things like "After you did that to me, I had no choice but to respond the way I did" or "She made me so mad when she said that" or "I have bad relationships with men because I had an emotionally distant father"? Don't all these statements affirm the underlying belief that other people have made us what we are?

Yet if our brother made us what we are, this means that we ourselves had no say whatsoever in the matter. Everything that *seemed* to make us what we are—our decisions, our actions, our reactions, all the things that happened to us, the world that shaped us—must have been under his control. He must have been the absolute puppet master, in complete charge of the entire process of our life and the world we live in. Do you know anyone who actually has such power? If the answer is no, then how could your brother have made you?

10. That you are what your brother made of you seems most unlikely. Even if he did, who gave the face of innocence to you? Is this <u>your</u> contribution? Who is, then, the "you" who made it? And who is deceived

> by all your goodness, and attacks it so? Let us forget the concept's foolishness, and merely think of this; there are two parts to what you think yourself to be. If one were [Ur: was] generated by your brother, who was there to make the other? And from whom must something be kept hidden? If the world be evil, there is still no need to hide what <u>you</u> are made of. Who is there to see? And what but is attacked could <u>need</u> defense?

The idea that our brother made us is, at the very least, "most unlikely." Yet let's assume for a moment that he did. We're claiming that our brother victimized us, which means he made the victim part of our self-concept. Who, then, made the face of innocence, the part that *masks* the victim part? Furthermore, why would there be a need to mask the victim part anyway? Whom are we trying to fool with the face of innocence? It looks like we're trying to fool the world with our "goodness," but if the world is evil—remember, the face of innocence sees itself as "good within an evil world"—who cares what the world thinks? Indeed, if the world is evil, why not be totally open about all the rotten ways it has victimized us? No, it must be someone besides the world that we're trying to fool. The question is: Whom?

> 11. Perhaps the reason why this concept [the victim level] must be kept in darkness is that, in the light, the one who would not think it true is <u>you</u>. And what would happen to the world you see [Ur: know], if all its underpinnings were removed? Your concept of the world <u>depends</u> upon this concept of the self. And <u>both</u> would go, if either one were ever raised to doubt. The Holy Spirit does not seek to throw you into panic. So He merely asks if just a <u>little</u> question might be raised.

All the Holy Spirit asks as we consider the victim self-concept is "if just a *little* question might be raised." Here are some little questions He raises: "Is it perhaps possible that the one you're hiding the victim level from, the one who would not believe it if it were brought to light, is *you*? Is it perhaps possible that you're not a victim of the world at all?"

This possibility is presented to us very gently, because it carries huge ramifications that might throw us into a panic if we really let them sink in. Our entire concept of the world depends on our self-concept—our victim self-concept goes hand in hand with a world that seems to constantly victimize us. Therefore, if either our self-concept or the world were seriously questioned, *everything* would go: our entire world and our very sense of who we are. Therefore, since the Holy Spirit doesn't want us to sink into the terror of "total loss of self," He asks if just *perhaps* we might consider just how unlikely it is that we could be a victim at the hands of a brother who made us.

> 12. There <u>are</u> alternatives about the thing that you must be. You might, for instance, be the thing you chose to have your <u>brother</u> be. This shifts the concept of the self from what is wholly passive, and at least makes way for active choice, and some acknowledgment that interaction must have entered in. There is some understanding that you chose for <u>both</u> of you, and what he represents has meaning that was given it by <u>you</u>. It also shows some glimmering of sight into perception's law that what you see reflects the state of the <u>perceiver's</u> mind. Yet who was it that did the choosing first? If you are what you chose your brother be, alternatives were there to choose among, and someone must have first decided on the one to choose, and let the other [Ur: others] go.

Having dispensed with the idea that we are solely what our brother made of us, Jesus now considers another alternative: Perhaps we are the thing we chose to have our brother be. This is somewhat confusing, but here is the basic idea:

- I chose to have my brother be a guilty victimizer of me.
- Therefore, if I am the thing I chose my brother be, *I* must be a guilty victimizer of *him*.

This theory is thus a curious amalgam of the bottom two levels this section has talked about: It retains the "enraged victim" level since it still includes our brother victimizing us, yet also plunges into the "pit of guilt" level, since it claims that we also victimized him. It says, in essence, that yes, my brother made me, but ironically, *I* made *him* into the one who made me. This alternative theory has a number of advantages:

- It shows I'm not a totally passive victim of my brother; I made an active choice.
- It shows there must have been interaction with my brother.

- It shows understanding that I chose for both of us.
- It shows understanding that my view of my brother reflects my state of mind.

Unfortunately, there is a big problem with this alternative theory. Do you see it? The theory basically says that I made my brother, who then turned around and made me. From his perspective, this would be reversed: He made me, then I turned around and made him. This process of each of us making the other keeps going and going as we interact with each other. The question is: *Who started all this?* What we have here is a classic "chicken or the egg" problem: Which came first? Did I choose to make my brother first, or did he choose to make me first?

> 13. Although this step has gains, it does not yet approach a basic question. Something must have gone <u>before</u> these concepts of the self. And something must have done the learning which gave rise to them. Nor can this be explained by either view. The main advantage of the shifting to the second from the first is that you somehow entered in the choice by <u>your</u> decision. But this gain is paid in almost equal loss, for now <u>you</u> stand accused of guilt for what your <u>brother</u> is. And you must <u>share</u> his guilt, because you chose it <u>for</u> him in the image of your own. While <u>only</u> he was treacherous before, now must <u>you</u> be condemned along with him.

The main advantage of the view that we are what we chose to have our brother be is one we've already seen: It means that we are no longer simply a puppet on his strings. However, it also contains a major disadvantage: It spreads the guilt around. In the view that our brother made us, only *he* stands condemned for what *we* are. But in the view that we made our brother who turned around and made us, *each* of us stands condemned for what the *other* is.

The central problem with both views, however, is this: There had to be something there *before* all this making took place. There had to be a prior "you" who generated these self-concepts and learned them—the same "you" we're trying to fool with the face of innocence, the same "you" who wouldn't believe it if he saw the victim level as it really is. This "you" is our actual *self,* the very thing these theories of the self-concept purport to explain, but actually overlook entirely. Indeed, these theories are designed for the very purpose of overlooking the "you" we really are.

> 14. The concept of the self has always been the great preoccupation of the world. And everyone believes that he must find the answer to the riddle of himself. Salvation can be seen as nothing more than the <u>escape</u> from concepts. It does not concern itself with content of the mind, but with the simple statement <u>that it thinks</u>. And what can think has choice, and <u>can</u> be shown that different thoughts have different consequence. So [Ur: And] it can learn that <u>everything</u> it thinks reflects the deep confusion that it feels about how it was made and what it is. And vaguely does the concept of the self appear to answer what it does not know.

The self-concept is indeed "the great preoccupation of the world." What is growing up but a process of trying to figure out who we are? And even when we think we've got that figured out, how often do we leave behind what we thought we were and go on a quest to "find myself"? Some of us may have come to the Course as part of this very quest for a more authentic self-concept.

Yet "Salvation can be seen as nothing more than the *escape* from concepts." Many Course students read this line as a repudiation of the intellect and ideas—"Get out of your head and into your heart"—but that's not what Jesus is saying here. After all, the Course itself is one long string of ideas that are meant to be studied. When Jesus speaks of concepts here, he is talking about our own *false* ideas. As Robert said in the last commentary, a *concept* is something we have *conceived*, something we made up—in particular, our made-up version of what we are. As we saw in the second paragraph, "A concept of the self is made by you." This concept above all is what must be escaped to find salvation.

Instead of being concerned with the specific content of these meaningless concepts in our minds, salvation is focused on these ideas:

- The mind can think.
- The mind can choose different thoughts.
- Different thoughts will have different consequences.
- The mind can learn that everything it now thinks reflects its deep confusion about how it was made and what it is.

Jesus is giving us that learning now, to replace the self-concept we've made to solve the "riddle" of what we are.

> 15. Seek not your Self in symbols. There can be no concept that can stand for what you are. What matters it which concept you accept while you perceive a self that interacts with evil, and reacts to wicked things? Your concept of yourself will still remain quite meaningless. And you will not perceive that you can interact but with yourself. To see a guilty world is but the sign your learning has been guided by the world, and you behold it as you see yourself. The concept of the self embraces all you look upon, and <u>nothing</u> is outside of this perception. If you can be hurt by <u>anything</u>, you see a picture of your secret wishes. Nothing more than this. And in your suffering of <u>any</u> kind you see your own concealed desire to kill.

The first two sentences here are another way of saying that salvation is the escape from concepts—in particular, self-concepts. None of our concepts can hold a candle to what we really are. And while we grimly hold on to *any* of the self-concepts described in this section— the "innocent" self in an evil world, the victim of an evil world, or the victimizer who made the evil world that then turned around and made us—we will see a self that interacts with an evil world in some sense.

Thus we will not recognize that our self-concept is actually meaningless and that we are interacting only with ourselves. We will not recognize that everything we react to "out there" is merely a projection of our self-concept. We will not recognize that our belief the world has hurt us is merely a projection of our desire to *be* hurt as punishment for our own desire to kill.

> 16. You will make many concepts of the self as learning goes along. Each one will show the changes in your own relationships, as your perception of yourself is changed. There will be some confusion every time there is a shift, but be you thankful that the learning of the world is loosening its grasp upon your mind. And be you sure and happy in the confidence that it will go at last, and leave your mind at peace. The role of the accuser will appear in many places and in many forms. And each will seem to be accusing you. Yet [Ur: But] have no fear it will not be undone.

Even though Jesus says that salvation lies in the total escape from concepts, that total escape doesn't actually happen until the very end of the journey. The journey itself is a process of constantly shifting our self-concept as learning progresses: As we advance on the path, our self-concept comes closer and closer to the truth.

Can you think of a time when you learned something that caused a significant shift in your sense of who you are? There is often a lot of confusion when this happens—our relationships, in particular, may never be the same again—but Jesus counsels us to be thankful, because this simply means "that the learning of the world is loosening its grasp upon your mind." Yes, that pit of guilt is still down there in the shrouded vaults of the mind, so we will continue to project accusers in various forms for a while yet. But we *are* making progress, and we can rest assured that one day *all* of our self-concepts will be totally undone and we will find peace.

> 17. The world can teach no images of you unless you <u>want</u> to learn them. There will come a time when images have all gone by, and you will see you know not what you are. It is to this unsealed and open mind that truth returns, unhindered and unbound. Where concepts of the self have been laid by is truth revealed exactly as it is. When every concept has been raised to doubt and question, and been recognized as made on <u>no</u> assumptions that would stand the light, then is the truth left free to enter in its sanctuary, clean and free of guilt. There is no statement that the world is more afraid to hear than this:
>
> > *I do not know the thing I am, and <u>therefore</u> do not know what I am doing, where I am, or how to look upon the world or [Ur: and] on myself.*
>
> Yet in this learning is salvation born. And What you are will <u>tell</u> you of Itself.

While the journey is a process of constantly shifting the self-concept to one that better reflects the truth, eventually the time will come when *all* self-concepts have been found wanting. It is then, and only then, that our minds will be fully open, and truth—our true Self—will dawn on them. Only when we recognize that we truly have not the slightest idea of what we are will we be ready to hear What we are tell us of Itself.

The world is terrified of this moment because it equates this moment with "total loss of self." The entire pageant of self-concepts is the world's attempt to stave this moment off. Yet it will come. Given all the pain our self-concepts have brought us, let us be thankful that they will all be set aside and the glory of our true Self will be revealed to us at last.

Application: Even though that moment of total open-mindedness won't come until the very end of the journey, we can bring it closer by practicing it. So first, bring to mind your own self-concept. Consider the following things:

- what you think you are
- what you do
- where you are
- how you look upon the world
- how you look upon yourself

Now, consider the possibility that you really have no idea about any of these things. Consider the possibility that your current self-concept bears no relation to What you really are. Repeat this paragraph's practice line with as much open-mindedness as you can muster:

> *I do not know the thing I am, and **therefore** do not know what I am doing, where I am, or how to look upon the world and on myself.*

Let What you are tell you of Itself.

VI. Recognizing the Spirit
Commentary by Robert Perry

1. You see the flesh or recognize the spirit. There is no compromise between the two. If one is real the other must be false, for what is real denies its opposite. There is no choice in vision but this one. What you decide in this determines all you see and think is real and hold as true. On this one choice does all your world depend, for here have you established what you are, as flesh or spirit in your own belief. If you choose flesh, you never will escape the body as your own reality, for you have chosen that you want it so. But choose the spirit, and all Heaven bends to touch your eyes and bless your holy sight, that you may see the world of flesh no more except to heal and comfort and to bless.

Everything I experience as real comes down to this one choice: Do I choose to "see the flesh or recognize the spirit"? When I look at my brother, do I choose to regard his body—how it looks and what it does—as real? Or do I choose the radiance and holiness of spirit as his reality? I usually overlook this choice—don't even notice it's there. Yet still, everything hinges on it, not only what I see in the world, but what I see as *myself*.

If I choose flesh, I have decided that flesh is *my* reality, that I am imprisoned by how my body looks, by what it does, by its state of health. I am alone with it, cooped up in its tiny box. If, however, I choose spirit, then I am no longer alone. Heaven will reach down and open my spiritual eyes, so that I see the spirit. I will be so caught up in this ecstatic vision that I won't even pay attention to the world of bodies anymore—except with one qualifier: I will pay attention to where and how I can help.

2. Salvation is undoing. If you choose to see the body, you behold a world of separation, unrelated things, and happenings that make no sense at all. This one appears and disappears in death; that one is doomed to suffering and loss. And no one is exactly as he was an instant previous, nor will he be the same as he is now an instant hence. Who could have trust where so much change is seen, for who is worthy

if he be but dust? Salvation is undoing of all this. For constancy arises in the sight of those whose eyes salvation has released from looking at the cost of keeping guilt, because they chose to let it go instead.

When you look around you, what you see is exactly what this paragraph describes. You see a bunch of separate, unrelated bodies caught up in senseless happenings. This person suddenly vanishes (dies). How does that make any sense? This person is doomed to a life of disability. How does that make any sense? How can you trust anything when everything is in flux? Moreover, behind the flux is a cruel gravity that tends to drag everything down, further undermining your ability to trust.

What you're seeing is a torture chamber in which everyone is paying for their guilt. But you only see this because *you* have chosen to look on the consequences of guilt. If you chose to let guilt go, you would see a different world, a world of *constancy*.

> 3. Salvation does not ask that you behold the spirit and perceive the body not. It merely asks that this should be your <u>choice</u>. For <u>you</u> can see the body <u>without</u> help, but do not understand how to behold a world <u>apart</u> from it. It is your world salvation will undo, and <u>let</u> you see another world your eyes could never find. Be not concerned <u>how</u> this could ever be. You do not understand how what <u>you</u> see arose to meet your sight. For if you did, it would be gone. The veil of ignorance is drawn across the evil and the good, and must be passed that both may disappear, so that perception finds no hiding place. How is this done? It is not done at all. What <u>could</u> there be within the universe that God created that must still be done?

Every time Jesus talks about seeing the spirit, something in our mind must be saying, "But how? How do I do that?" Given that, this paragraph should be a massive reassurance. "Be not concerned with how," it says. After all, we don't even know how we are seeing the world in front of us now. All we need to concern ourselves with is the *choice*. If we simply choose to see the spirit, the world we see now will be undone for us, and sight of the real world will be *given* us. "How is this done?" The answer is that God has done it already.

Now we have no excuses left. Nothing is stopping us. We have the power to make choices, and so we have the power to make *this* choice.

4. Only in arrogance could you conceive that <u>you</u> must make the way to Heaven plain. The means are <u>given</u> you by which to see the world that will replace the one you made. Your will be done! In Heaven as on earth this is forever true. It matters not where you believe you are, nor what you think the truth about yourself must really be. It makes no difference what you look upon, nor what you choose to feel or think or wish. For God Himself has said, "Your will be done." And it <u>is</u> done to you accordingly.

It's amazing how many conventional ideas this brief paragraph turns on their heads. First, we think that somehow we have to make the way to Heaven plain; we have to give ourselves vision. This may seem humble, but it's really arrogant. In reality, we just do our small part. We just make the choice. However, we then worry that our choice won't be enough, that there will be some disconnect between the light switch we flip and the light bulb going on. Jesus counters this with "No, your will is always done."

This leads us into his remarkable reversal of the Lord's Prayer. Traditionally, we were taught to pray to God, "Thy kingdom come. Thy will be done, on earth as it is in Heaven." We were signifying our hope that God's Will would be done on earth like it's done in Heaven. But now Jesus turns that around. He has God saying these lines to us—a rather amazing idea all by itself! Further, God is talking about our will being done in *Heaven* as it is on *earth*—the reversal of the traditional order. Finally, He's saying it not as a hope, but rather as an acknowledgment of what is always true.

Application: Ask yourself the question that must surely have crossed your mind at some point: "Even if I choose to see the spirit, how can I know that my choice will have its desired results?" Then hear God say to you personally:

"Your will be done," [name].
"In Heaven as on earth this is forever true."

5. You who believe that you can choose to see the Son of God [yourself] as you would have him be, forget not that no <u>concept</u> of yourself

will stand against the truth of what you are. Undoing truth would be impossible. But concepts are not difficult to change. One vision, clearly seen, that does not fit the picture as it was perceived before will change the world for eyes that learn to see, <u>because the concept of the self has changed</u>.

We see what we want to see, but the illusions we choose to see cannot stand forever. In the end, they will fall before the truth. This includes our illusion of ourselves. Eventually, we will become weary of holding onto this false self-concept. Our grip will tire and then relax. We will let go of that ancient self-concept. Then we will see a new world, and this joyous sight will spread to the eyes of others, causing them to see what we see.

> 6. Are <u>you</u> invulnerable? Then the world is harmless in your sight. Do <u>you</u> forgive? Then is the world forgiving, for you have forgiven it its trespasses, and so it looks on you with eyes that see as yours. Are <u>you</u> a body? So is all the world perceived as treacherous, and out to kill. Are you a spirit, deathless, and without the promise of corruption and the stain of sin upon you? So the world is seen as stable, fully worthy of your trust; a happy place to rest in for a while, where nothing need be feared, but only loved. Who is unwelcome to the kind in heart? And what could hurt the truly innocent?

Self-concept determines worldview. This is because you see the world in terms of how it affects you, and how it affects you is a product of your concept of "you." This paragraph mentions three ways in which this happens. First, what you think you are determines how the world *can* affect you (whether it can hurt you or not). Second, what you think you have done to the world determines how the world (apparently) *deserves* to affect you (whether it should punish you or not). Third, your mindset and your nature (as you see it) become the lens through which you see the world. In all three ways, your concept of yourself determines how you see the world, especially how you see it treating you.

Application: Reflect on the following questions; make them personal:

> *If I cannot be hurt, then how could the world **not** look harmless?*
> *If I forgive the world, then won't I see a world that forgives me?*

If I am a fragile body, then how will my world not look dangerous?
If I am a stable spirit, then won't I see a world that is similarly stable and deserves my trust?
*If I am truly kind in heart, then how will everyone **not** be welcome to me?*
*If I am genuinely innocent and thus deserve no hurt, could anything **really** hurt me?*

7. Your will be done, you holy child of God. It does not matter if you think you are in earth or Heaven. What your Father wills of you can never change. The truth in you remains as radiant as a star, as pure as light, as innocent as love itself. And you *are* worthy that your will be done!

I get the impression (from putting this paragraph together with the previous one) that my self-concept determining my worldview is an example of the idea that my will is done. In other words, because my will is always done, if I will just let go of my self-concept, I will *also* see a new world.

Application: Again ask yourself, "Is my choice to see the spirit truly enough to guarantee that I really do see the spirit?" Then hear Jesus speaking to you personally, saying this:

> "Your will be done, [name].
> The truth in you remains as radiant as a star,
> as pure as light,
> as innocent as love itself.
> And you *are* worthy that your will be done!"

VII. The Savior's Vision
Commentary by Robert Perry

1. Learning is change. Salvation does not seek to use a means as yet too alien to your thinking to be helpful, nor to make the kinds of change you could not recognize. Concepts are needed while perception lasts, and changing concepts <u>is</u> salvation's task. For it must deal in contrasts, not in truth, which has no opposite and cannot change. In this world's concepts are the guilty "bad"; the "good" are innocent. And no one here but holds a concept of himself in which he counts the "good" to pardon him the "bad." Nor does he trust the "good" in anyone, believing that the "bad" must lurk behind. This concept emphasizes treachery, and trust becomes impossible. Nor could it change while you perceive the "bad" in you.

We are not ready for changelessness. We are not ready to dive into the truth. All we are ready for now is a change of concepts, new concepts. True, concepts are like paintings—they are representations, not the thing represented. But all we can handle right now are *better* concepts. Look at the third sentence, which is a nice little bit of rhyming iambic pentameter:

Concepts are needed while perception lasts,
and changing concepts is salvation's task.

The question now becomes "what concept are we supposed to change?" Answer: the concept of ourselves as *bad*. This concept dominates our thinking, though most of us don't realize it. We are all hoping that our good will pardon our bad—the bad we have done and the bad in us. We are doing good all the time in the hope that it will erase some of the black marks on our record.

We also project this concept of our self as bad onto others. Now we think the bad is what they are really about, while the good is just a façade. How, then, can we trust them? But all we are seeing in them is what we think is true about ourselves.

Application: Think of something good you've done recently. It may help to write it down. Then ask yourself,

What am I hoping this good thing will pardon me for?

Try to get in touch with an answer. I've done this with a class before. When most of them asked themselves, "What am I hoping this good thing will pardon me for?" they started out somewhat skeptical that anything would be there. Yet, almost the instant they asked, something leapt into their mind. It may have been something clearly related to the good thing they did, or apparently unrelated—just some general sin they are trying to pay off. But in most cases, it seemed, *something* was there. Which means that the good deed was, at least in part, secretly driven by a hoped-for pardon.

> 2. You could not recognize your "evil" thoughts as long as you see value in attack. You <u>will</u> perceive them sometimes, but will <u>not</u> see them as meaningless. And so they come in fearful form, with content [of nothingness] still concealed, to shake your sorry concept of yourself and blacken it with still another "crime." <u>You</u> cannot give yourself your innocence, for you are too confused about yourself. But should *one* brother dawn upon your sight as wholly worthy of forgiveness, then your concept of yourself <u>is</u> wholly changed. <u>Your</u> "evil" thoughts have been forgiven with his, because you let them all affect <u>you</u> not. No longer do you choose that you should be the sign of evil and of guilt in him [thus letting your "evil" thoughts not affect you]. And as you give your trust to what is good in him [thus letting his "evil" thoughts not affect you], you give it to the good in you.

It's just not going to work to keep attacking and then forgive ourselves. There are two problems with this (unfortunately popular) approach. First, we won't really see our attack thoughts. This is because our investment in attack will make our attacks seem real. This will make our attack thoughts seem like real crimes, cruel confirmations that we really are bad. As a result, we'll keep them safely buried. And even when they squeak through into consciousness, we won't see them for what they really are: innocent mistakes.

Second, we cannot give ourselves our innocence. Gifts to ourselves are always a bit suspect, aren't they? We suspect they are ego-driven, and we are probably right. And ego-driven innocence is an oxymoron.

The real solution is not to try to give innocence to ourselves, but to give it to our brother, to see the good in him through forgiveness. This will transform our own self-concept (which says we are bad), again for two reasons. First, we don't allow the bad in us to cloud our view of our brother, thus making the bad in us seem powerless, irrelevant. Second, we give our trust to the good in our brother, and since he is probably not too different from us, this implies that we should trust the good in ourselves as well.

> 3. In terms of concepts, it is thus you see him <u>more</u> than just a body, for the good is <u>never</u> what the body seems to be. The actions of the body are perceived as coming from the "baser" part of you, and thus of him as well. By focusing upon the good in him, the body grows decreasingly persistent in your sight, and will at length be seen as little more than just a shadow circling round the good. And this will be your concept of <u>yourself</u>, when you have reached the world beyond the sight your eyes alone can offer you to see. For you will not interpret what you see without the Aid That God has given you. And in His sight there *is* another world.

Trusting the good in our brother (rather than seeing it as a deceptive façade) is how we see him as more than a body. This sounds odd at first, but it makes sense. The body's actions seem to come from the baser part of him, do they not? His body runs around driven mostly by the needs of the body and of the ego. Think what this means: If we focus on the good in our brother, we will automatically deemphasize the importance of his body and its actions, until at last we see his body as just a faint shadow circling round the radiant orb of the good in him. Kind of like faint rings around a holy Saturn. And when we see him that way, we will see ourselves that way.

Application: Think of someone you are inwardly struggling to love, and say:

> *Your body has done a lot of petty things.*
> *But that doesn't matter.*

301

> *I trust the good in you as what is real, even if it only sometimes*
>   *expresses through your body.*
> *I see your body as just a shadow circling round the good.*

> 4. You live in that world just as much as this. For <u>both</u> are concepts of yourself, which can be interchanged but never jointly held. The contrast is far greater than you think, for you will love this concept of yourself, <u>because it was not made for you alone</u>. Born as a gift for someone <u>not</u> perceived to be yourself, it has been given <u>you</u>. For your forgiveness, offered unto him, has been accepted now for <u>both</u> of you.

Now we see the contrast mentioned in the first paragraph. It is the contrast between our self-concept in this world and our self-concept in the real world, between ourselves as bad and ourselves as good. We currently have no idea just how vast this contrast is, for we can barely conceive of genuinely *loving* our self-concept. Indeed, we will only love it when we fashion it first as a gift to someone else, a gift that says, "What you are is purely good." Only when we hand this gift to another will we then receive it for ourselves.

> 5. Have faith in him who walks with you, so that your fearful concept of yourself may change. And look upon the good in him, that you may not be frightened by your "evil" thoughts because they do not cloud your view of him. And all this shift requires is that you be <u>willing</u> that this happy change occur. No more than this is asked. On its behalf, remember what the concept of yourself that now you hold has brought you in its wake, and welcome the glad contrast offered you. Hold out your hand, that you may have the gift of kind forgiveness which you offer one whose need for it is just the same as yours. And let the cruel concept of yourself be changed to one that brings the peace of God.

What a beautiful paragraph! We need to have faith in our brother, to trust the good in him. We must not let our "evil" thoughts dictate our view of him, for this will make them seem to be the ruling power in us, and that will scare the hell out of us. Instead, we must hold out our hand and give him "the gift of kind forgiveness," recognizing that he needs it just as deeply as we do. And recognizing that when we give it to him, we receive it for ourselves. As we receive it, our fearful self-concept will be changed to one that brings the peace of God. For this miraculous change to occur, all we need is just to want it, to be willing to let it happen. We will gain this willingness quickly, if we just remember all the pain that our self-concept has brought us.

> 6. The concept of yourself that now you hold would <u>guarantee</u> your function here remain forever unaccomplished and undone. And thus it dooms you to a bitter sense of deep depression and futility. Yet it need not be fixed [set], unless you choose to hold it past the hope of change and keep it static and concealed within your mind. Give it instead to Him Who understands the changes that it needs to let it <u>serve</u> the function given you to bring you peace, that you may offer peace to have it yours. Alternatives are in your mind to use, and you <u>can</u> see yourself another way. Would you not rather look upon yourself as <u>needed</u> for salvation of the world, instead of as salvation's enemy?

This paragraph is all about our function of extension to others, our part in the world's salvation. This function is a deep impulse within. It is the call of our being, a call that cannot be denied. We simply will not be content until we are a channel of blessing to everyone; a pure force of good in the world.

And herein lies the problem with our self-concept. It makes our function impossible. It says that we are salvation's *enemy*, not its instrument. Have you ever had a purpose you knew you were supposed to fulfill but felt unable to? Think of the sense of futility and depression which that spawned. Well, that's what our self-concept is doing to us now. We think, "I *have* to fulfill this purpose. I was born to fulfill this purpose. My very being cries out for it. But I can never do it. I am the enemy of that purpose."

The good news is that this self-concept can be changed. Thank God! We can give it to the Holy Spirit and He can refashion it into a self-concept that actually serves our function, rather than makes it impossible.

> 7. The concept of the self stands like a shield, a silent barricade before the truth, and hides it from your sight. All things you see are images, because you look on them as through a barrier that dims your sight and warps your vision, so that you behold nothing with clarity. The light is

kept from everything you see. At most, you glimpse a shadow of what lies beyond. At least, you merely look on darkness, and perceive the terrified imaginings that come from guilty thoughts and concepts born of fear. And what you see is hell, for fear *is* hell. All that is given you is for release; the sight, the vision and the inner Guide all lead you <u>out</u> of hell with those you love beside you, and the universe with them.

Look around at the place you are in. It seems as if you are simply seeing what is there. What you don't realize is that you are looking through a shield you are holding up before you. This shield is your self-concept. It says, "I'm bad, but I hope to do enough good that I'll finally be pardoned for all the bad."

The shield you are holding up is not entirely opaque. Rather, it is made of a dark, semi-translucent material that is actually somewhat moody about the light that it lets through. At its best, some light gets through and you see dim shadows of what lies on the other side. Often, the images get warped as they pass through the shield's curvature and deformities, and so the vague shapes you see are gross caricatures of what's really out there. At worst, no light gets through at all and you see nothing from the other side. But you still see shapes and colors on the shield's (inside) surface as you hold it up. You just don't realize these shapes are projected by your mind, by your guilt and fear; they're not coming from the other side at all.

Right now, as you look out at your world, you are looking through (and at) the shield of your self-concept. Take a moment and imagine that. What you especially do not realize is that what lies out there beyond the shield are not shapes and movement at all, but rather the undifferentiated light of truth. This is what the shield is there to shield you *from*. That is why what you see on the shield is hell—the opposite of the light that's out there.

You could say that this shield image is the Course's (much darker, more complex, and psychologically sophisticated) version of Plato's cave analogy.

> 8. Behold your role within the universe! To every part of true creation has the Lord of Love and Life entrusted <u>all</u> salvation from the misery of hell. And to each one has He allowed the grace to be a savior to the holy ones especially entrusted to his care. And this he learns when first he

looks upon <u>one</u> brother as he looks upon himself, and sees the mirror of himself in him. Thus is the <u>concept</u> of himself laid by, for nothing [no shield] stands <u>between</u> his sight and what he looks upon, to judge what he beholds. And in this single vision does he see the face of Christ, and understands he looks on everyone as he beholds this one. For there is light where darkness was before, and now the veil [the shield] is lifted from his sight.

To each and every one of us, God has entrusted the role of leading those we love out of hell, with the whole Sonship beside them. This is your function while on earth. Try to let that sink in. When do you step into this function? When you see one brother as yourself, when you make a deliberate choice in which you do not see someone else's interests as apart from yours (M-1.1:3).

Why is this the beginning of our function? Because it means the lowering of the shield that was described in paragraph 7. That shield was the self-concept which says, "I'm bad," and which causes us to look on everything through its virtually opaque wall of judgment. This shield, in other words, separates us from everything we see. Thus, when we really see another person as ourselves, we have dropped the shield. Then we see the face of Christ in front of us, and seeing that face is what gives us the power to save others.

> 9. The veil across the face of Christ, the fear of God [the final obstacle to peace] and of salvation, and the love of guilt [part of the first obstacle] and death [third obstacle], they all are different names for just <u>one</u> error; that there is a space between you and your brother, kept apart by an illusion of yourself that holds him off from you, and you away from him. The sword of judgment is the weapon that you give to the illusion of yourself, that it may fight to keep the space that holds your brother off unoccupied by love. Yet while you hold this sword, you <u>must</u> perceive the body as <u>yourself</u>, for you are bound to separation from the sight of him who holds the mirror to another view of what <u>he</u> is, and thus what <u>you</u> must be.

The shield of the self-concept and the obstacles to peace are all different names for the idea "that there is a space between you and your brother." Now, while still holding our shield, we also wield our sword. We use the sword of judgment to "fight to keep the space that holds off your brother unoccupied by love." What an image! Just imagine you swinging your sword of judgment, making sure you keep your brother away from you, lest he, and love with him, cross the gap and join with you. Yet if you dropped your sword and shield and looked at your brother, you would see him quietly holding up a mirror. Imagine him holding this mirror at arm's length from him, at an angle, so that as you looked in it, you beheld in it his true face, the face of Christ, and understood that at the same time you were also looking at your own true face.

> 10. What is temptation but the <u>wish</u> to stay in hell and misery? And what could this give rise to <u>but</u> an image of yourself that <u>can</u> be miserable, and remain in hell and torment? Who has learned to see his brother <u>not</u> as this <u>has</u> saved himself, and thus <u>is</u> he a savior to the rest. To everyone has God entrusted all, because a <u>partial</u> savior would be one who is but partly saved. The holy ones whom God has given you to save are but everyone you meet or look upon, not knowing who they are; all those you saw an instant and forgot, and those you knew a long while since, and those you will yet meet; the unremembered and the not yet born. For God has given you His Son to save from every concept that he ever held.

The theme of temptation has been running throughout this chapter. Here, Jesus says that the temptation to give in to the ego, in any form, is really "the *wish* to stay in hell and misery" (Urtext version). And this wish to be in hell gives rise to an *image* of ourselves that can be in hell. When we stop seeing our *brother* as such an image, we save ourselves, and thus acquire the ability to save others.

The question is, which others? Paragraph 8 mentioned "the holy ones especially entrusted to his care." Who are these holy ones? The fifth sentence answers that, in a simply astonishing way.

Application: Repeat the following to yourself:

> *The holy ones whom God has given me to save are:*
> *everyone I meet, such as [someone you've met recently], the strangers I look upon, such as [a stranger you have seen recently], all those I saw an instant and forgot, all those I knew a long time ago, such as [someone from your past], and those*

I will yet meet,
the unremembered and the not yet born.
For God has given me His Son to save from every concept that
  he ever held.

11. Yet while you wish to stay in hell, how <u>could</u> you be the savior of the Son of God? How would you know his holiness while you see him apart from yours? For holiness is seen through holy eyes that look upon the innocence within, and thus <u>expect</u> to see it everywhere. And so they call it forth in everyone they look upon, that he may be what they expect of him. This is the savior's vision; that he see <u>his</u> innocence in all he looks upon, and see his own salvation everywhere. He holds <u>no</u> concept of himself between his calm and open eyes and what he sees. He <u>brings</u> the light to what he looks upon, that he may see it as it really is.

However, as long as we give in to the temptations of the ego, we want to stay in hell. How, then, could we lead God's Son *out* of hell? The only way to lead our brothers out is to drop the shield of our self-concept, to hold nothing in between our calm and open eyes and what we see. As long as we hold that shield in front of our eyes, we will see our brother as separate from us. Yet the vision that saves is the vision of holiness. How does that vision work? Holy eyes first look on the holiness within and then look out and "expect to see it everywhere." Seeing it in others will then actually call it forth in them. They, in other words, become more likely to manifest holiness if we *expect* to see it in them.

12. Whatever form temptation seems to take, it <u>always</u> but reflects a wish to be a self that you are not. And <u>from</u> that wish a concept rises, teaching that you <u>are</u> the thing you wish to be. It will remain your concept of yourself until the wish that fathered it no longer is held dear. But while you cherish it, you will behold your brother in the likeness of the self whose image has the wish begot of <u>you</u>. For seeing <u>can</u> but represent a wish, because it has <u>no</u> power to create. Yet it can look with love or look with hate, depending only on the simple choice of whether you would <u>join</u> with what you see, or keep yourself apart and separate.

Here is another angle on the temptation to give in to the ego: Temptation is "a wish to be a self that you are not," a wish to not be

God's Son. That wish then gives rise to the self-concept, the concept that "I am bad." Then you hold this concept in front of your eyes and see your brother through its smoky glass. Now he appears to be the same thing you believe you are: bad.

Application: Think of someone whom you see as, to be blunt, *bad*. Then realize that you hold a self-concept that says that, underneath your good façade, *you* are bad. Picture yourself holding this self-concept up before your eyes like a shield, to shield your eyes from the blazing light that this person really is. Now you see him or her only through the shield's dim glass, and this is what makes this person seem bad. Without your self-concept, you would instantly see that this person is holy, regardless of what he or she displays on the outside.

> 13. The savior's vision is as innocent of what your brother is as it is free of any judgment made upon yourself. It sees no past in anyone at all. And thus it serves a wholly open mind, unclouded by old concepts, and prepared to look on <u>only</u> what the present holds. It cannot judge because it does not know. And <u>recognizing</u> this, it merely asks, "What is the meaning of what I behold?" Then is the answer given. And the door held open for the face of Christ to shine upon the one who asks, in innocence, to see <u>beyond</u> the veil of old ideas and ancient concepts held so long and dear <u>against</u> the vision of the Christ in you.

Application: Think of the same person that you used in the previous application. See yourself lower the shield of your self-concept (though don't try to picture what is on the other side of it just yet). Then say,

> *I am prepared to look on only what the present holds.*
> *I cannot judge because I do not know.*
> *I ask to see beyond the veil of old ideas.*
> *I ask the Holy Spirit, "What is the meaning of what I behold?*
> *What is the real meaning of this brother (or sister)?"*

Then see a door open in front of you,
and see the face of Christ shining there behind the doorway.

This is who this person really is.
See this serene, radiant face shine on you,
and reveal the Christ in you.

14. Be vigilant against temptation, then, remembering that it is but a wish, insane and meaningless, to make yourself a thing that you are not. And think as well upon the thing that you would be instead. It is a thing of madness, pain and death; a thing of treachery and black despair, of failing dreams and no remaining hope except to die, and end the dream of fear. *This* is temptation; nothing <u>more</u> than this. <u>Can</u> this be difficult to choose *against*? Consider what temptation is, and see the real alternatives you choose between. There <u>are</u> but two. Be not deceived by what appears as many choices. There is hell or Heaven, and of these you choose but <u>one</u>.

When you are tempted to be afraid, to judge, to be worried, realize that this is actually an insane wish to be someone other than yourself (which is God's Son). And what are you wishing to be instead? Earlier in the section, Jesus used the word "bad." Now he expands on that: "a thing of madness, pain and death; a thing of treachery and black despair, of failing dreams and no remaining hope except to die, and end the dream of fear." This sounds extreme, but think about each item. Don't you feel a little crazy at times? Don't you experience pain and aren't you heading toward death? Do you feel entirely trustworthy, or can you be treacherous at times? Have you ever had moments of black despair? How many of your dreams have failed? Have you had moments where hope was so absent that death would be a relief? Maybe Jesus' list is not so extreme, which makes his question all the more important: "Can this be difficult to choose *against*?"

15. Let not the world's light, given unto you, be hidden from the world. It <u>needs</u> the light, for it is dark indeed, and men despair because the savior's vision is withheld and what they see is death. Their savior stands, unknowing and unknown, beholding them with eyes unopened. And <u>they</u> cannot see until he looks on them with seeing eyes, and offers them forgiveness with his own. Can you to whom God says, "Release My Son!" be tempted <u>not</u> to listen, when you learn that it is <u>you</u> for whom He asks release? And what <u>but</u> this is what this course would teach? And what <u>but</u> this is there for you to learn?

309

Look around you and you will see a great deal of darkness. People are in despair because everywhere they look they see different forms of death. Perhaps it is a quiet, stoic despair. Perhaps it is masked by hollow laughter and shallow smiles. Or perhaps the despair is obvious and desperate. But it's there. As you look around at these people weary with hopelessness, you hear a quiet but authoritative voice, apparently directed at no one in particular, that says, "Release My Son!" Of course, you think—someone needs to release these people from their chains. Someone needs to see the light in them, the radiance which will shine away their despair.

Then the Voice speaks again: "Release My Son!" This time you realize that it is directed at you. *You* are the person who is being called on to see the light in these people. You are the one appointed to be their savior. Yet the eyes in you that can see this light are closed. In effect, then, their savior stands before them with eyes unopened. You, their savior, are "unknowing and unknown."

The Voice speaks one more time: "Release My Son!" Now you realize that it is talking about you. *You* are His Son. The Voice is calling you to release these people as *the way* to release yourself. Given this, can you be tempted not to listen?

VIII. Choose Once Again
Commentary by Robert Perry

Jesus now ends the Text of *A Course in Miracles*, and does so with an absolutely masterful section. He has asked us to choose many times in this text. Now he asks us to choose one more time, to choose whether we will yield to the temptation to believe we are a weak, frail body, or whether we will claim the strength of Christ, which gives us power to assume our true role as a savior of the world. He then ends the section with a moving prayer to God, in which he doesn't ask God to *help* us choose again, but rather thanks God that we *will* choose again, and will lead the entire world back to where we started, back to God.

> 1. Temptation has <u>one</u> lesson it would teach, in <u>all</u> its forms, <u>wherever</u> it occurs. It would persuade the holy Son of God he is a body, born in what must die, unable to escape its frailty, and bound by what it orders him to feel. It sets the limits on what he can do; its power is the only strength he has; his grasp cannot exceed its tiny reach. Would you <u>be</u> this, if Christ appeared to you in all His glory, asking you but this:
>
> > *Choose once again if you would take your place among the saviors of the world, or would remain in hell, and hold your brothers there.*
>
> For He *has* come, and He *is* asking this.

The previous section said that all temptation to give in to the ego is "a wish to be a self that you are not" (T-31.VII.12:1). Now Jesus gets more specific. It is a wish to believe that you are a body. Look at the following list—drawn from the third and fourth sentences—and see how many items describe your experience of yourself:

- I have been born into a body that will inevitably die.
- I cannot escape its frailty and vulnerability.
- I have to feel the pains and pleasures it tells me to feel.
- I can only do what it is able to do.

311

- Its power is the only strength I have.
- I can reach no farther than its fingertips.

These seemingly obvious facts of your existence were actually things you taught yourself, bit by bit, by giving in to temptation.

Now picture Christ Himself, the true Self of every living thing, coming to you in person, and laying before you a fundamental decision: "Choose once again, [hear Him speak your name], if you would take your place among the saviors of the world, or would remain in hell, and hold your brothers there." Notice that the choice is not between being a savior and being ineffectual. It's between leading your brothers to Heaven or *holding* them in hell.

If you chose to lead them to Heaven, would you want to be a mere body? As a body, wouldn't you feel terribly inadequate for the task you had chosen?

If Christ came to you, if He really did, and asked you this personally, what would you answer—honestly? Now realize that He *is* here, right now, asking you this very thing.

> 2. How do you make the choice? How easily is this explained! You always choose between your weakness and the strength of Christ in you. And what you choose is what you think is real. Simply by never using weakness to direct your actions, you have given it no power. And the light of Christ in you is given charge of everything you do. For you have brought your weakness unto Him, and He has given you His strength instead.

How do you choose to take your place among the saviors of the world? By choosing to let Christ's strength direct your actions. For only with His strength are you able to take on such a world-embracing role.

Application: Think of a choice facing you right now, either big or small. Say to yourself,

> *I will not let my body dictate what I choose.*
> *I let the strength of Christ in me choose.*
> *Through His strength I can be a savior of the world.*

VIII. Choose Once Again

Does a certain choice come to mind from saying this?

3. Trials [which tempt you] are but lessons that you failed to learn presented once again, so where you made a faulty choice before you now can make a better one, and thus escape all pain that what you chose before has brought to you. In every difficulty, all distress, and each perplexity Christ calls to you and gently says, "My brother, choose again." He would not leave one source of pain unhealed, nor any image left to veil the truth. He would remove all misery from you whom God created altar unto joy. He would not leave you comfortless, alone in dreams of hell, but would release your mind from everything that hides His face from you. His holiness is yours because He is the <u>only</u> Power that is real in you. His strength is yours because He is the Self That God created as His <u>only</u> Son.

We make a lot of faulty choices. We often choose our weakness instead of His strength. And then life gets hard. Having chosen weakness, we seem to lack the needed strength to face life's challenges. The difficulty, though, doesn't come from the outside circumstances. It comes from us choosing weakness.

The good thing, though, is that the basic scenario in which we made the faulty choice always comes up again, so that this time we can make another choice. The pain we experience as it comes up again is the direct result, not of the situation, but of our own previous choice. Yet there is a doorway out of that pain, and this comes not from our choices, but from Christ. He is always there in the midst of each trial and tribulation, quietly whispering, "My brother, choose again. Choose My strength. Take your place." To us, these repetitions of past challenges are like the repetitive dripping of the Chinese water torture. But to Him, they are like the keyhole passing in front of our face once more, giving us a chance to insert the key.

He wants us to have these chances, because He wants to not only deliver us from misery; He wants to pull aside all the veils across His face, so that we at last look on Him and realize He is our Self.

4. The images you make cannot prevail against what God Himself would have you be. Be never fearful of temptation, then, but see it as

it is; another chance to choose again, and let Christ's strength prevail in every circumstance and every place you raised an image of yourself before. For what appears to hide the face of Christ is powerless before His majesty, and disappears before His holy sight. The saviors of the world, who see like Him, are merely those who choose His strength instead of their own weakness, seen <u>apart</u> from Him. They will redeem the world, for they are joined in all the power of the Will of God. And what they will is <u>only</u> what He wills.

The landscape of your life is like a field dotted with stone idols. Each one is a statue of you, depicting you as a tiny, frail body. They are false images of who you are. They block out the sight of your real Identity as the Christ.

Your life is a process of revisiting each idol, repeating each situation in which you gave in to temptation and chose a false image of yourself. As you stand before the situation once more, you feel heavily tempted to make the same choice that you did before. However, do not fear this temptation. See it instead as a blessed chance to choose again. See it as a chance to let the idol go down to dust, to be replaced instead with your reality as Christ. See it as a chance to learn that no image can "prevail against what God Himself would have you be."

Now that you have chosen Christ's strength instead of your own weakness, you will finally have the strength it takes to be a savior of the world.

> 5. Learn, then, the happy habit of response to <u>all</u> temptation to perceive yourself as weak and miserable with these words:
>
> *I am as God created me.*
> *His Son can suffer nothing.*
> *And I **am** His Son.*

Thus is Christ's strength <u>invited</u> to prevail, replacing all your weakness with the strength that comes from God and that can <u>never</u> fail. And thus are miracles as natural as fear and agony <u>appeared</u> to be before the choice for holiness was made. For <u>in</u> that choice are false distinctions gone, illusory alternatives laid by, and nothing left to <u>interfere</u> with truth.

Jesus introduced the term "response to temptation" back in section III. Now he gives us an actual response to temptation practice (which he wants us to make into a "happy habit"), a kind of foreshadowing of scores more such practices in the Workbook (including this very one again in Lesson 110). So let's go ahead and practice it.

Application: Think of some trial you are facing now, some situation in which you feel tempted to let your body and its weakness decide for you. Realize you are standing before a false image of yourself that you raised in a similar situation in the past. Don't be afraid; this is your chance to undo that false image. Say with confidence,

> *I am as God created me.*
> *His Son can suffer nothing.*
> *And I **am** His Son.*

6. You *are* as God created you, and so is every living thing you look upon, <u>regardless</u> of the images you see. What you behold as sickness and as pain, as weakness and as suffering and loss [in those living things], is but temptation to perceive <u>yourself</u> defenseless and in hell. Yield <u>not</u> to this, and you will see <u>all</u> pain, in <u>every</u> form, <u>wherever</u> it occurs, but disappear as mists before the sun. A miracle has come to heal God's Son [your brother], and close the door upon his dreams of weakness, opening the way to his salvation and release. Choose once again what you would have him be, remembering that every choice you make establishes your own identity as you will see it and believe it <u>is</u>.

Here we have one of the primary forms of temptation: the temptation to perceive others as weak, sick, suffering bodies. Little do we know it, but this is actually the temptation to perceive *ourselves* "defenseless and in hell." If we only realized that, wouldn't we choose again?

If we acknowledge that our brother is as God created him, two things will happen. First, his pain, "in every form, wherever it occurs" (notice the parallelism with the first line of the section), will "disappear as mists before the sun." I have always loved that image. We will heal him with a miracle. Second, this will dictate how we see our own identity. We will believe that we too are still as God created us.

7. Deny me not the little gift I ask, when in exchange I lay before your feet the peace of God, and power to bring this peace to everyone who wanders in the world uncertain, lonely, and in constant fear. For it is given you to <u>join</u> with him, and through the Christ in you unveil his eyes, and let him look upon the Christ in him.

All Jesus asks is that we respond to temptation with the happy acknowledgment that we, and everyone else, are as God created us. Then we dispense with the false image of ourselves as weak, and we accept Christ's strength instead (as a gift that Jesus lays at our feet in tribute—what an image!). Now we have the strength to be a savior. Now we have the power to go up to anyone who walks this world alone and afraid, and "unveil his eyes, and let him look upon the Christ in him." What would we do with power like this? Or, more like it, what *wouldn't* we do?

8. My brothers in salvation, do not fail to hear my voice and listen to my words. I ask for nothing but your <u>own</u> release. There is no place for hell within a world whose loveliness can yet be so intense and so inclusive it is but a step from there to Heaven. To your tired eyes I bring a vision of a different world, so new and clean and fresh you will forget the pain and sorrow that you saw before. Yet this a vision is which you must <u>share</u> with everyone you see, for otherwise you will behold it not. To <u>give</u> this gift is how to make it yours. And God ordained, in loving kindness, that it <u>be</u> for you.

Here, as he closes his masterwork, the Text of *A Course in Miracles*, Jesus breaks into a moving plea for us to listen to what he's been telling us. We stand back and fold our skeptical arms, thinking he is asking us to sacrifice our precious happiness. Yet all he wants is to release us from our self-imposed chains. We don't have to feel weak and miserable and in hell. Our experience here can be almost Heaven. We can accept from him a vision that will heal our tired eyes. And our eyes *are* tired, aren't they? Tired of seeing friends separate in hate. Tired of seeing images of emaciated corpses bulldozed into mass graves. Wouldn't we love "a vision of a different world, so new and clean and fresh" that we will forget all the pain and sorrow we have witnessed? This vision is held out to us. It is for us, yet we will only claim it when we give it to *everyone* we see.

9. Let us be glad that we can walk the world, and find so many chances to perceive another situation where God's gift can once again be recognized as ours! And thus will all the vestiges of hell, the secret sins and hidden hates be gone. And all the loveliness which they concealed appear like lawns of Heaven to our sight, to lift us high above the thorny roads we travelled on before the Christ appeared. Hear me, my brothers, hear and join with me. God has ordained I cannot call in vain, and in His certainty I rest content. For you *will* hear, and you *will* choose again. And in this choice is everyone made free.

With our current vision, it can be so hard to walk the world and see all the hurting people. But our new vision includes the power to heal all those hurting people. Now we can actually *be glad* when we see them, for here we will see another chance to give God's gift, and giving it away will make it ours. And as we do, the curtain of hell we see before our eyes will lift, and we will look upon a landscape of aching loveliness. Instead of a thorny road stretching before us, we will see the lawns of Heaven, with Heaven's gate only a short walk away.

Why, then, would we not listen to Jesus? Again he makes his plea: "Hear me, my brothers, hear and join with me." Then he switches from the topic of *attractiveness* to that of *inevitability*. He tells us that sooner or later, we *will* hear him and we *will* choose again. God has ordained that it is so. This raises the fateful question: If we are going to do it eventually, why not just do it now?

10. I thank You, Father, for these holy ones who are my brothers as they are Your Sons. My faith in them is Yours. I am as sure that they will come to me as You are sure of what they are, and will forever be. They will accept the gift I offer them, because You gave it me on their behalf. And as I would but do Your holy Will, so will they choose. And I give thanks for them. Salvation's song will echo through the world with every choice they make. For we are one in purpose, and the end of hell is near.

Now Jesus breaks into a prayer to his Father. This is clearly meant to echo the prayer in John 17 that concludes the famous Farewell Discourse (John 14-17). There, as he is about to leave this world, he prays on behalf of his followers, "that they may have my joy fulfilled in themselves" (John 17:13). Here, the idea is very similar. As he is about to close his text, he prays to God on behalf of his followers.

However, he does not pray for us to choose again. Rather, he thanks God for the fact that we *will* choose again. He expresses the same absolute faith in us that our Father has. He expresses his certainty that our choice will be just like his, and that salvation's song will thereby echo through the world, signaling the end of hell.

How does it feel if you accept this as an *honest* prayer, not one that is staged for us, but one that really captures the private sentiments that Jesus shares with his Father?

> 11. In joyous welcome is my hand outstretched to every brother who would join with me in reaching past temptation, and who looks with fixed determination toward the light that shines beyond in perfect constancy. Give me my own, for they belong to You. And can You fail in what is but Your Will? I give You thanks for what my brothers are. And as each one elects to join with me, the song of thanks from earth to Heaven grows from tiny scattered threads of melody to one inclusive chorus from a world redeemed from hell, and giving thanks to You.

In the back of my mind, I project a whole different picture onto Jesus. I picture him like the frustrated coach of the worst team in the world. The players don't listen to him. They fight amongst each other. They often don't show up for games. And they always lose.

What a different picture he conveys here! He is stretching out his hand in joyous welcome. He is sure that we will take it and join him. He thanks God for us. He can't stop thanking God for us (this is the third time!). And he looks forward in confidence to more and more brothers taking his hand, so that the song of salvation grows from just a few scattered voices into the entire earth uniting as one vast choir lifting its voice in thanks to God: "Thank You, Father, for rescuing us from hell." Just imagine a six billion-member Mormon Tabernacle Choir!

His optimism is almost unbearable. Can he really be seeing things that way? And if he can, what does that mean for us? Doesn't that mean that things really *are* that way?

> 12. And now we say "Amen." For Christ has come
> to dwell in the abode You set for Him
> before time was, in calm eternity.

The journey closes, ending at the place
where it began. No trace of it remains.
Not one illusion is accorded faith,
and not one spot of darkness still remains
to hide the face of Christ from anyone.
Thy Will is done, complete and perfectly,
and all creation recognizes You,
and knows You as the only Source it has.
Clear in Your likeness does the Light shine forth
from everything that lives and moves in You.
For we have reached where all of us are one,
and we <u>are</u> home, where You would have us be.

I have laid this final paragraph out in iambic pentameter, simply to accentuate its beauty. Early on, when Helen asked how she would know when the Course was done, Jesus told her, "When you hear the final 'Amen.'" As it turned out, this wasn't the final amen, but it was a very significant one. It closes the Text, which comprises over sixty percent of the Course's total volume of words.

To fully appreciate this final paragraph, we need to see it in light of the previous ones. There, Jesus spoke of us hearing him and joining with him as saviors of the world. And he envisioned a process whereby more and more of us would do that, so that the entire world would eventually join in "one inclusive chorus," singing its song of thanks to God for redeeming it from hell.

What happens when all of us have joined in that "inclusive chorus"? That's when the big "Amen" is said, not the one that closes the Text, but the one that closes the *universe*. At that point, our entire journey through time and space is over. We have come full circle, back to where we started. We have retraced all our steps, so that each step has been undone and the journey itself has vanished. "No trace of it remains." It's been erased from the books.

Just like the journey of the prodigal son, our journey was one big denial of our Father, one gigantic act of turning our back on Him. Time and space themselves were a denial of our Father. His Will of unity appeared to be constantly thwarted by our collective fragmentation. His role as the only Source was constantly contradicted by all the other sources we saw around us.

Yet now that denial, that turning of our back, has been undone. We are facing our Father again. The "Amen" that ends our journey is, paradoxically, the one that *begins* the real prayer, the real time of communion with our Father. Now we acknowledge *Him*, not the world, as the only Source we have. We shine with *His* likeness, not our ego's. We live and move in *Him*, not in time and space. We allow *Him*, not our childish fantasies, to determine our dwelling place. And therefore, at last, we are where He would have us be. We are home.

About the Circle's
TEXT READING PROGRAM

An Unforgettable Journey through the Text in One Year

The Text is the foundation of *A Course in Miracles*, yet many students find it hard going. This program is designed to guide you through the Text, paragraph by paragraph, in one year.

Each weekday, you will receive an e-mail containing that day's Text section, along with commentary on each paragraph, written by Robert Perry or Greg Mackie. The readings contain material edited out of the published Course as well as exercises for practical application. This is the material that has been presented now in book format in our series *The Illuminated Text*.

By signing up for our online program, you will also receive:

- Weekly one-hour class recordings led by Robert Perry and Greg Mackie that summarize that week's sections and answer students' questions
- An online forum for sharing with others in the program
- Related articles on key Text sections e-mailed directly to you
- Your personal web archive, with access to all your commentaries and class recordings
- An unlimited "pause feature" for pausing your program while you're away

Want to learn more? Call us today on 1-888-357-7520, or go to www.circleofa.org, the largest online resource for *A Course in Miracles*!

We hope that you will join us for this truly enlightening program!

ABOUT THE AUTHORS

 Robert Perry has been a student of *A Course in Miracles* (ACIM) since 1981. He taught at Miracle Distribution Center in California from 1986 to 1989, and in 1993 founded the Circle of Atonement in Sedona, Arizona. The Circle is an organization composed of several teachers dedicated to helping establish the Course as an authentic spiritual tradition.

One of the most respected voices on ACIM, Robert has traveled extensively, speaking throughout the U.S. and internationally. In addition to contributing scores of articles to various Course publications, he is the author or co-author of nineteen books and booklets, including the hugely popular *An Introduction to A Course in Miracles*. Robert's goal has always been to provide a complete picture of what the Course is—as a thought system and as a path meant to be lived in the world on a daily basis—and to support students in walking along that path.

Robert has recently authored his first non-ACIM book, *Signs: A New Approach to Coincidence, Synchronicity, Guidance, Life Purpose, and God's Plan*, available on Amazon sites internationally.

 Greg Mackie has been a student of *A Course in Miracles* since 1991. He has been teaching and writing for the Circle of Atonement since 1999, and has written scores of articles for A Better Way, the newsletter of the Circle of Atonement, as well as other ACIM publications. He is the author of *How Can We Forgive Murderers?* and co-taught, along with Robert Perry, the Text Reading Program and the Daily Workbook Program, which consisted of 365 recordings.

CPSIA information can be obtained
at www.ICGtesting.com
Printed in the USA
FSOW01n2233280116
16269FS